I0074995

MEDICARE'S VICTIMS

How the U.S. Government's Largest Health Care Program
Harms Patients and Impairs Physicians

Medicare's Victims Copyright © 2015 by The National Center for Public Policy Research

All Rights Reserved. No part of this book may be reproduced or transmitted in any form by electronic or mechanical means now known or to be invented, including photocopying, recording, or information storage and retrieval systems, without permission in writing from the publisher, except by a reviewer who may quote brief passages in a review. Nothing herein should be construed as necessarily reflecting the views of the National Center or as an attempt to aid or hinder the passage of any bill before Congress.

The National Center for Public Policy Research
501 Capitol Court NE, Suite 200
Washington, DC 20002
Telephone: 202-543-4110 Fax: 202-543-5975
Website: www.nationalcenter.org

Portions of chapter nine were originally published as "Rx for a Crisis" in *The New Individualist*, a publication of The Atlas Society. They are re-printed here with permission of The Atlas Society, www.atlassociety.org.

Cover design and image by Tadd Foote, www.taddfoote.com
Formatting by Custom-Book-Tique, www.custom-book-tique.com

LCCN: 2015940131
ISBN: 978-0-692-41532-0

MEDICARE'S VICTIMS

How the U.S. Government's Largest Health Care Program
Harms Patients and Impairs Physicians

DAVID HOGBERG

NATIONAL CENTER
FOR PUBLIC POLICY RESEARCH

CONTENTS

To my Mom and Dad: May your years on Medicare be healthy ones.

Acknowledgements

It's wonderful to be writing the acknowledgements section. It means that the work on this book is all but over.

I think it is best to start by thanking the people who reviewed and edited the various chapters. This includes Linda Gorman, Matthew Vadum, Greg Scandlen, Sherrie Gossett, Scott Alford, Jonathan Hanen, and Sean Higgins. Michael F. Cannon offered very helpful advice early on in the process, and James Reschovsky's criticism was indispensible to my re-working the final chapter. Others who gave me much needed advice, especially on the chapter about the disabled, include Stephen A. Moses, Juliette Cubanski, Gary Gilberti, and Henry Claypool.

I also owe enormous thanks to my wife, Laura, and my mom, Nancy, who went over the chapters with a fine-tooth comb looking for typos and making sure the book was accessible to the intelligent layperson.

My wife and mom also provided much needed moral support through this process, as did my dad, Bill, and my brother and sister-in-law, Doug and Melissa. Others who provided encouragement were Amy and David Ridenour, Justin Danhof, David Almasi, Ed Carson, Jed Graham, and Kimberly Sexton.

Before I mention the physicians and patients who spoke with me, let me first thank the people who helped put me in touch with them. Jason Connors was very helpful in assembling a group of seniors to interview at Greenspring. Diane Coleman and Amber Smock were indispensible in introducing me to the group ADAPT where I met most of the disabled patients that I spoke with. Greg Shenk, Andrea Squitieri, and David Brandt were very generous in letting me post an announcement on a special list-serve for physicians. After I did that, my phone rang repeatedly in the following weeks from physicians interested in speaking with me. Finally, thanks to Sonya Colberg of *The Oklahoman* who helped me reach Donna Dennis and thanks to Jeffrey Lord who put me in touch with Amy DiFrancesca.

Next, thanks to both Representative Gene Green and former-Speaker of the House Dennis Hastert for taking time out of their busy schedules to do interviews with me.

I am very grateful to Drs. Juliette Madrigal-Dersch, John Slatosky, Dariush Saghafi, Thomas Tkach, Thomas Janssen, David Holden, Mark Pascale, Daniel Fass, Scott Braddock, and Eric Logan for not only doing an interview with me but allowing me to follow them around as they treated patients and to include those experiences as part of this book. I spoke to numerous physicians, most of whose stories, sadly, I could not include in these pages. Still, I am thankful that they took time out of their busy schedules to speak with me: Todd Stewart, Jay Crutchfield, Hooman Sedighi, John Dietz, Richard Armstrong, Smiley Thakur, George Watson, Margaret Lewin, Joe Marshall, Paul Sisk, Daniel Jones, Gary Mohr, Tony Shaia, Susan Dean, Mike Lininger, William Jones, Cary Kaufman, Brian Kopeikin, David Baron, Richard "Buz" Cooper, Kathleen Brown, Michael Hall, Harold Glickman, Blake Curd, and Ralph Brindis. Also thanks to Mark Galliart, the CEO at McBride Orthopedic Hospital, and Bruce McCall and Lori Kelly of the Napa Valley Physical Therapy Center for sharing their expertise with me.

I am most grateful to the patients and their families and friends who agreed to participate. This no doubt caused them to revisit very painful episodes in their lives, and their willingness to do this took courage. I am forever in their debt. They include Maureen and Marie Daly, Jack and Robbie Lentz, Ellen Gale, James Upp, Don Giles, Mary Noon, Jeff and Rudy Fox, Ben Barrett, Sean and Shari Lynne Denton-Plomann, Laura Johnson, Donna Dennis, Mitch Lesever, James Reiss, Joe Kopytek, Sandra and Robert Klos, and Amy DiFrancesca. I hope that Clay Bell, Dolores Reiss, and Francine English are receiving my thanks up in Heaven. My biggest regret with this book is that they passed away before it was completed.

Other patients and family who spoke to me included Jim Wacker, Donna Lauinger, B.J. Stasio, Ernest Severino, and Cherie Boen. Unfortunately their stories could not be included here, but their willingness to talk with me is immensely appreciated. There were other patients who spoke with me but, ultimately, declined to go on the record. Nevertheless, I thank them for taking the time to speak with me.

I am solely responsible for any errors that remain in this book.

1. INTRODUCTION

Maureen Daly described her mother Johanna as a vibrant, outgoing 64-year-old woman. She had lived in Brooklyn, New York, all of her life. At the time mother and daughter were running a medical billing service.

"You'd find her very involved in life," said Maureen. "She was a lifelong volunteer, very involved with family and friends."

She was happily married to Daniel Daly for 43 years.

"They were still corny and in love," Maureen recalls. "My dad had just retired and he and my mom were having a great time. They liked nothing better than to get in their car and begin driving and stop at any little town that attracted them. Their goal was to see all 50 states. They had seven to go before she died."

On January 9, 2004, Johanna decided to go shopping at a local mall. She wanted to get some new clothes for a trip she was taking to Disney World with Maureen and her other daughter, Marie. After shopping Johanna went out for lunch. Upon leaving the restaurant, she slipped on some ice on the sidewalk and injured her shoulder.

Her family took her to the emergency room. X-rays revealed her shoulder had been badly broken. To Johanna the injury was a minor nuisance.

"When she found out it was broken she said, 'All right, all right, we might have to postpone Disney World, but once I get it set, we can go. We'll drive down and we'll still have a great time,'" said Maureen.

Johanna wasn't entirely certain surgery was worth the trouble. She asked her physician if her shoulder would heal if she left her arm in a sling. Her physician told her that unless she had surgery, she would be unable to raise her arm above her head for the rest of her life. "You don't want your husband to have to brush your hair," the physician told her.

"Frankly, it didn't really matter to her," Marie laughed. "She had a husband and two daughters, she figured she'd have all the help she'd need."

But Johanna relented to her physician and agreed to surgery to put a prosthetic joint in her shoulder at the Hospital for Joint Diseases in New York.

Johanna was initially scheduled to have the surgery on Friday, January 16. Her primary care physician was worried that the injury had caused her to lose some blood, so in the hospital paperwork, known as a "clearance," he asked that a transfusion be done before Johanna went into the operating room.

It was at this point that Maureen began to feel some unease.

"Apparently no one at the hospital bothered to read the clearance," said Maureen. "It wasn't until that morning [when she entered the hospital] that I asked them, when is she getting the transfusion? They asked me what I was talking about. No one there had read the clearance."

In the end, the hospital decided to give her the transfusion that Friday and then reschedule the surgery for the following Monday.

"Inside something said to me that they weren't giving her the best care," Maureen said. "But we didn't know what else to do. This hospital has a great reputation, and my mom needed the surgery."

Johanna had the surgery on Monday, January 19, which just happened to be Martin Luther King Day. That may have been to her detriment. On this holiday, the operating room had a skeleton crew, so Johanna may not have received all due care.

Nevertheless, Johanna's surgery went off without a hitch, and two days later she was discharged from the hospital.

Before she left the hospital, a physician came into her room to change the dressing on her wound. He didn't wash his hands or put on gloves.

"I knew he should have put on gloves. I should have said something, but I didn't," lamented Maureen. "He just seemed to be rushing through his day."

As Johanna prepared to leave, she found the old dressing in her bed. It was covered with blood and betadine, an antiseptic solution. She held it up and said to Maureen, "Do you see how little I matter to these people? Please get me home while I'm still alive."

Her first few days at home were uneventful other than visits from a nurse and a physical therapist.

Her first post-operative visit was scheduled for five days after her discharge. On the day before, she started to complain that her shoulder was causing her more pain that it had at any point since the operation.

Her nurse and physical therapist examined Johanna and could find nothing wrong. They both agreed that it was likely due to the physical therapy, which Johanna had been working very hard at. The physical therapist told Johanna they would work more slowly.

Marie, who is also a nurse, gave her mother another examination later that evening.

"She did not at that time have any clinical signs of infection," Marie said. "She was not running a fever. The arm was no more swollen than it had been. It wasn't hot to the touch."

At home, Johanna had been recuperating in a bed in the downstairs of her house. Daniel and Maureen took turns staying with her. That night it was Maureen's turn.

Around 1 am Maureen heard Johanna crying. Marie was terrified. Her mother did not cry easily.

"Mommy, what's wrong?" Maureen asked.

"Oh, the pain, it just hurts so bad," Johanna said through tears.

Maureen and her father discussed what to do. Maureen felt that calling an ambulance and taking Johanna to a local hospital wouldn't do much good. She wanted her mom to be seen by the surgeon who had operated on her at the Hospital for Joint Diseases.

They decided to wait for the follow-up appointment that was set for 8 a.m. Johanna cried about the pain through the early morning hours. Maureen gave her pain medication. It had little effect.

When Johanna arrived for her follow-up appointment she was so weak that she could barely speak. She needed a wheel chair to make it into the surgeon's office.

When her surgeon removed the bandage on Johanna's shoulder, a green fluid started oozing out of her wound.

"The smell of that fluid, that disgusting smell will stay with me for the rest of my life," said Maureen. "It's hard to describe; it just smelled like a bunch of rotten eggs. My dad started to gag and had to leave the room."

The surgeon said, "Oh this is not good." He said that he would schedule her for surgery and clean out the wound.

Maureen took him aside and asked, "Will she lose her arm?"

The surgeon replied, "Oh, you worry too much."

In retrospect, that would have been a small price to pay.

Maureen and her dad accompanied her mother across the street to the urgent care center. Johanna was admitted and put on a gurney where another surgeon examined her.

"I have to cut this open," he said.

"Yeah, they are going to do that tonight," Maureen said.

"No," he replied. "She might not make it to surgery. This could kill her. I need to get as much of this rotten flesh as I can out of her now."

Maureen protested, asking why they couldn't wait for an operating room to open up so that her mother could have the operation under anesthetic.

"No, there isn't time," the surgeon said. "I cannot leave her. I can't admit her to the hospital and have her wait for the surgery. I have to take care of this now. I'm telling you her life is in danger."

Maureen told her father to leave the room, that she didn't want to him to see what was coming. Johanna then told Maureen to leave, but Maureen refused, insisting she'd stay with her mom through the end.

4

With Maureen holding Johanna down, the surgeon cut open the wound and squeezed on the arm to get the fluid to come out.

Johanna kicked and screamed, begging Maureen to make the surgeon stop.

"Mommy, I'm sorry," Maureen cried. "But we need to do this. They said you could die."

Maureen doesn't recall how long it took the surgeon to finish. When it was done, both Johanna and Maureen's clothes were covered with the green fluid.

Later that evening Johanna had a second operation to clean out the infection.

Maureen met the surgeon afterward to ask how the operation went.

"It went great," he replied. "We cleaned everything up. We got the infection out, it's been cut out of her. She's going to be good."

"Are you sure?" Maureen asked.

"I am," he replied.

Johanna came out of recovery and seemed to be doing well. Maureen and her father stayed with her that night.

The next day they decided to take shifts staying with Johanna. Her father took the first shift, and Maureen left to go home at 2 p.m. It was a 40-minute drive back to her house.

"I didn't even get into the house," Maureen recalled. "I was parking when my cell phone rang. It was my father. He said, 'Maureen, your mother can't breathe. You need to come back.'"

Her mother was being transferred into the intensive care unit by the time Maureen returned to the hospital. She contacted Marie, who arrived at the hospital just in time to see Johanna being put on a ventilator.

A few hours later Maureen and Marie sent their father home to get some rest. Not long after, the physician in charge of the intensive care unit gave Maureen and Marie grim news.

"I have to tell you, your mom has taken a turn for the worse," he said. "We got the labs back and she has multiorganism sepsis. She's running a fever in excess of 106."

"Should I call my dad back in?" Maureen asked.

"Yes. Anyone who wants to see her should come now," he said.

Maureen and Marie went in to see her.

"As we approached the bed we could feel the heat coming off of her," Marie said.

Against the odds, Johanna pulled through.

One of the bacteria that infected Johanna was Methicillin-resistant Staphylococcus aureus (MRSA). It is an especially dangerous type of bacteria because it is highly resistant to many antibiotics. However, MRSA is not difficult to prevent with proper screening, sanitizing surfaces, and hand washing.

While Marie believed that it was possible that her mom contracted the infection as a result of the physician not washing his hands before changing the dressing, she thought it far more likely that her mom was exposed to MRSA in the operating room.

"As a former operating room nurse myself, for the infection to have been that virulent, I think something had to have been contaminated in the operating room," she said. "For it to be MRSA, that implies the operating room wasn't cleaned properly."

The infection ravaged Johanna's nervous system and she began to lose the ability to move her body. By Valentine's Day she was unable to move from the neck down.

Eventually, Johanna wanted to return home. Maureen and Marie wanted that as well.

But Daniel was unable to accept that his wife would be paralyzed for the rest of her life. He insisted that they move her to a rehabilitation center. Arguments ensued between the daughters and their father.

Eventually Daniel told his daughters, "If your mother ever asks me why I didn't try something like rehab, I want to be able to say that I tried everything I could." They agreed to send her to a rehabilitation center.

After two weeks at the rehabilitation center, the physical therapists had a meeting with Johanna's family. They informed them that there was nothing they could do for Johanna. It was time to take her home.

But shortly before Johanna was to be taken home she started having trouble breathing again. An ambulance was called, and she was moved back to a hospital. She had contracted pneumonia.

On May 28, 2004, the Sunday before she was to go home, Johanna passed away from heart failure.

Daniel lived another five years, but he was never the same. He had retired a few years before Johanna's death. In retirement, his day began when Johanna got up in the morning—literally. He'd make coffee and wait until he heard her wake. Then he would ask her what she wanted for breakfast. During breakfast, they would discuss what they were going to do for the rest of the day.

"Once she was gone, he tried so hard to go on, but they were meant to be together," said Maureen. "The way she died—it was such a horrible shock for him. They were truly one and part of him was gone."

Marie felt betrayed by her profession. "As a nurse I had always given my best to take care of other people's parents. Why didn't these people take care of my mother?"

For four months she was unable to work as a nurse. She contemplated quitting, but eventually went back. Her mom's death has had a huge impact on how she practices as a nurse.

"I always felt that I was careful about hygiene when I dealt with patients. Now I'm fanatical about it," Marie said. "I think it has also made me more compassionate toward patients and their families. I know what it's like to be on the other side now."

For Maureen it meant fulfilling a promise she made to her mom.

"At one point my mom said to me, 'You have to make sure this doesn't happen to anyone else.'"

About a year later, she heard about the Committee To Reduce Infection Deaths (RID), a non-profit organization that works to make hospitals take more preventive measures against infection.

"When I heard that RID existed, I said to myself, well, that's what I'll try to do," said Maureen.

In the end, she did far more than try. She sold her business to volunteer for RID full time. While she finds the work rewarding, at times it is very difficult.

"We get too many calls from far too many families who have lost someone due to an infection from a hospital," she said.

Paying For Infection

There is plenty of blame to go around for Johanna's death, from the surgeon who changed her bandage, to the team that handled her shoulder-replacement surgery, to possibly even hospital administrators who may have tolerated lax hygiene procedures. But there is one culprit that is less obvious. It's Medicare, the federal government's health care program for seniors age 65 and older and the disabled.

Until recently, Medicare paid hospitals to treat infections that were acquired in the hospital. In effect, Medicare was paying hospitals to correct their errors.

"My mom's hospital bill for the broken shoulder was about $40,000," said Maureen. "At the time of her death, her bills were $600,000. It certainly looked like the hospital was compensated for its mistake...It appeared to me that the hospital was the only one who benefited from the infection."

She points out what would happen if other businesses were financially rewarded for their mistakes.

"If I bring my car in to have the oil changed, and the mechanic breaks the windshield, I don't pay for the windshield. The mechanic does." That provides the mechanic with the incentive to avoid making mistakes. But what if mechanics were paid to fix their mistakes? They would face little cost for being careless. Could there be any doubt that cars would be far more likely to suffer damage when customers brought them in for repairs?

Until recently, hospitals enjoyed exactly those incentives from Medicare. Since they faced no penalty if a patient contracted an infection while in the hospital, hospitals had far less incentive to institute measures to limit infections.

The Centers for Disease Control (CDC) has been tracking hospital-acquired infections since 1970. A decade later the CDC began developing a series of guidelines for the prevention of hospital-acquired infections. Yet in 2003 the Society for Healthcare Epidemiology of America reported that "there has been little evidence of [infection] control in most facilities" in the U.S.[1] According to the CDC, somewhere between 75,000 and 100,000 patients die from hospital-acquired infections every year. Despite this, Medicare's payment policy regarding infections did not begin to change until 2005.

The groups that lobby on behalf of hospitals had qualms about changing it. They argued, not unreasonably, that some hospital-acquired infections are not preventable. Nevertheless, ample research showed that preventive measures could reduce hospital-acquired infections. It wasn't until groups like the Committee to Reduce Infection Deaths, the Consumers Union and others began campaigning to change Medicare's policy that Congress acted.

In 2006 Congress passed legislation requiring Medicare to change its payment policies regarding preventable conditions acquired in a hospital. In 2007 and 2008 the Centers for Medicare and Medicaid Services (CMS) identified a list of such conditions that Medicare would stop paying for, including infections associated with the use of catheters and surgery.[2] However, CMS decided against including MRSA in that list. Groups representing hospitals successfully argued that (1) many catheter-related infections that Medicare was no longer paying for would account for many MRSA infections, and (2) it would be difficult to determine if the patient already had the infection before he was admitted to the hospital.[3] However, the change in policy does not appear to have diminished the number of hospital-acquired infections.[4] Although Medicare will not pay for infection related to use of a catheter, many hospitals get around this by failing to indicate that a catheter was related to an infection when they bill Medicare.[5]

Unfortunately, a hospital that fails to take proper precautions will harm more than just Medicare beneficiaries. Even people like Johanna, who are not eligible for Medicare, can be harmed.

But more often the people harmed by Medicare's policies *are* Medicare recipients themselves. Those who die, or suffer illness or financial hardship because of Medicare are the program's victims.

They are people like the disabled, who must endure a two-year waiting period to qualify for Medicare. They are also the disabled who, once on Medicare, are impoverished by the program's cost sharing.

They are people who are on the Medicare prescription drug program—Part D—and fall into the "donut hole" and do not have sufficient income to pay the full cost of their prescription drugs.

They are the patients who grow sicker because Medicare's policies result in inadequate treatment. They are also the patients who, because of Medicare's price controls, receive unnecessary treatment that causes harm.

Ironically, these are the people for whom Medicare is supposed to provide the most protection. When signing Medicare into law in 1965, President Lyndon Johnson said, "No longer will older Americans be denied the healing miracle of modern medicine. No longer will illness crush and destroy the savings that they have so carefully put away over a lifetime so that they might enjoy dignity in their later years."[6]

The notion that Medicare provides good care for all of its beneficiaries has crystallized into an article of faith among many advocates of a government-run health care system who argue that we should open up Medicare to everyone. As one advocacy group puts it, "There is a single solution to the challenges of providing coverage to the 50 million who are uninsured, that would curb out-of-control costs and provide a human standard of care to all who enter the medical system. That solution is an improved Medicare-for-All, single payer system."[7]

It's a hollow promise. Medicare can't even ensure those things for the people who are currently eligible for the program. Expanding it to cover all Americans would only exacerbate its shortcomings for patients.

Patients are not the only ones who struggle with Medicare. Medicare also impairs many physicians. An increasing number of physicians, especially ones who work in primary care, find it difficult to make ends meet with what Medicare pays. They have stopped taking new Medicare patients or have dropped out of the program altogether.

Medicare also interferes with physicians who try to provide better quality care. Medicare's payment system actually pays less to physicians who have longer visits with their Medicare patients than to physicians who have shorter visits. Thus, physicians who try to improve the care they provide by spending more time with Medicare patients are penalized.

Finally, Medicare can be used by powerful political interests to squash smaller competition. As we shall see in the case of physician-owned specialty hospitals, physicians who innovate in ways that threaten large, politically-connected medical providers will see politicians try to drive them out of business.

It would be tempting to say that many of these problems could be solved if taxpayers spent more money on Medicare. But chances are lack of money is not the problem. Rather, the problem is that Medicare dollars are spent ineffectively or, in the jargon of economists, "misallocated." Decisions on where and under what circumstances to spend the money are made in large part by members of Congress and bureaucrats at CMS. Were the decisions on how to spend Medicare funds left almost entirely with patients, the funds would be allocated in a much better way.

Ultimately, the victimization of patients and physicians is the result of too many Medicare-related decisions being taken out of their hands. Congress and CMS have tremendous influence over decisions such as which treatment to use, where the treatment should take place and the price to pay for it. Yet those decisions are best left with patients and their physicians since they have the greatest incentive to make correct decisions about their medical care given that they are the ones who will pay the greatest cost if wrong decisions are made. Putting those decisions in the hands of politicians and bureaucrats—that is, in the hands of people who pay little to no cost for being wrong—is a recipe for bad outcomes and, on occasion, disaster.

Political Neglect

So why does the fact that Congress and CMS control Medicare lead to some patients and physicians becoming victims of the program? The employees at CMS, of course, get their funding from Congress. Thus, they have ample incentive—i.e., keeping the funds flowing—to make decisions that keep members of Congress happy. As such, understanding why some patients and physicians are victimized by Medicare requires understanding what motivates representatives and senators. Federal lawmakers are chiefly motivated by a desire to get reelected, so they will design Medicare's policies in ways that enhance their reelection prospects. Groups that can influence lawmakers' reelection chances are likely to get good treatment under Medicare. Those groups that cannot are far more likely to be neglected by Congress.

There are many ways to influence the reelection chances of members of Congress. The most effective, obviously, is the ability to turn out thousands if not millions of people to vote on election day. There are other ways, of course, such as giving campaign contributions or providing politicians with specialized expertise so they can make more informed policy decisions. But nothing quite gets members' attention like the threat that a lot of unhappy voters will show up at the voting booth.

This explains why most of the elderly are pleased with Medicare. Seniors aged 65-74 vote at higher rates than almost any other demographic group. (They are exceeded only by those aged 55-64.) Furthermore, millions of seniors belong to the lobbying group known as the AARP, making it one of the most influential organizations in Washington, D.C., especially on the issue of Medicare.

Thus, members of Congress are going to pay attention to seniors' concerns on Medicare. They will shy away from making changes to

Medicare that upset the elderly. Rather, members of Congress often add new benefits to Medicare. (See Table 1 in the appendix for a list). Then, when Congress is not in session, representatives and senators will visit the retirement communities and senior centers in their districts and states and talk up the new benefits.

By contrast, Medicare's victims lack such political clout. For starters, they tend to lack the numbers necessary to effect elections. Very few people are even *potential* victims of Medicare in any year because very few people become seriously ill. For example, only a small percentage of beneficiaries each year were ill enough that the cost of their medication caused them to fall into Part D's donut hole. Or consider the disabled. At any given time there are about 1.2-1.8 million disabled people waiting to get on Medicare, a small number when compared to the over 42 million seniors already in the program. And, of course, not all of those disabled people will suffer hardship while in the waiting period. In short, the relatively small number of Medicare's victims limits the impact they might have on election day.

The fact that they are ill results in other political disadvantages. People who are ill are generally not engaging in the networking, meetings and other activities necessary to form effective political organizations. Since they often have relatively low incomes they are also not going to be contributing money to organizations that can lobby on their behalf.

A final disadvantage is that Medicare's victims may be completely unaware how Medicare policy has harmed them. A beneficiary harmed by overtreatment is probably unaware that Medicare may overpay for the treatment that caused the harm. When harm befalls a Medicare patient, he is likely to blame the physician, nurses and others who treated him. He is unlikely to realize that Medicare played a part, and chances are slim anyone will ever tell him. Obviously, people are not going to be politically active on issues about which they are completely ignorant.

Since Medicare's victims have little impact on the reelection prospects of members of Congress, Congress will neglect them. As a result, Medicare policies that cause harm can take years to change, if they ever change.

This is not necessarily a moral indictment of members of Congress. Congress doesn't neglect Medicare's victims because representatives and senators are indifferent or corrupt (although, granted, there is no shortage of corruption on Capitol Hill.) Rather, members of Congress face incentives and constraints just like everyone else. They won't spend much time catering to people who are of little to no help in pursing their most important objective, which is getting reelected. Instead they will focus their attention on people who are crucial to helping them avoid their biggest fear, getting booted from office. Surely, members of Congress have other goals as well, such as helping their constituents, changing public policy or achieving power and fame. But all of those other goals are contingent on winning reelection.

It follows that members of Congress will make policy that, whatever else it is supposed to accomplish, will cater to groups that are crucial to them winning another term in office. As history shows, Medicare was that type of politicized program from the start.

2. GREENSPRING VOTES

Greenspring is a 108 acre retirement community located in Fairfax County, Virginia, about a dozen miles from Washington, D.C. In January 2010, a small group of Greenspring residents agreed to discuss their experiences with Medicare.

For the most part, these seniors were college educated and had professional careers before retiring. They not only had Medicare, each one of them had private supplemental insurance, often called "Medigap," that paid for the cost sharing required by Medicare.

These seniors couldn't be classified as "Medicare's victims." Indeed, a few of them objected to the title of this book. For the most part, they were pleased with their Medicare experiences. One theme that emerged in the conversation was how well Medicare usually covered their expenses.

Ellen Gale grew up in both New York City and Richmond, Virginia before settling and raising a family in Northern Virginia. She achieved a master's degree in economics and worked in the field of both criminal justice and social services.

Not long ago she had a hip replacement. "That worked fine," she said. "[In general], Medicare's been prompt and fairly painless so I didn't have to think much about it."

Robbie Lentz expressed similar thoughts.

"I really don't remember negative experiences," she said. "I've had a pacemaker and various procedures and Medicare has been my primary insurer. I have positive feelings about it."

Robbie was a homemaker who raised three sons. She was born and raised in Cincinnati, Ohio and studied philosophy at Ohio Wesleyan

College and the University of Cincinnati, where she met her husband, Jack.

"We met in a Spanish class. She didn't think much of me," he joked.

Jack, who studied languages and accounting in college, is a World War II veteran who landed at Normandy on D-Day. He later pursued a career in the Central Intelligence Agency and, after retiring from the CIA, taught English as a second language.

A few years ago, he had triple-bypass surgery.

"It began with unease at night, no dramatic pains or anything," he said. "I thought it was a dill pickle I'd had for dinner that had caused the unrest."

The rooms in Greenspring have emergency cords that, when pulled, alert the security personnel. Jack pulled the cord in his apartment. The security personnel showed up promptly and, after checking Jack out, sent him to the Inova Health Center.

"When I got there, they told me I was in the midst of a heart attack. 'Let's get you to Fairfax Hospital,' they said," Jack said.

He had surgery within hours and was back home in about three days.

Regarding Medicare's role he said, "Everything was paid beautifully."

Another Greenspring resident, James Upp, had also gone through major heart surgery.

"I applied for Medicare about the time I needed an aortic valve replacement, post haste," said the Ohio State graduate and 22-year Air Force veteran. "Next thing I know, I'm scheduled for open-heart surgery at Fairfax Hospital. All within less than a month."

James spent four days in the hospital and then recuperated for six weeks at home.

"I came out like a peach," he said. "There was never a question of a charge. I got a statement from Fairfax Hospital. I saw nothing on the bill that troubled me."

James, because of his Air Force career, was covered in the military's TriCare system until he went on Medicare.

16

"Compared to TRICARE Prime, Medicare has been a blessing in proportion to what it can do," he said.

James's sentiment is one likely shared by millions of seniors. They have received care when they needed it, and Medicare and Medigap have paid the cost of that care with minimal hassle.

If President Lyndon Johnson were alive and listening to these Greenspring residents, he'd probably conclude Medicare was working out much as he had planned.

What's $400 Million Between Friends?

The standard history of the creation of Medicare focuses on the political acumen of Representative Wilbur Mills, then the chairman of the powerful Ways and Means Committee in the House of Representatives. There is little doubt that Mills was shrewd, with a keen sense of which way the political wind was blowing. Although he later received credit as the architect of Medicare, in the early 1960s he opposed Medicare due to a serious election threat in his Arkansas district from a candidate opposed to government expansion. And when, a few years later, he first expressed support for Medicare, he was less than keen on it covering anything beyond hospital services.[1]

From his perch as chairman of the powerful Ways and Means Committee in the House of Representatives, Mills won passage in 1960 of a far more modest health care program called Medical Assistance to the Aged (MAA). It provided state governments with the funding to help low-income seniors pay their medical bills. By the end of 1964, 39 states and the District of Columbia had enacted some version of MAA. But enrollment was tiny, with only 148,000 by 1963.[2] MAA never really got off the ground, probably because officials in the Department of Health, Education and Welfare—who supported a much larger health care program—actively undermined it.[3]

With the landslide election of President Johnson in 1964 resulting in expanded Democratic majorities in Congress, presumably Mills realized that the pressure to pass Medicare was about to become immense. Ultimately, Mills decided he could best control the outcome by taking control of the legislation. After a few months of hearings on the issue, Mills released a bill that surprised many observers. It included not only coverage of hospital services, but also the coverage of physician services included in a Republican alternative called "Bettercare," and coverage of the poor included in an American Medical Association alternative and supported by more liberal Democrats called "Eldercare" (and now called Medicaid.) By combining all three, Mills had co-opted most of the potential opposition to Medicare. It passed Congress with relative ease, and President Johnson signed the bill into law on July 30, 1965.

Yet, many of Mills actions were taken at the behest of President Johnson who by late 1964 was already having dinners and phone calls with Mills to impress upon him the importance of passing Medicare.

Tapes of Johnson's phone calls show that adding the physician component of Medicare was probably his idea. In early 1964, Mills told Johnson he was thinking about pushing a bill that included a Social Security cash benefit, Medicaid, and the hospital portion of what would ultimately become Medicare. "Johnson agreed and then upped the ante, saying 'I'd be for all three of those if you could put that fourth one [the physician component] in it.' Johnson was pushing for a bigger, more complete Medicare package, perhaps even physician coverage, while deferring to Mills on the details."[4]

After the 1964 election, Mills and Johnson had another conversation about Medicare. This time it was Mills who urged the importance of covering physician services. He "told Johnson…that he was afraid that legislation covering only hospital services would deeply disappoint elderly Americans, who were expecting much more. Mills recalled Johnson's reply: 'Well, do what you want to do about it, then, and develop it as you want to develop it.'"[5]

Mills would later say about adding physician service to Medicare, "We planned that, yes. Oh, yes."[6] They planned it not only as a way to co-opt Congressional Republicans into supporting the bill, but also as a way to improve Medicare's support among seniors. Including physicians' services would made it easier to pass the bill quickly since seniors would find Medicare much more appealing if it paid for visits to the doctor.

Moving Medicare through Congress more quickly was politically crucial for the president according to Johnson's point man on Medicare, Wilbur Cohen:

> It was the end of January, probably the beginning of February 1965 when [Johnson] called all of the people who were handling legislation...together...And he said..., "Now look. I've just been reelected by the overwhelming majority. And I just want to tell you that every day while I'm in office, I'm going to lose votes. I'm going to alienate somebody...We've got to get this legislation fast. You've got to get it during my honeymoon."[7]

Johnson also assuaged Mill's concern that adding physician services would add $400 to $500 million to the cost of Medicare. "I'll take care of that, I'll do that," Johnson told Mills. Later, Johnson compared it to an old Texas judge who was told "that he might've abused the Constitution and he said, 'What's the Constitution between friends?' And I say, tell Wilbur that 400 million's not going to separate us friends when it's for health..."[8] Many commentators have suggested that Johnson actively worked to hide the true cost of Medicare to facilitate its passage. It's unclear if he did, although politicians always find it easier to sell the public on new programs when the proposed cost is relatively low. Nevertheless, actuaries in the Johnson Administration badly underestimated the cost of Medicare. The initial estimates said that the hospital portion of Medicare would cost $9 billion in 1990; the actual cost was $66 billion.[9]

The coverage of hospital services became known as Medicare Part A. Mills financed Part A using a "trust fund," which would collect the new Medicare payroll tax and pay out benefits. Participating in Part A is all but mandatory. Seniors can only decline Part A benefits if they forego Social Security benefits as well.[10]

Bettercare became known as Medicare Part B, and it covered outpatient services such as doctor visits, ambulance services, medical supplies and X-rays. About 75 percent of Part B's costs are financed primarily through income taxes.

For the benefit structure of Medicare, Mills borrowed heavily from Blue Cross/Blue Shield practice at the time. Part A required beneficiaries to pay a deductible for the first 60 days of hospitalization; in 2015, that deductible had grown to $1,260. The next 90 days in the hospital required daily co-payments from beneficiaries; in 2015 days 61-90 required a daily co-payment of $315 and days 91-150 a co-payment of $630. Beneficiaries are responsible for all costs beyond day 150.

Part B also required a deductible, albeit a much smaller one; in 2015 it was $147. Beneficiaries would also have to pay 20 percent of the cost of any service provided under Part B. Finally, beneficiaries would have to pay a monthly premium for Part B; in 2015 it was about $104.90.* Monthly premiums currently finance about 25 percent of Part B.

In one other political move, Mills garnered the support of insurance companies by allowing them to cover Medicare's cost sharing. Prior to Medicare, health insurance companies sold private insurance to seniors. By one estimate, 60 percent of seniors had health insurance by 1962, although the quality of that coverage is a matter of debate.[11] Health insurance companies would lose that business with the enactment of Medicare. To compensate, Mills permitted insurance companies to sell "supplemental insurance" that is now usually referred to as Medigap. It covers Medicare's cost sharing including Part A deductibles and co-payments and the Part B deductibles and the 20 percent of Part B services. Today, about 75 percent of seniors purchase some form of Medigap coverage.[12]

---

* Premiums are now based on income. Those seniors at the very top of the income scale now pay slightly higher premiums.

In some ways, Johnson and Mill's strategy was brilliant. It limited opposition to Medicare and maximized support especially among seniors, resulting in its ultimate passage. But, in other ways, it was irresponsible if not dishonest. By throwing caution to the wind on costs, Johnson was putting a substantial financial burden on future generations. He was also setting in motion a powerful political constituency that would often demand more from Medicare, thereby making subsequent attempts to rein in its costs that much more difficult.

Inconveniences

Of course, not all Greenspring residents were so pleased with their Medicare experiences. Medicare and Medigap do have gaps in coverage, and sometimes those gaps can result in substantial out-of-pocket spending. Take another member of the Greenspring group, Don Giles. In 2008, Giles, a Naval Academy graduate, came back from a summer vacation in terrible pain, unable to move his head and neck.

"They took me to the hospital and found out that my blood pressure was down, my glucose level was down. I was a hell in a hand-basket, so to speak," he said. "They couldn't figure it out, so they kept me there for a couple of weeks."

After many tests, the diagnosis was severe dehydration and acute arthritis.

"Medicare picked up everything they said they were going to. But the rest [of the bill] went to the secondary insurance, and they didn't," he complained. Don seemed a bit annoyed and perhaps disappointed, but not angry—although he could have been forgiven if he had been.

"We were left with a $1,500 bill to pay," he said.

After paying the bill, Don switched to a Medigap policy that in the future would cover such costs.

Jack recently had two cases of melanoma on the back of his neck treated, one at Arlington Hospital and the next at Fairfax Hospital.

"And that's worked well," Jack said. "My only complaint with that is to get in the hospital, you have to re-do a full blood scan, the whole works."

Under the hospital rules, a patient must have the tests re-done if more than thirty days have passed since the last time the tests were conducted.

"I've always complained because in a couple of cases it was close to thirty," Jack said. "I said, 'This is expensive.'...I mean this was unreasonable; those expenses are not cheap."

In one instance, Jack had had a physical in between hospital visits, but the hospital wouldn't accept that in lieu of the blood tests either.

Yet Medicare and Medigap still came through for Jack.

"They paid for it, so it didn't cost me anything," he said. Repeating the tests "was just the annoying feature of that experience."

Mary Noon had a more dramatic story of repetitive care.

Mary Noon was born in Cincinnati, Ohio and grew up in New Haven, Connecticut. She worked as a secretary most of her life, eventually being recruited by the General Services Administration. She worked her way up and became secretary for the General Counsel at GSA. The General Counsel of GSA took her to the office of General Counsel of the Navy, where she stayed for nineteen years.

A few years ago, Mary spent four days in the hospital for a bleeding colon. "The doctor's said, 'It popped,'" she said.

She was on a liquid diet for three days and then, on the fourth day, she received a colonoscopy to determine if her colon was healing. She was sent home on the fourth day.

"I didn't have to pay anything for it," she said.

But one aspect of the way her physicians behaved bothered her.

"The first day I was in the hospital my doctor came to see me," she said. "The second day walked in one of his partners; the third day walked in [another] of his partners; the fourth day walked in [another] of his partners. And they all did the same thing. They stood at the bottom of the bed...and stared at me like I had two heads and repeated exactly what my doctor had told me [on the first day]. They think it was just lack of blood to that section of the colon, it burst out, and that was what the bleeding was. And when they got me clear, they'd do a colonoscopy."

None of the doctors, according to Mary, spent more than 10 minutes speaking to her. At first it seemed like a minor annoyance to her. Then she got the "explanation of benefits" from Medicare and her Medigap policy.

"I got a bill from both Medicare and Blue Cross/Blue Shield for four doctor's visits!" she exclaimed. "They'd stand there, repeat this stuff, look at me, never come near me, never took a pulse, never looked at me like I was a human being."

"Did they read your chart?" asked Ellen.

"They must have before they came in because they all repeated exactly what my doctor had told me the very first day," replied Mary.

"How much were the individual bills?" Jack asked.

"They were upwards of $2,000, each one," Mary said. "Just to stand there and talk to me."

"That sounds ridiculous," said James. He then recounted the six years of intensive care his late wife had for emphysema, heart failure and chronic obstructive pulmonary disease. She was usually treated by a group of practitioners.

"One of them, the Northern Virginia Pulmonary Associates, had eight. And those were the eight best doctors I think I've run into as a group that treated her over that period of time," he said. "But the point is, when they would treat her, it would be an inpatient visit for $175. That's what struck me, when you said $2,000."

"Oh yeah, they were in the thousands, each one," replied an exasperated Mary. "It wasn't even a consultation because I said nothing! I was waiting for (the doctors to explain) some sort of magical solution! They didn't do anything. They didn't even take my temperature."

"I got $175 worth every time then!" James chuckled.

In the grand scheme of things, these experiences with Medicare aren't that serious. While these seniors faced inconveniences and, in the case of Don, a significant financial burden, none of them can be classified as victims. To the extent that these seniors are representative of Greenspring residents, then Greenspring residents get rather good medical treatment under Medicare.

Greenspring Votes

So why do Greenspring residents receive relatively good treatment under Medicare? Perhaps it is the result of excellent hospitals and physicians. Inova Hospital, which many Greenspring residents use, is ranked as one of the top hospitals in Virginia. There are many top-notch physicians in the area as well.

But that's a partial explanation at best. Patients on Medicaid, the health insurance program for the poor, might have much different experiences. According to one study, about 24 percent of physicians in Virginia refuse to see Medicaid patients because Medicaid's reimbursement rates are too low.[13]

Medicare pays better than Medicaid and one reason is that seniors vote at rates higher than just about any other group as displayed in Table 2.1.

Table 2.1 Voter Turnout for Seniors vs. All Citizens		
	Age 65 and Over	All Citizens
2012	72.0%	61.8%
2010	60.7%	45.5%
Source: Census Bureau		

Seniors vote at a rate of 10 percentage points higher than the general population in a presidential election. In an "off-year" election like 2010, the difference is an even larger 15 percentage points.

Greenspring numbers are also impressive. There are about 2,000 residents in Greenspring. In 2012, 1,407 of them voted for a turnout rate of 70.4 percent, and in 2010, 1,304 voted for a turnout rate of 65.2 percent.[14]

Greenspring's numbers are even more impressive when turnout for the U.S. House of Representatives is examined. Greenspring, which is in the 11th House District in Virginia, puts the rest of Fairfax County to shame.

Table 2.2: Turnout for Presidential vs. Off-Year Election in Viriginia House District 11			
	2012	**2010**	**Difference**
Greenspring	1,407	1,304	-7.3%
Fairfax County	251,955	139,076	-44.8%
Source: Viriginia State Board of Elections			

While only about seven percent fewer people voted at Greenspring in 2010 when compared to 2012, nearly 45 percent fewer people did in the entire Fairfax County portion of the 11the district. Greenspring is going to be an important source of votes for anyone running for office in that area of Virginia. Politicians will show up regularly there to try to win the support of the residents. Congressman Gerry Connolly, who represents the 11th District, has visited Greenspring at least eight times between 2009 and 2012.

Greenspring residents receive good coverage from Medicare because their voting behavior gives them political clout. If they have serious problems with Medicare, it won't be long before Representative Connolly hears about it. In turn, Connolly knows that to maximize the support he receives from Greenspring means keeping the seniors there satisfied with their Medicare coverage and, if possible, expanding the benefits they receive under Medicare. One isn't going to find many complaints about Medicare among Greenspring residents.

Exactly how many retirement communities there are in the U.S. is not known. However, retirement communities that include medical facilities like nursing homes—known as Continuing Care Retirement Communities—number about 2,000. Senior centers—places where seniors can gather for socialization and support—number about 11,000. Not only do seniors vote, because so many live in retirement communities and visit senior centers, they are easy to organize should the need arise. With that degree of political power, seniors are seldom denied the services they want in Medicare.

Unfortunately, this comes at a cost. As the Baby Boomers head for retirement, Medicare will consume ever-larger portions of the federal budget and the economy. In 1975, Medicare consumed about 3.9 percent of the federal budget and about one percent of gross domestic product (GDP). In 2014, those numbers were 14.4 percent and 2.9 percent, respectively. By 2035, Medicare could consume 17.1 percent of the federal budget and 4.3 percent of GDP.[15] Unless substantial change is made to Medicare, taxpayers will have a harder and harder time paying for it in the years to come.

Another consequence is that Congress members' attention on Medicare is largely consumed by the concerns of seniors with political clout. As such, Medicare beneficiaries who are sick and lack political clout will often suffer. Any change to Medicare must find a way to ameliorate this problem too.

3. Medicare's Second-Class Citizens

Meeting Jeff Fox is a bit like stepping into a time warp. His long, somewhat stringy brown hair and bushy beard suggest an era that ended over four decades ago.

His story of how he came to be in his wheelchair is also something of a "trip."

Born and raised in Wisconsin, he graduated from high school and was apprenticing to be a carpenter in 1977.

"I was riding my bike on a nice spring morning and got hit by a car three times in one day," he says.

Seriously?

"I was nineteen years old, I was indestructible," he said.

Jeff was riding his sister's Schwinn, which he had borrowed, from his place to his parents' home, where he had left his brand new, $700 Fuji bicycle. When he got there, he discovered that the front tire on the Fuji was flat, and he had no way to fix it. So, he took the front tire off the Schwinn and put it on the Fuji. He then strapped the front tire of the Fuji to his back.

Jeff had the first accident on his way back to his home.

"The first time I got hit in the second lane of traffic," he said. "When I woke up there was a car bumper right above my head and when I turned to the right, there was the front tire," he said.

Jeff wasn't seriously hurt, and he and the driver agreed not to get the police involved as long as the driver agreed to pay for any damage to Jeff's bicycle.

"I went home and my bike was fine," Jeff said. "I thought, 'Gee whiz, it's a beautiful day for a bike ride.'" He strapped the Fuji tire on his back again in order to take it to the bicycle store.

"So I rode a few blocks from my home, and a girl pulling out of a restaurant did the same thing," he said.

Again, Jeff landed on the ground with the front tire of the car a few feet from his head. Just like the first accident, Jeff and the driver decided not to involve the police and the driver agreed to pay for the damage to his bike.

Jeff got back on his bicycle. He was riding on the sidewalk of a bridge, and when he reached the end of the sidewalk a car pulled out in front of him.

"I t-boned the car, did a head plant on the hood, and the bicycle and I landed 10 feet on the other side of the car. My spine was completely severed."

The accident had severed the spinal cord between his sixth and seventh vertebrae. He was paralyzed from the waist down.

Jeff spent nearly eleven weeks in the hospital recuperating. They put him in a ward with old stroke patients instead of people closer to his age.

"They didn't want me to get depressed because I was never going to walk again. The other young people, they were going to get better. In the minds of the hospital folks, it was better for me if I was with old and dead stroke patients who couldn't talk," Jeff said.

Did it work?

"Yeah, I ran away from the hospital," he said.

He contacted an old girlfriend from high school who agreed to meet him at the door that led to the hospital kitchen. He was able to slide out of his wheelchair and into the front seat of her car. The girlfriend asked if his wheelchair folded up so they could put it in the car. Jeff said that it probably did. She then asked him how to fold it up.

"I don't know," replied Jeff. "I've never been in a chair before!"

As Jeff and his former girlfriend struggled with the chair, a security guard walked around the corner.

"Are you guys having some problems?" he asked.

"We said, yeah, we can't get this damn chair to fold up," Jeff said.

The security guard showed them how to pull the pin underneath the wheelchair and fold it up. He then asked, "Would you like me to put this in the trunk for you?"

"And we said, sure, that would be wonderful!" said Jeff. "And so off we went. We went to a bar and had a good time."

Jeff has been on Social Security Disability Insurance (SSDI) most of his adult life. However, at various times, he has volunteered as an accountant for his church and worked as a director at a home for the disabled. He currently volunteers with ADAPT, a grass-roots organization of disabled people that fight for disabled rights and are willing to use civil disobedience.

He married his wife, Rudy, in 1982 and had a daughter that same year. She has given him two grandsons. They live in a small house in Gordon, Wisconsin. At the initiative of Rudy, years ago they began helping abused women and children, at times willing to shelter them in their home

Two years after going on Social Security Disability Insurance (SSDI), Jeff went on Medicare. However, he is not one of Medicare's victims and for good reason.

He avoids using it if he can, referring to it as "MediScare."

"MediScare has a lot of goofy rules," he said. "And if you don't do it exactly by the letter, they're going to deny you."

Medicare has made it more difficult for Jeff to get a new wheelchair. Years ago, he needed to get an authorization from a physician, and then he could go to the medical supply store and place an order. Not long ago, the procedures changed

Jeff griped, "I was telling the people at the store what I wanted, and they told me, 'You have to go back to the doctor and have him schedule you an appointment with the occupational therapist so he can measure you for your chair.'"

How long has he been in a wheelchair?

"About thirty-three years," Jeff said.

Doesn't he know what kind of chair he needs at this point?

"You would think so. This long, this high," he said as he motioned with his hands.

Jeff went through the hoops only to find out that the store wanted him to pay for the new chair up front.

"They were having so many problems getting paid by MediScare, the only way they would order me a wheelchair was if I came up with the whole $2,600 first. Then they would bill Medicare for it, and Medicare would give me back the 80 percent," he said. "I said, 'Come on, I'm disabled! I was hoping we could set up a payment plan for the $600 [the 20 percent copay]. Now you want me to come up with another $2,000? It's not going to happen. I don't have that kind of cash."

Jeff decided it wasn't worth the effort. Instead, he turned to Wisconsin's wheelchair recycling program.

"So I'd go down there and buy a chair," he said. "I paid $250 for my chair and the seat cushion. It was out of my own pocket. MediScare didn't pay a dime. If I had ordered a chair through a supplier, my MediScare payment would have been $600."

Another unusual feature about his wheelchair is that it doesn't have the standard, gray-colored tires. Instead, Jeff uses bicycle tires.

"The gray ones are $32 a piece," he said. "My co-pay would be about $6. Well, that's how much a bike tire costs."

Making it difficult to get a wheelchair is not the only frustration Jeff suffers. Medicare also interferes with how he goes to the bathroom.

"Originally, I would get my leg bags and my bed bags and my Texas catheters as I needed them. I would get a gross [144] of Texas catheters. All of sudden I was told I could only get those thirty at a time," he said. "I'm sorry, but I'm only going to use them one at a time as I need them. It's not like you're going to get addicted to Texas catheters."

Jeff also has to manually stimulate his bowel movements.

"I used to use latex gloves for that," he said. "All of a sudden I was told that I couldn't get latex gloves anymore. I asked why I couldn't, and I was told that those were only for people with hemophilia or blood diseases. I was denied latex gloves because I didn't have a blood disorder."

Most of us take for granted that we will be able to meet our bathroom needs as we see fit. But most of us would quickly feel the indignity if a government program were to suddenly interfere, telling us which products we can and cannot use to urinate and defecate.

Fortunately, Jeff has only suffered indignities with Medicare. Other disabled people are not so lucky. Many must endure a two-year waiting period to qualify for Medicare and if they are unable to afford health care during that time, the wait can be a harrowing one. Once on Medicare, they must face the program's cost sharing. That can mean high levels of medical debt for those disabled with low incomes and no means of covering Medicare's cost sharing.

A Curious Feature

If one of the purposes of a government health care program is protecting the sick and the poor, then Medicare's treatment of the disabled fails in some substantial ways. Its flaws can be traced back to the legislation that allowed the disabled access to Medicare in 1973. The historical record suggests that Congress didn't put a good deal of thought into how the disabled would fare on Medicare when it passed the legislation. That is probably due to the fact that the main purpose of the bill was actually welfare reform.

By the early 1970s, government welfare costs at both the state and federal level had exploded, thanks largely to changes made during President Lyndon Johnson's "Great Society" in the mid-1960s. For example, the Aid to Dependent Children program, begun in 1935, didn't reach $1 billion in cost until 1960. A mere eight years later, the cost had ballooned to $1.5 billion.[1] By the late 1960s, members of Congress, state governments, and many interest groups were clamoring for "welfare reform."

At that time, though, welfare reform meant spending *more* money on welfare programs, not less. In 1969, the administration of President Richard Nixon put forward a welfare reform bill that included a national guaranteed minimum income of $1,600 annually to a family of four (about $10,320 in 2014 dollars.) The Senate Finance Committee held a hearing on the bill in 1970, but the bill never made it out of committee due to differences among the members.

In late 1970 and into 1971, the House of Representatives held its own hearings on the matter. Later in 1971, it passed a bill that included an annual guaranteed minimum income of $2,400 (about $14,028 in 2014 dollars). The bill also increased Social Security benefits and made changes to Medicare, including adding the disabled to the program.

The Senate took up the House bill in 1972. The reason the U.S. does not have a guaranteed minimum income came down to $200. The Nixon Administration supported the House bill, including the $2,400 guaranteed minimum income. However, it refused to go any higher. Senator Abraham Ribicoff, a liberal representing Connecticut, insisted on $2,600 and refused to go any lower. Many of Ribicoff's liberal allies in the Senate supported his position. Many conservative senators representing southern states wanted nothing to do with any guaranteed minimum income. The two groups combined had enough power to block the bill.

In the end, many senators decided passing the Social Security and Medicare portions of the bill would be better than passing nothing at all, so they succeeded in removing all of the welfare provisions, including the guaranteed minimum income. In late 1972, the Senate passed the bill, the House soon followed suit, and President Nixon signed it.

The legislation required the disabled to endure a two-year waiting period between the time they qualified for SSDI and when they would be admitted to Medicare. It was a curious feature given that, presumably, the reason for giving the disabled access to Medicare was that they were sick and needed considerable help affording their medical bills. Why make them wait two years for help that they might need immediately?

Cost was likely one factor. At the time, Elliot Richardson, then-Secretary of the Dept. of Health, Education and Welfare, testified that the cost was "the chief roadblock" to giving the disabled access to Medicare.[2] A waiting-period would, theoretically, lower the cost in that some disabled persons might regain their health before they ever entered Medicare.

Congress was also worried about minimizing "crowd out" and disability fraud. Some members of Congress were concerned that if the disabled with private insurance had quick access to Medicare they would drop their private insurance for Medicare, a phenomenon known as "crowd out." Further, they wanted to "ensure that only those with long-lasting disabilities were given access to the benefits. Congress was also concerned about creating greater incentives for workers to exit the workforce and apply for SSDI benefits."[3]

Congress has made some exceptions to the two-year waiting period. People who are suffering from kidney failure or amyotrophic lateral sclerosis (Lou Gherig's Disease) do not have to endure the waiting period. Nevertheless, at any given time between 1.2 million and 1.8 million disabled people are enduring the two-year waiting period for Medicare, depending on the estimate.[4] However, referring to it as a "two-year" waiting period is somewhat misleading, because the waiting period begins on the day a person qualifies for SSDI. It usually takes at least five months to qualify for that, so the actual wait for Medicare is closer to 29 months.

That, of course, assumes that an applicant is approved for SSDI on his or her first try. About 75 percent of applicants are denied the first time. In some extreme cases that results in a much longer wait. A Texas woman with multiple sclerosis and rheumatoid arthritis waited four years for Medicare to start because she was repeatedly denied SSDI.[5]

Sean Plomann waited four years as well, even though he was given access to SSDI on his first attempt.

Scars That Light Up

Sean Plomann's difficulties with Medicare can be traced back to 1989, when he was 12 years old.

At that time, Sean began experiencing pain in his left leg and developed a slight limp. He also began coming home from school increasingly fatigued, a disturbing sign for a child who had been energetic to the point of being hyperactive.

His mom, Laura, took him to a pediatrician, who ordered an X-ray on his leg. The radiologist who examined the X-ray said that Sean was fine.

But Laura wasn't convinced. Her experience as an oncology nurse, perhaps combined with her "mother's intuition," compelled her to take Sean back to the pediatrician two weeks later.

"I just kept getting a sinking feeling in my stomach that something was wrong," she said.

On the second visit, the pediatrician referred Sean to a pediatric orthopedist. This new physician ordered additional X-rays, and after examining them, broke the news to Sean and Laura.

"I remember him saying, 'There's no way to sugar coat this. Sean has cancer. We just have to figure out which one,'" Sean recalled.

A biopsy was performed, and in January 1990 Sean was diagnosed with Ewing's Sarcoma in his left femur.

"It affects the lower extremities," Sean explained. "People who are likely to get it are young, white males, often in adolescence."

Sean would need an operation to remove his left femur and would then undergo chemotherapy. He did not want to lose his leg, so the physicians agreed to take the bone in the back of his left shin, the fibula, and put it where his femur had been.

The chemotherapy rid Sean of his cancer. At age 33, when this interview was conducted, the cancer had not returned.

But the operation that put his fibula in his thigh proved a disaster. The femur is the heaviest, thickest bone in the human body, designed to carry a human's weight. By contrast, the fibula is a thin bone. Its primary function is to provide an attachment for leg muscles.

Sean refers to the new bone that was in his thigh dismissively, as a "twig." It would break 10 times in the next eight years. His left leg became about three inches shorter than his right, necessitating a lift to be put on his left shoe.

When Sean was 17, surgeons broke the fibula in Sean's thigh in an attempt to get his left leg to be the same length as his right one. He had to wear a contraption on his leg known as an "Orthofix" that was supposed to help the bone grow back together.

"I had it on for a year and a half, but the bone wasn't filling in," Sean said. "I made the decision to have it taken out, and they put in a metal rod to hold the bone together."

Sean tried to hold down some part-time jobs during this time, in the hopes that they might get his mind off the pain. "That only made the pain worse," he said.

Sean qualified for SSDI in 1998. He was now entering the two-year waiting period for Medicare with no access to other insurance. His parents divorced when Sean was in his late teens, leaving them at loose ends for a while. It wasn't just a matter of not being able to afford insurance for Sean; they were unable to afford visits to the pain clinic at the University of Illinois-Chicago, which cost about $150 plus the cost of a prescription for pain medication.

Although most people on SSDI wait about two years to qualify for Medicare, for Sean it turned into a four-year ordeal. While he qualified for SSDI in 1998, for reasons that no one can seem to explain, it wasn't until 2002 that he qualified for Medicare Part B, the portion of Medicare that would pay for his visits to the pain clinic. One Medicare expert suggested that Sean at one point might have wanted to maximize his SSDI benefits and, thus, inadvertently opted out of Medicare Part B so that the Part B premiums were not deducted from his SSDI checks. Sean isn't sure, although concedes that it is possible.

Sean's memory of this time is somewhat hazy stemming from the pain in his left leg. Without medication, the pain from his left leg was nearly unbearable. For nearly four years Sean endured what he calls a "constant, dull, throbbing, aching" pain in his leg.

"A lot of the time it felt like I was having my surgeries all over again, but this time it was without any anesthetic and without any pain meds," said Sean. "There were rarely any breaks in the pain."

The scars from the operation only added to Sean's misery. Sean described them as "lighting up."

Pain medication was expensive, at least relative to alcohol. So, to deaden the pain, Sean drank.

"It started out with beer. I would go through a 40-ounce beer, and I didn't care if it was cheap. The cheaper the better, since I didn't have a lot of money. I just wanted to dull the pain."

Eventually, Sean developed a tolerance for beer, so he moved on to whiskey. As best as he can recall, he would go through a fifth of whiskey in under a week. By the end of the waiting period, he was occasionally using marijuana, provided by friends.

"I never wanted to drink to control the pain," Sean said. "I didn't have a lot of choice."

Sean managed to apply to college at the University of Illinois-Chicago, and he was admitted in the Fall of 2002. He qualified for the university health care plan for students, enabling him to pay for pain medication. A few months earlier he had entered Medicare Part B and was able to pay for visits to the pain clinic. Able to get proper pain treatment, Sean soon stopped drinking. But it had an after effect.

"My mom and my younger brother thought I was an alcoholic, that I was drinking just to drink," Sean said. "I tried to explain to them why I was drinking, but nobody really believed me. It took a while to convince them that I was just drinking for the pain."

Sean completed his Bachelor's Degree at the University of Illinois-Chicago and is now close to finishing a Master's Degree. In between, though, he decided to have his left leg amputated. Doing so got rid of most the pain and also eliminated the chances his cancer would ever return, at least in his left leg.

He still struggles with pain from phantom leg syndrome, but that is not as severe and is controlled with pain medication. But the experience has changed Sean's personality. He suffers from depression and an anxiety condition.

"He used to be such a happy kid, and it's sad to see him be such a worry wart all the time now," said Laura.

Lack of Data on Lack of Insurance

Surprisingly, there is scant research on how many beneficiaries in Medicare's two-year waiting period endure hardships similar to Sean's.

Both the Commonwealth Fund[6] and the Christopher Reeve Paralysis Foundation[7] have produced reports telling the stories of other people who have struggled during the waiting period. Yet, the reports are, at best, anecdotal. They don't tell us how many people are unable to afford medical treatment and suffer debilitating health effects or die because they can't afford medical treatment while in the waiting period.

One estimate found that about 16,000 people die annually while on the Medicare waiting period.[8] Yet, it reveals little else. Did they die because they lacked health insurance to help pay for medical treatment? It is a tricky question because many people who apply for SSDI have illnesses such as cancer and heart disease that kill regardless of insurance. To know what impact health insurance has on those who die while in the waiting period requires knowing both their insurance status and their health status. So far, no study has examined that.

Three studies have examined the insurance status of the disabled in the waiting period. Their findings are summarized in Table 3.1.

Unfortunately, two of the studies listed in the table have serious limitations. The Riley study used data from 1994-1996, and so may be out of date.[9] The Short-Weaver study examines only people ages 55-64 who entered the two-year waiting period and probably cannot be generalized to the entire population that is in the waiting period.

Table 3.1: Insurance State of Disabled During Medicare Two-Year Wait Period			
Study	Uninsured	Medicaid	Other*
Riley	25.8%	21.8%	52.4%
Short	24.0%	17.1%	58.9%
Livermore (1-12 months)	23.3%	17.1%	59.6%
Livermore (13-24 months)	17.4%	20.5%	62.1%
*Other includes coverage such as private insurance and military coverage.			

The Livermore study examines the entire disabled population in the waiting period and uses more up-to-date data.[10] It also breaks down the data on insurance coverage into the first and second years of the waiting period.

This study yields some surprising findings. For example, under federal law an employee can continue on his employer's insurance plan for six months after leaving his job. Assuming that some of the disabled made use of that option, we would expect the number of uninsured in the waiting period to increase over time, as those six months ran out. But the Livermore data shows that the number of uninsured actually decline, from about 23 percent in the first year to 17 percent in the second. Medicaid may account for part of that, as the number on Medicaid increases from the first to second year.

Unfortunately, the Livermore study doesn't reveal how long people are uninsured for during the waiting period. How many people uninsured during the first year are the same people who uninsured during the second? Do people in the waiting period experience frequent changes in insurance status, sometimes enduring brief periods of being uninsured? Or are more of the uninsured like Sean Plomann who are uninsured during the full time? We don't yet have answers to such crucial questions.

There is some data about disabled persons' access to medical care during the wait period. The Riley study found that those who were uninsured during the waiting period were more likely than the insured to need care that they could not afford, need a prescription drug they couldn't get and delay seeking medical care because of the cost.[11]

The Livermore study found that about 10 percent of those in the first year of the waiting period needed care but were unable to get it; that dropped to just under eight percent in the second year. About 21 percent delayed getting care due to cost in the first year, dropping to just over 18 percent in the second year.[12] Unfortunately, the Livermore study did not break out that data by insurance status, so it is impossible to know the extent to which being uninsured accounted for those access problems.

The data also fails to answer even more serious questions, such as did the beneficiaries who were unable to access needed care experience serious health effects like severe pain? If they were unable to receive medical care because of cost, did their condition worsen? If so, did it worsen to the point that they had to be admitted to the hospital?

Because of inadequate research, getting a good, accurate picture of the experiences of those who must endure Medicare's two-year waiting period is simply not possible. Fortunately, explaining why the two-year waiting period has not been changed since it was first instituted in 1973 is considerably easier.

Waiting Period versus Donut Holes

Estimates of the cost of eliminating the waiting period vary, from about $5.3 billion to about $13.9 billion annually.[13] Another estimate suggests that while eliminating the waiting period would cost Medicare even more, the government would save money on the Medicaid program.[14]

Representative Gene Green of Texas has been trying to eliminate the waiting period since 2002. Each Congressional session, he introduces the "Ending the Medicare Disability Waiting Period Act." First elected in 1992, Green noticed that over the years he had a constituency that would benefit greatly if the waiting period was eliminated.

"I have a blue collar district in Houston," he said while sitting in his D.C. office. "We have refineries, chemical plants—people are outside, doing hard work…we've had lots of cases in our district where people get hurt and going through the disability system is difficult. And even when you get your award, you have to wait 24 months for Medicare.

"I thought our chance was during the health care bill [in 2009]," said Green.

The odds seemed good as Green wasn't the only one pushing for an end to the Medicare waiting period. When Congress first started discussing an overhaul of the health care system in late 2008 (what would later be known as "ObamaCare"), Senator Max Baucus of Montana released a "white paper" on reform that called for "eliminating the requirement that disabled individuals wait two years to enroll in Medicare."[15] As chair of the Senate Finance Committee, which has jurisdiction over Medicare in the Senate, Baucus was going to have a great deal of influence over the final health care bill and would be in an ideal position to eliminate the waiting period.

Yet, a provision to phase out the waiting period for the disabled never made it into any version of the health care overhaul introduced into Congress. What happened?

Ultimately, "sticker shock" happened. In July 2009 the Congressional Budget Office (CBO) estimated what the first version of the health care overhaul—Representative Charlie Rangel's "Affordable Health Choices Act"—would cost. It found that Rangel's bill would add $239 billion to the budget deficit over 10 years if Congress passed it.[16] No bill that added that much to the deficit had a chance of passing. Indeed, getting the cost of the bill down so that it actually *reduced* the deficit (at least on paper) became crucial, especially as the popularity of the health care reform legislation declined in public opinion polls during the Fall of 2009.

"We just couldn't come up with the money," Rep. Green said of ending the Medicare waiting period. "I ran with an amendment [to eliminate the waiting period] in committee, and I had a lot of support, but if you had an amendment you had to come up with the money for it. So we ended not having a vote on the amendment."

Green would not put his colleagues in the position of voting for an amendment that added to the budget deficit. According to the CBO, eliminating the Medicare waiting period for everyone who qualified for SSDI would be expensive, costing about $113 billion over 10 years. However, there were options that were cheaper. Eliminating the waiting period only for those who did not have access to either private insurance or Medicaid would cost about $28 billion over 10 years.[17] Yet Congress could not find the money to do even that.

However, Congress did find money to eliminate the "donut hole" in Medicare Part D—the coverage gap in Medicare's prescription drug benefit. That would cost about $38 billion over 10 years, more than the cost of some proposals to eliminate the two-year waiting period for the disabled. Indeed, almost every version of ObamaCare that came before Congress included a provision to close the donut hole.

The reason money was found for one but not the other came down to political influence.

To pass a major piece of legislation like ObamaCare requires building a large coalition of groups willing to support it. Democrats were going to need as many key groups on board as possible, from physicians, nurses and hospitals to insurance companies, drug manufacturers and medical device makers. Getting seniors and the disabled into the coalition would add to its power.

But when the price tag of the bill became too large, Congress had to decide which parts of the bill could be eliminated. This also meant deciding which groups of the coalition could be jettisoned without jeopardizing passage of the bill. Democrats, it seemed, had decided that groups representing seniors, like the AARP, were needed to pass ObamaCare while groups representing the disabled were expendable.

And they were right.

"Seniors were much more identifiable. Their numbers are huge," said Green. "Not everybody has Part D, but a huge number do. That was more of a higher level political issue to deal with than the 24-month disability period."

As noted in the previous chapter, seniors vote at rates higher than just about any other demographic group. As Table 3.2 shows below, seniors[18] vote at much higher levels than the disabled.[19] Indeed, the turnout rate for the disabled is even lower than the entire voting age population.

Table 3.2: Voter Turnout for Seniors and Disabled in Off-Year Election (1998)			
	Population	**Voters**	**Turnout Rate**
Seniors, 65 and up	32.7 million	19.4 million	59.5%
Disabled, 18-64	33.1 million	7.1 million	21.4%
Total Population, 18 and up	202.6 million	84.8 million	41.9%
Sources: Census Bureau; Jamieson, Shin and Day			

When members of Congress must make a choice between spending money to improve Medicare for seniors or the disabled, the numbers suggest it is not a difficult choice. The disabled are at a serious disadvantage at the ballot box, and that's where it matters most when it comes to getting Congress to change Medicare.

The disabled have an additional political disadvantage. Seniors have only two federal programs that concern them, Social Security and Medicare. The interest groups that represent them, which include AARP and a few others, have little trouble focusing their efforts.

By contrast, there are over 20 different federal agencies administering nearly 200 programs for the disabled.[20] Interest groups that lobby for the disabled have a plethora of policies that concern them. Getting them to concentrate their efforts around any one policy for any length of time is difficult.

When it comes to the political power necessary to change Medicare, the disabled do not have as much of it as seniors do.

Unfortunately, the difficulties that the disabled experience with Medicare are not limited to the waiting period.

Disabled and in Debt

Francine English is sitting in her power wheelchair near the receptionist's window at Dekalb Medical's Surgical Weight Loss Center in Decatur, Georgia, filling out some paperwork when a Dekalb County police officer walks in. He sits down in a chair next to her with his legs spread apart.

There is something obviously wrong, and Francine soon notices it. She writes a quick note on a piece of paper and hands it to him.

The trooper turns slightly red, then laughs and says something in reply. That causes Francine and some of the other women sitting near her to laugh.

Shortly thereafter, Francine wheels her way back to her adult daughter who is sitting across the room.

"What did you do?" her daughter asks.

"I wrote him a note saying there was a hole in his crotch—what do you think I did?" Francine replies.

"And what did he say to you?" her daughter asks.

"That because of county cutbacks he can't afford a new pair of pants!" Francine chuckles.

Francine needs a wheelchair because the cartilage in her knees has deteriorated from osteoarthritis. However, she can't get knee replacements because she is also seriously overweight. She's come to the Surgical Weight Loss Center for her first visit in what she hopes will lead to bariatric surgery. Before she can have the surgery, though, she'll also have to meet with a psychologist, pulmonologist, dietician, and cardiologist.

She's unsure which of these her Medicare Advantage plan, administered through WellCare, covers. She picks up her cell phone and starts dialing one of the numbers on her insurance card. The police officer is lucky that Francine only noticed something wrong with him—he didn't irritate or frustrate her. The customer service people at WellCare won't be so fortunate.

"No, that's not what I'm asking," she says into her phone. "Does anyone there have an answer? Okay, fine, I'll call that number."

Francine starts to dial another number.

"WellCare has farmed out their call center to a place in the Philippines," she says, her voice elevated as she raises the phone to ear. "Do you have any idea what it is like to get information on your Medicare benefits from people in the Philippines? They don't know shit for shinola!"

But then a slightly confused look comes over her face followed by a broad smile. This time her call has not been routed to another country.

"I'm so happy to talk to someone in the U.S.," she laughs into the phone. "Did you kick the people in the Philippines to the curb? I swear, they can't buy a clue."

The woman on the other end is also unable to answer her question, but gives her another number to call.

Francine dials another number. Her joy deflates; her feistiness rises. She's been routed back to the Philippines.

"Look, I'm just trying to find out if you pay for me to see the dietician. Yes, the dietician...No, that's not what I said! You're not listening...You don't need to know my phone number. I'm using someone else's phone anyway. That's got nothing to do with the price of groceries!"

As Francine barks into the phone, her daughter gives a tired smile and wearily shakes her head.

Indeed, it's possible that the presence of her daughter is making Francine extra feisty today, although with Francine it is hard to tell. The reason has nothing to do with mother-daughter relations. Francine loves her children—three daughters and a son—very much.

It's that her daughter is at the Center to pay the $25 co-pay that Francine cannot afford. Francine does not like to have her children paying her medical bills.

"It bothers me," Francine said softly over a lunch earlier in the day. "I've always been the strong one in the family. My oldest daughter, when I didn't have the money for some medication two months ago, she asked me, 'Why didn't you say something?' I said, 'I just don't like asking people for anything.'"

WellCare requires a $25 co-pay every time Francine sees a specialist, a $10 co-pay when she sees a primary care physician, and a $50 co-pay for emergency room visits. Co-pays for other treatments and tests vary. Prior to WellCare she had a different Medicare Advantage plan through United Health Care. Prior to that she had regular Medicare, with its 80% coverage and 20% cost sharing.

WellCare has reduced her out-of-pocket costs more than any of her other Medicare options. Yet for the month of August 2010 she has co-pays of $10 for a primary-care visit, $25 for a cardiologist visit, $100 for a stress test, and $75 for a cardiogram, totaling $210.

"The insurance will send you a $200 co-pay all at once," she says. "You can't shake that money off a tree. But I try to give what I can every month."

That's not easy for her. Being disabled, she is currently on SSDI which pays her $930 a month, $11,160 annually.

Sometimes the doctors' offices and hospitals make the mistake of calling Francine to complain that she hasn't paid all of her bills.

"I tell them I don't need them to call me with an attitude, make me mad and get my blood pressure up," she says. "Then I'll just end up right back in the doctor's office. I pay them what I can when I can."

She estimates that she has over $2,000 of outstanding medical bills accumulated over the last three years—nearly 20% of her annual income.

Born in 1949, Francine grew up in New York City. Her mom died when she was young, and she was raised by her father. In her late teens she became a civil rights worker. For years she was active in politics in New York City. She held various jobs such as a social worker and a toll taker.

In 1993 she visited her eldest daughter in Georgia.

"I fell in love with the culture," she said. "I loved the fact that the buses and trains weren't dirty like they were in New York, and I didn't have to duck bullets. And my daughter asked me to come down and help with her kids."

In 1995 she moved down and worked for various temporary agencies.

Not long after, her health problems began. First it was high-blood pressure and heart disease. She is currently on four medications for those conditions.

In the late 1990s, she developed osteoarthritis in her knees. Being a degenerative condition, she was still able to walk for many years, albeit in considerable pain.

By May of 2005, her knees had degenerated to the point that she had to increasingly use a manual wheelchair. At that point, she applied and was approved for SSDI. She qualified for Medicare in 2007.

Francine's monthly bills leaves little left over for out-of-pocket medical expenses. Francine's rent is $500. That keeps her in a small, one-bedroom apartment in a relatively crime-free neighborhood about half-an-hour east of Atlanta. Her electrical bill is about $40 and food is about $150. Her phone (a land-line that includes internet service) is about $47.

She has some expenses that, at first glance, she could probably do without such as life insurance, internet and cable, a cell phone, and car insurance. But it's not clear how "unnecessary" those things are.

The life insurance costs her about $69 a month.

"It costs over $6,000 to bury a person," Francine says. "If something happens to me, I don't want my kids running around here going, 'Can you donate to Francine's funeral?' I, as a black woman, don't want anyone going around here begging for money to bury me."

What about the internet? She could get rid of that and reduce the monthly bill she gets for the land line to help pay some of her medical bills.

"Do you know how many times you call a politician or an agency and they'll say, 'Do you have access to the internet so we can email you something?'" she asks. "It's the superhighway of information." She also uses it to download coupons that help her save money on food.

Her car insurance costs about $65 a month. There is bus transportation, but she can't use it.

"The housing authority has a bus that takes the seniors shopping every Tuesday, but they will not accommodate my wheelchair. That's discrimination!" she exclaims. "So I have to use my car, and you can't be driving around in no city without car insurance or you can go to jail. I don't look good in an orange jumpsuit!"

Francine recently qualified for food stamps that also qualified her for a government-subsidized cell phone known as "TracFone." It was a relief for her, otherwise she would have kept her regular cell phone which was costing her about $68 a month.

"I keep that cell phone with me when I go into the shower," she says. "If I fall, I can call my daughter. She has a key and can come and help me up."

One can certainly quibble with Francine over some of her expenses (although do so gently). Yet, Medicare would have left her with debt even if she had reduced her expenses. Were she to free up, say, another $100 per month, it would still take her 20 months to pay off her accumulated medical debt, and that's not counting any additional medical expenses she'll have in the future.

The "Perfect Storm" for Medical Debt?

There are three reasons to think that there is widespread debt due to medical bills among the disabled on Medicare.

First, they tend to have relatively low incomes, and incomes that are generally lower than seniors on Medicare. "Medicare's disabled are twice as likely as seniors to live under the federal poverty level (45 percent vs. 20 percent)," according to a survey from the late 1990s.[21] A study conducted a few years later found that the 43 percent of the disabled have annual incomes of $10,000 or less versus 24 percent of seniors.[22]

Second, on average, they use a lot of medical care. One survey found 9 out of 10 disabled patients had been to see a physician at least once in the last six months, and just under six out of 10 had been at least four times. One-third had been to the emergency room in the last six months, and 18 percent had been two or more times. Forty-five percent of those with a physical disability use some form of equipment, such as a wheelchair, to manage their daily needs.[23]

Finally, the disabled on Medicare are more likely to incur medical debt because they are less likely than the elderly to have supplemental insurance (Medigap) that covers Medicare's cost sharing. Some disabled on Medicare have incomes low enough that they also qualify for the government health care program for the poor, Medicaid. If they do, then Medicaid will pay for Medicare's cost sharing. (People who qualify for both Medicare and Medicaid are often known as "dual-eligibles.")

But others have income high enough that they do not qualify for Medicaid. For example, Francine's monthly income of $930 was too much for her to qualify for Medicaid in Georgia where, through 2010, the cut-off was $923 per month. However, while the disabled like Francine have incomes too high for Medicare, they have incomes too low to cover Medicare's cost sharing by purchasing a private Medigap plan, which usually run a few hundred dollars a month.

About 20 percent of the disabled do not have supplemental coverage, as opposed to only eight percent of the elderly.[24] Since there are about 9.4 million disabled on Medicare, just under 1.9 million lack supplemental coverage. Furthermore, over three-fourths of the disabled without supplemental coverage have incomes of $20,000 or less.[25]

In summary, there are about 1.9 million disabled on Medicare who lack supplemental coverage, millions who have low income, and millions who use a lot of health care. It seems like the "perfect storm" for a high rate of medical debt. Yet, surprisingly, no study has examined medical debt among the disabled on Medicare. Thus, there is no way to know exactly how many of the disabled on Medicare are in debt and to what extent they are in debt.

The three factors listed above should cause not only great indebtedness among the disabled on Medicare, but also more difficulty among the disabled in actually affording health care. For that, there is considerable evidence.

A study from the early 1990s found that 17 percent of the disabled on Medicare reported not receiving health care as opposed to only six percent of the elderly. Among the disabled, 71 percent cited cost as the main reason they didn't receive care.[26] In the KFF survey mentioned above, 33 percent of the disabled reported major or minor problems paying for health care in the previous year as compared to only 13 percent of the elderly. Forty-six percent of the disabled reported delaying or not obtaining a health care service because of cost versus only 16 percent of the elderly. As a result of having higher rates of putting off or not getting care, the disabled experienced higher rates of stress and anxiety, physical pain, and the worsening of a medical condition or problems that eventually required medical attention.[27]

Disabled Medicare beneficiaries whose incomes are too high to qualify for Medicaid but too low to afford Medigap seem most prone to struggle with the following problems:

> Among disabled Medicare beneficiaries under age sixty-five, those with some form of supplemental coverage are at a substantial advantage in surmounting cost-related barriers to care. Medicare beneficiaries without supplemental coverage through either a private source or Medicaid were significantly more likely than those having coverage sources to report problems on...cost-related outcome measures...Those relying solely on Medicare were almost seven

times more likely than those with supplemental coverage to postpone care because of cost. They were also about five times as likely as those with private supplemental coverage and about three times as likely as those with both Medicare and Medicaid to go without health care necessities because of cost.[28]

Yet no one has sought to investigate the indebtedness of the disabled on Medicare.

Nevertheless, it is a phenomenon that deserves to be thoroughly researched. If Medicare is leaving a significant number of its beneficiaries vulnerable to medical debt, then policymakers need to address it. But only when we have relatively precise estimates of how many of the disabled on Medicare have medical debt and how much medical debt they have will we know the extent of the problem.

4. Donut Hole

The Medicare Prescription Drug, Improvement and Modernization Act that passed in 2003 (more commonly known as Medicare Part D) was not the first time Medicare offered coverage for pharmaceuticals. Congress had previously included prescription drug coverage in the Medicare Catastrophic Coverage Act (MCCA) of 1988.

Congress attempted to deal with many of Medicare's shortcomings with the MCCA. Not only did it give seniors prescription drug coverage, it also provided them with coverage for long-term hospitalizations, skilled-nursing facilities and home health care. The MCCA imposed a surtax on more affluent seniors to help pay for the new Medicare benefits. Congress passed it by overwhelming margins and President Ronald Reagan signed it into law on July 1, 1988.

There was only one problem. No one had asked what seniors thought about it. Many were up in arms when they found out that their taxes would go up to pay for it.

The backlash created a great deal of difficulty for members of Congress, none more so than Representative Dan Rostenkowski. Rostenkowski, then chairman of the powerful House Ways and Means Committee, had played a significant role in crafting the MCCA.

On August 17, 1989, Rostenkowski was visiting a senior center in his Chicago-area district. Upon leaving, he refused to meet with group of seniors who were angry about the MCCA. He got in his car to go, but many of the seniors surrounded the sedan yelling "You're Wrong!" "Bum!" and "Impeach Him!" One elderly woman, Leona Kozien, even leaned over the hood of the car and put her hand on it while shouting at the Congressman.

Since running over little old ladies seldom generates favorable press, Rostenkowski decided not to let his driver start the car. Instead, he got out and headed down the street, pursued by seniors and the media. Like many politicians who have been in power for many years, Rostenkowski was dismissive of his constituents' complaints.

"I don't think they understand what the government is trying to do for them," he told a reporter. "It's a problem, but it's always been a problem."[1] As he approached a gasoline station, his driver pulled up in the car ahead of the crowd. Rostenkowski quickly got in and they drove off.*

The opposition to the new law stemmed, in part, from the fact that seniors had not been well informed about the tax portion of the MCAA, due largely to a lack of media coverage.[2] The surtax was set at 15 percent of a senior's federal tax liability. This would impose a larger burden on more affluent seniors as tax liability tends to rise as income increases. Initially, at least, most Medicare beneficiaries wouldn't pay the surtax. According to the Congressional Budget Office, just under 36 percent seniors would pay an average surtax of $285 in 1989. But it would rise quickly to more than 42 percent of seniors and $506 by 1993.[3]

Another problem was that 70 percent of seniors had Medigap plans that already covered many of the benefits in the MMCA.[4] Without providing many new benefits, the MMCA was not going to generate enthusiasm from seniors in the amounts necessary to offset the opposition to the new taxes.

As the opposition grew, many members of Congress dismissed the elderly as "selfish," "ungrateful," and "greedy." Many in the media echoed those sentiments.[5] However, members of Congress were not willing to

---

* The author tried to interview Rep. Rostenkowski for this book, but he passed away before that could happen. Apparently, while dead people often vote in Chicago, they do not grant interviews.

indulge their attitudes at the risk of millions of angry seniors showing up at the ballot box. In late November 1989, Congress repealed the MMCA.

While the MMCA was dead, the lessons from it lived on. First, keeping the support of a large majority of seniors is crucial to passing any major change in Medicare. And second, the best way to keep that support is to offer new benefits while requiring most seniors to pay very little of the cost. Congress took those lessons to heart when crafting a prescription drug benefit for Medicare about fifteen years later.

Donut Holes

Whenever Congress creates a new entitlement, cost is always a major issue. Adding a prescription drug benefit to Medicare—what became known as Part D—was no exception. During his 2003 State of the Union speech, President George W. Bush announced that the budget he was putting forward that year would commit an additional $400 billion over the next decade for Medicare, the bulk of which would go toward adding a prescription drug benefit. That same year, President Bush would push an additional tax cut and add the cost of a war in Iraq to the one already going on in Afghanistan. That only added to the pressure to limit the ten-year cost of Part D to $400 billion.

Keeping the cost down would leave a major "gap" in the coverage offered by Part D. The first hint that the design would leave a big gap for beneficiaries with high drug costs came not under President Bush but President Bill Clinton. Clinton first proposed a prescription drug plan for Medicare in June 1999. It was limited, paying only for 50 percent of the first $5,000 in Medicare beneficiaries' drug expenses. Beyond that, a beneficiary would have to find a way to pay for his drugs.

In February 2000, Vice President Al Gore released his own Medicare drug plan as part of his campaign for the presidency. Under the Gore plan, beneficiaries would pay a monthly premium of $44 to join the program. Just like Clinton's plan, it would cover the first 50 percent of a beneficiary's drug expenses up to $5,000. A beneficiary would then enter a gap of $1,500. In the midst of that gap, a beneficiary would have to pay for all of his prescription drugs out-of-pocket. After going through the gap, Medicare would pay for all drug costs.

Not wanting to lose the senior vote, Republicans in the House of Representatives proposed their own plan in April 2000. The bill actually passed the House by three votes in June, but stalled in the Senate. It had all of the main elements of the prescription drug bill that would eventually pass Congress and would be signed into law by President Bush in 2003. It paid private insurance companies to provide beneficiaries with prescription drug coverage. Beneficiaries would be able to choose the private plan through which they would receive their prescription drug benefits. It had a $250 deductible, after which it would pay for 50 percent of a beneficiary's drug costs up to $2,100. It, too, had an out-of-pocket gap of $3,400.

The gap would soon become known as the "donut hole." It would become the most conspicuous and controversial feature of the Part D benefit, largely because it was so unusual. At the time, Robert D. Reischauer, former director of the Congressional Budget Office, said the donut hole "defies rational policy analysis" and was not found in commercial insurance.[6] Usually, although not always, out-of-pocket costs decline as a patient's costs rise under private coverage.

In a 2010 interview, Dennis Hastert, who was Speaker of the House in 2003, said, "We would have liked to not even have had a donut hole, but the donut hole kept the costs down…All of it was a function of making the numbers match."[7]

In 2009, the last year before ObamaCare began closing the donut hole, the standard Part D benefit included a $295 deductible after which there was the level of cost sharing. In the cost sharing level the insurance company paid 75 percent of prescription drug costs and the beneficiary paid 25 percent until $2,995 in drug expenses was reached. The beneficiary then entered the "donut hole" where he or she was responsible for 100 percent of the cost of prescription drugs until $4,350 in total out-of-pocket drug expenses was reached. Beyond the donut hole is "catastrophic coverage" where beneficiaries paid 5 percent for their drugs while Medicare and the insurance company paid the other 95 percent. The Centers for Medicare and Medicaid Services (CMS) increased these amounts most years using a formula based on per-capita prescription drug costs of Medicare beneficiaries and inflation. Some Part D plans did provide coverage for the donut hole, but premiums for those plans were usually more than double what they were for standard Part D plans.

Three Strokes

Donna Dennis is the type of woman who easily fits the ideal mold of a grandmother: patient and kind, with gray hair and a warm smile.

Her disposition makes it hard to believe that she has suffered three strokes. It is even more difficult to believe that her youngest son committed suicide in 2010, a victim of bipolar disease. Understandably, she still sometimes speaks about him in the present tense.

She lives in a small duplex just outside of Oklahoma City. She was born into a family of famers in Oklahoma near the end of the Dust Bowl. Her father went into the service, after which he went to work for Boeing Aircraft in Wichita, Kansas. She grew up there, married and had two sons. She moved back to Edmond, Oklahoma when her husband received a job there. After twenty years of marriage, they divorced.

Then in her forties, she went to work in the food-service industry. She was attracted to the social aspect of it.

"People need to eat, and I love to be around people," she said.

She eventually ended up working at a chain known as Petro Truck Stop. That took her to Memphis, Tennessee, Shreveport, Louisiana and West Memphis, Arkansas.

"Upon reaching the age of 60, I told the company that I wanted to go back home to Oklahoma," she said. "I didn't want to retire in the South."

"So, they brought me back to Oklahoma City, and I had three strokes after I got back home," she laughs.

She had her first stroke shortly after she turned 61.

"After being reassured I wouldn't have another stroke, six months later I had a second one," Donna said.

About three years later Donna had her third stroke.

"At that time I was turning 65, so I thought I should hang it up."

She quit working at Petro Truck Stop—temporarily.

"I stayed home for about two months, and one morning I looked in the bathroom mirror and I said, 'Donna, you are no longer a domestic diva, so why don't you go back to work?"

She says Petro Truck Stop has been very supportive of her.

"They've made room for me. I now cashier three days a week and keep active and keep my brain going," she said. "It is a wonderful place to interact with people which is something you need after you've had a stroke and as you get older."

When Donna received her prescription drug plan through Part D in 2006, she was aware of the donut hole. She didn't really think it would be a serious problem for her.

The Rise of Prescription Drugs

One section of the health care overhaul Congress passed in 2010 (a.k.a. "ObamaCare") gradually closes the donut hole. Beneficiaries will pay a percentage of their drug costs when they reach the donut hole instead of paying the full cost. That percentage declines each year until 2020 when it reaches 25 percent.

However, even with the donut hole disappearing, the sickest beneficiaries still face greater difficulty compared to other beneficiaries. The law that created Part D gives insurance companies flexibility in designing the cost sharing level. Most Part D plans do not use the standard 75/25 percent cost sharing. Rather, they use a system of "tiered co-pays" that encourage enrollees to use cheaper drugs.[8] The tier with the lowest co-pay is the one for generic drugs. The next tier is for brand-name drugs that the insurance company has on its "preferred list," known as a formulary. Following that is the tier for brand-name drugs that are not on the preferred list. For example, the Humana Gold plan charged a flat co-pay of $7 for a monthly supply of drugs in the generic tier. It charges a $40 co-pay for preferred brand-name drugs and an $80 co-pay for non-preferred.

There is one additional tier, known as the "specialty tier," that applies to drugs that cost $600 or more per month. The majority of plans use a co-insurance rate of 33 percent for drugs in the specialty tier.[9]

The top drugs that tend fall into the specialty tier include ones that treat multiple sclerosis (Copaxone), rheumatoid arthritis (Enbrel and Humira), anemia (Procrit), pulmonary arterial hypertension (Tracleer), HIV (Truvada), and cancer (Thalomid). The lowest amount of cost sharing for those drugs is Truvada at $285; the highest is Thalomid at $1,916.[10] The people who get hit with such high co-insurance costs are ones with serious illnesses. In short, the specialty tier is another way in which Part D results in the sickest beneficiaries getting hit with the highest out-of-pocket costs.

It seems ironic that Part D leaves the sickest beneficiaries exposed to such high out-of-pocket costs given that it was seniors' complaints about rising drug costs that was the impetus to create a Medicare prescription drug benefit in the first place. Yet very few seniors use specialty drugs, not enough to cause politicians any headaches.

There had been attempts to include prescription drugs under Medicare long before Part D and even before Rostenkowski was chased down a street. For example, during the debate over including the disabled under Medicare in 1972, Senator Joseph Montoya of New Mexico offered an amendment that would establish Medicare prescription drug coverage. The bill that initially passed the Senate included Montoya's amendment. However, during the conference committee to iron out the differences between the House and Senate versions of the bill, the amendment was jettisoned.

These early efforts were unsuccessful because, prior to the 1990s, politicians weren't hearing about the high cost of prescription drugs from their senior constituents. In fact, the percentage of total health care spending in the U.S. on prescription drugs had declined over time, from about 10 percent in 1960 to less than five percent in the mid 1980s.[11] They were still just over 5 percent when Rostenkowski had his unpleasant day in 1989.

But in the next decade, Congress would feel more and more pressure to add prescription drug coverage to Medicare as the cost of drugs exploded. In real dollars, the U.S. spent $40 billion on prescription drugs in 1990; by 2000 it was $120 billion. As a percentage of total health care spending, prescription drugs rose from 5.6 percent to 8.9 percent during that same time.[12]

What precipitated the rise in drug costs was a revolution in the pharmaceutical industry. Advances in microbiology and new computer techniques such as magnetic resonance imaging made studying the effect of drugs much easier. A faster approval process at the Food and Drug Administration made it easier to bring new drugs to market. A profit-driven industry to conduct clinical drug trials developed, greatly increasing the efficiency of such trials. Finally, insurance companies and pharmacy benefit managers became sources of large amounts of data on the effect of drugs, making it easier to conduct drug studies.[13]

The result of this revolution was new and more effective treatments for ailments such as heart disease, diabetes, osteoporosis, and mental illness. It also resulted in more drugs that treated disease the same as older drugs but with fewer side effects. These new drugs resulted in cost savings elsewhere in the health care system:

> H2 antagonists (Tagamet and other drugs that suppress stomach acid secretion) reduced the costs of surgery of gastrointestinal ulcers by more than half. The use of "clot-busters" in treating strokes has reduced health care costs by about four times as much as the cost of the drug (not to mention the benefits to patients and families). Schizophrenia drugs costing about $4,500 per year avoided about $73,000 a year in institutional treatment costs.[14]

The trade-off was that we spent more on pharmaceuticals, ones that were usually more expensive than older drugs. The burden of this cost fell disproportionately on seniors since they tend to consume more prescription drugs. By 1997, about 2.3 million seniors spent at least 10 percent of their income on prescription drugs annually.[15] Average out-of-pocket drug spending among those aged 65-and-older grew by an average of 7 percent annually from 1992-2000.[16]

In addition, insurance coverage of drugs was deteriorating for seniors. The Medicare+Choice program (a precursor to Medicare Advantage) was one source of drug coverage for seniors. Changes Congress made in 1997 to Medicare+Choice resulted in a lot of private insurers leaving the program in the following two years. Many people who had drug coverage under Medicare+Choice were unable to find drug coverage elsewhere when their Medicare+Choice policies were discontinued.[17] Some Medigap policies also provided drug coverage, but those policies became less affordable as rising drug costs resulted in average annual premium increases of more than 10 percent.[18]

By the late 1990s, members of Congress were hearing from their senior constituents about the cost of prescription drugs. "It may be the single most potent issue we have back home," claimed Representative Martin Frost of Texas.[19]

The 2000 election campaign was the seminal one for a Medicare prescription drug benefit. After Gore released his drug plan in February, he spent much of the summer attacking the Republican Presidential nominee, Texas Governor George W. Bush, on the issue of Medicare prescription drug coverage. Bush had little choice but to respond lest he risk losing a substantial share of the senior vote. He released his own plan in September.

With both sides offering drug plans going into the November election, it was all but guaranteed that the next president would have to push hard to pass a Medicare prescription drug benefit. After a controversial election that ended only when the Supreme Court stepped in, Bush became the next president.

Shortly after assuming office, Bush put forward the Medicare plan he had proposed during the campaign. Any chance that Congress and the President had of passing a drug benefit by the end of 2001 was derailed by the terrorist attacks of September 11. It wasn't until early 2003 that a Medicare prescription drug benefit again took center stage.

Bush got the Part D ball rolling again in his 2003 State of the Union speech in which he proclaimed, "Medicare is the binding commitment of a caring society. We must renew that commitment by giving seniors access to the preventive medicine and new drugs that are transforming health care in America."

A few days earlier the Bush Administration had released some details of Bush's Medicare plan. It included a prescription drug benefit with a $275 deductible, 50 percent cost sharing up to $3,050, a donut hole to $5,500 after which Medicare would pay 90 percent of the cost of a beneficiary's prescription drugs.

The Administration also hinted that a beneficiary would not be able to receive the drug benefit if he or she stayed in traditional Medicare. Rather, beneficiaries would have to join a private insurance plan, paid for by Medicare, to receive drug coverage.

Members of Congress quickly objected, including Republicans. Senator Charles Grassley of Iowa, chair of the powerful Senate Finance Committee, stated that drug coverage should be available to all Medicare beneficiaries, not just those joining private plans. Senator Olympia Snowe, a moderate Republican and also a member of the Finance Committee, said, "I am concerned that the president's focus on ways to reform Medicare could hamper our efforts to pass comprehensive prescription coverage."[20]

Any chance Bush had of requiring beneficiaries to join private plans in order to receive drug coverage was likely dead when then-policy director of AARP John Rother announced, "Drug benefits must be available to all beneficiaries, including those who want to stay in the traditional Medicare program."[21] To pass a Medicare prescription drug benefit Congress would need to keep the AARP, the largest of the organizations that lobby on behalf of seniors, on board. For example, in June of 2003, the House of Representatives passed a Medicare prescription drug bill that included means testing. The amount of prescription drug costs covered by Medicare would begin to decline once a beneficiary's annual income reached $60,000. The AARP's opposition to that provision was a big reason it was not part of the final bill.

The pharmaceutical industry was the other interest group that Congress had to appease. In the late 1990s, the rising cost of drugs made the drug companies a convenient whipping boy for politicians. The industry responded by becoming more active in lobbying and election campaigns. According to OpenSecrets.org, the Pharmaceutical Research & Manufacturers of America, the main trade association for pharmaceutical makers, more than tripled its efforts, from spending just over $5 million on lobbying in 1990 to $16 million in 2003. In the 1990 election, the pharmaceutical industry donated $2.3 million to political campaigns, with about $1 million going to Democrats and $1.3 million to Republicans. After getting attacked by Clinton and the Democrats in the late 1990s, the pharmaceutical industry's contributions skyrocketed to $21.9 million in the 2000 election. Republican received the bulk of it, $17.4 million.

Many Democrats preferred a Medicare program that purchased prescription drugs directly. Pharmaceutical companies worried this would lead to price controls that would cut into their profits. Republicans controlling both Congress and the White House in 2003 all but guaranteed that the drug benefit would be administered by private insurance companies, with whom the drug companies could negotiate prices.

In July, both chambers of Congress passed a version of a Medicare drug benefit. The Senate passed its version 76-21, with 35 Democrats joining 40 Republicans and one Independent in voting yes. The House bill was a far more partisan affair, passing by a one-vote margin with only nine Democrats voting yes.

There were stark differences in the bills that took months of negotiations to bridge. The biggest concerned the provisions in the House bill that would require the entire Medicare program to compete with private insurance. It would give beneficiaries the option of joining a private plan that Medicare would pay for. To force traditional Medicare to compete with those plans, the bill would raise the premiums for traditional Medicare so that they would be comparable to those of private plans.

The other major difference was Health Savings Accounts, something not directly related to Medicare. The bill would allow those people under age 65 in private insurance the option of purchasing a plan with a high deductible that they could pay for by putting tax-free money into a Health Savings Account.

By and large, House Republicans supported those provisions, while Democrats in both the House and Senate opposed them. In the end, the final bill was much closer to what House Republicans wanted. The Health Savings Accounts remained, as did giving beneficiaries the option of choosing private plan, what became known as Medicare Advantage. However, the provision that would force traditional Medicare to compete by raising its premiums was limited to a demonstration project in six cities.

In November, the Senate approved the final bill, this time by a much closer 54-44, with only 11 Democrats joining 42 Republicans and one Independent in supporting it. The House passed it by an even narrower margin, 220-215. The House Republican leadership went into the vote not having enough votes to pass the bill—many GOP members were unwilling to add a huge new expense to the federal budget. The Speaker of the House, Dennis Hastert, used a controversial maneuver to get the votes he needed. Most votes on the House floor last fifteen minutes. Hastert kept this one open almost three hours until he had persuaded enough Republicans to vote yes.

Hastert justified it by saying that fifteen minutes was a *minimum* amount of time for a vote, not a maximum.[22] That is true. But Democrats were quick to remind Republicans about an incident sixteen years earlier, when Democrats controlled the House and then-Speaker Jim Wright held a budget vote open an extra 30 minutes. Dick Cheney, then a member of the House, called it the "most arrogant, heavy-handed abuse of power in the 10 years I've been here."[23]

Another controversy arose a few months later when the official actuary of Medicare, Richard Foster, released an estimate showing that Part D would cost closer to $534 billion over 10 years, not the $400 billion estimated by the Congressional Budget Office.[24] Foster revealed that he was pressured by the Bush Administration—specifically, by then-director of CMS Thomas Scully—to keep the estimate under wraps until Part D had passed. Foster did consult a lawyer at the Department of Health and Human Services who informed him that under the law Scully did have the authority to keep Foster from sharing the estimate.[25] Whether Scully behaved ethically was, at the very least, debatable.

Nevertheless, Congress and the President had designed a benefit that, on paper at least, held down drug costs for the government. Now beneficiaries who were the sickest would have to find a way to hold down their own drug costs.

Almost Number Four

Donna Dennis woke up in Deaconess Hospital in November of 2009 with her primary care physician looming over her. According to Donna, he's the size of a football player. What he had to say that morning only made him more intimidating.

"'Young lady, did you know you could have died?'" Donna recalls him saying.

Donna, who was 70 at the time, had suffered restricted blood vessels in her brain. Fortunately, she was rushed to the hospital in enough time so that the restriction didn't result in what would have been her fourth stroke.

At the time, she took 10 medications: Fexofenadine for allergies, Nexium for acid reflux disease, Levothroid for a thyroid condition, Fosamax for osteoporosis, Wellchol for high cholesterol, Amlodipine, Benecar, and Metoprolol for high blood pressure, Janumet for diabetes, and Plavix to help prevent further strokes.

Between Social Security and Petro Truck Stop, Donna made about $1,617 monthly after taxes.

Until 2011, her monthly expenses included $500 for rent, $200 for groceries, $170 for gas and electric, $50 for water, $50 for her phone, $23 for a cell phone, $33 for life insurance, and $9 for a newspaper.

She was also making a $339 monthly payment on her car. Car insurance was $135 and she spent about $40 for gas.

"There is so little bus transportation here and my son lives about 30 miles east of here, so I need the car for work," she said. "I need it to visit my doctors and go to grocery store."

And there are her medical expenses. In an average month, she has $175 in drug co-pays and, on average, about $25 in co-pays for doctor's visits. Her total monthly expenses, $1,749, exceed her income.

"I do some powerful, powerful juggling," said Donna "I'd extend the bills from one month to another, sometimes paying them late. I'd also do a lot of creative shopping. I get my food from Aldi and toiletries from Dollar General. I keep an eye on sales and coupons."

Donna receives her benefits from a Medicare Advantage plan called Secure Horizons. The Part D section of her plan waives the deductible.

In both 2008 and 2009, she fell into the donut hole in June. In 2009, total out-of-pocket costs had to reach $4,350 before a beneficiary would reach the catastrophic coverage level. When Donna reached the donut hole, she had made about $875 in co-pays. Thus, her donut hole was $3,475.

In both years, she found ways to supply most of the drugs she needed. The one exception was Plavix. It didn't harm Donna in 2008. In 2009, she wouldn't be so lucky.

In November of that year, she was at work, beginning her shift.

"I was in the back office, counting down my cash drawer," she said. "Suddenly, my right arm went to sleep. I thought, 'Good Lord, do I have a pinched nerve?'"

But the numbness quickly progressed up her shoulder to her collar bone and then to her jaw.

"My tongue felt like it was three times its size," she said. "I thought to myself, 'What in the world!' I didn't know what was going on, because each one of my other strokes had begun in different ways. They are not predictable."

She counted her drawer down and then went to see her boss.

"I tried to tell him something was wrong. I got the first part of the sentence out, but I couldn't finish the latter part."

Frustrated, she went back to the cash register. After serving three customers, she knew something wrong.

"I turned to the assistant manager and indicated that something was wrong and that I needed someone to get my son up here," she said.

The assistant manager called her son and he showed up promptly.

She looked at her son and said, "I need to go to..." She couldn't finish the sentence.

Her son asked, "Is it the hospital we went to last time?"

She was able to say "yes." Her son took her to Deaconess Hospital. The nurses immediately gave her Plavix. She was given both a CAT scan and an MRI. By getting to the hospital when she did, another stroke was prevented.

After she got out of the hospital, she went to her primary care physician for a follow up visit.

Her physician told her, "You know, you have significant damage to your brain due to your strokes."

"You think?" Donna retorted.

Looking back on her strokes, Donna says, "I was very fortunate that none of them were major ones. God has kept me on this earth for some purpose."

Indeed, she doesn't complain of the maladies that have resulted from her strokes but talks about them matter-of-factly. She tires more easily now and can no longer "multi-task." She has permanent damage to her eyesight for which she wears special eyeglasses. The strokes have also upset her equilibrium. She now uses a cane to keep her balance. Three or four times a year she takes a "nasty spill," as she puts it. Thus far, none have caused her any serious harm.

At the beginning of 2010, she took steps to lower her drug costs, switching what drugs she could to cheaper generics. It stretched out her drug coverage some, but she still fell into the donut hole in late August.

Donna can afford to pay for the five generic drugs she takes when she reaches the donut hole. Amlodipine, Metoprolol, Fexofenadine, Fosamax, and Levothroid in total cost about $150 a month.

But the brand-name drugs she takes are too expensive. Fortunately, she has managed to find ways to supply most of them while she is in the donut hole. Her primary care physician gave her enough free samples of Benecar to last her until the end of the year. She is able to get her Janumet through an assistance program set up by pharmaceutical companies called RxCrossroads. A state program called Oklahoma County Pharmacy supplies her with Nexium.

However, she was unable to find a way to supply Wellchol while she was in the donut hole, so she takes red yeast rice pills, a supplement that helps lower cholesterol.

Most disturbing was that she was still playing Plavix Roulette.

"I got some Plavix from my diabetes doctor and some more when I went to apply for it from RxCrossroads," Donna said. "It's been back and forth. Right now, I'm not taking it."

Adding to her frustration was her experience trying to qualify for one of the state government programs to help her get Plavix while in the donut hole.

"I was told that I make $16 too much a month," she said. "That floored me. I told the gentleman at the program, 'Do I have to quit my job, go to a shelter, and be on the streets in order to qualify for your program?' And he replied, 'Honey, I'm sorry, but that's just about the way it is.'"

Donna's voice is strained as she continues. "How humiliating! For someone who is trying to stay off of welfare, who is trying to help herself, I'm going to be penalized for this? I just could not see the sense in it. At that point I just felt like I was fumbling around, wondering where do I go now?"

One possibility is her family members who live close by. Her eldest son is married and has given her four grandchildren. She also has an aunt who is about nine years her senior and a cousin who is about ten years her junior.

So why doesn't she reach out to them for help paying for her drugs?

"My older son, he and his wife have children, they have expenses and they are building a home," she said. "Pride keeps you back from that. My aunt, she said, 'Any time you need it I've got it. But...'"

Donna's voice chokes up and tears come to her eyes.

"I'm one who likes to make it on her own. I like to feel like I can do it. And there will be a time when I won't be able to. But right now...that's why I work."

Sickest Fall the Fastest

Donna has good reason to be frustrated that her income makes her ineligible for certain government prescription-drug assistance. If she made less money, she would qualify for the Low-Income Subsidy (LIS) Program under Part D. Those who qualify for LIS do not pay Part D premiums or the deductible, nor do they face any donut hole. They do have to make co-pays for drugs, but no co-pay is more than six dollars.

To qualify for LIS, Medicare beneficiaries must either be poor enough that Medicaid covers their cost sharing; or they must be receiving Supplemental Security Income (Social Security for disabled people with no work history); or they must have an income below 150 percent of the federal poverty level (FPL), about $17,505 for a single person in 2014.

There are about 8 million Medicare Part D enrollees who are on the LIS Program.[26] One of the drawbacks is that beneficiaries on LIS have fewer Part D plans to choose from.[27] However, they have lower out-of-pocket costs and are less likely to skip medications because of cost than beneficiaries whose income—151 percent-200 percent FPL—puts them just above the LIS threshold.[28]

An article published just as Part D was getting underway warned that "low income seniors who do not receive subsidies would still have relatively high drug costs compared with their incomes."[29] The "danger-zone" occurs at roughly 151 percent-200 percent FPL. Seniors at that income level are the most vulnerable to the impact of high-out-of-pocket drug costs. They are just as likely to spend at least $100 a month out-of-pocket on drugs as those seniors whose incomes are above 200 percent FPL. However, more than 43 percent of them have three or more chronic conditions as compared to less than 15 percent of those over 200 percent FPL. And they are more likely than those above 200 percent FPL to not fill or delay filling a prescription due to cost—25.9 percent vs. 14.7 percent.[30] With an income that is just above 200 percent of FPL, Donna was right on the cusp of the danger-zone.

To be fair, Part D did provide relief to many beneficiaries. Supporters of Part D hoped that it would provide coverage for those previously without it, that its structure would lead to many choices for beneficiaries and that the competition would hold down costs. And to a large degree those hopes were realized.

In 2003, 27 percent of seniors in Medicare, about 9.5 million, had no prescription drug coverage.[31] By 2010, only about 4.6 million did not have coverage.[32]

Beneficiaries had a wide array of plans to choose from. In 2014, there were a total of 1,169 Part D plans, with at least 28 plans offered in every state.[33] The competition also appears to have saved on costs. Between 2007 and 2012, the actual cost of Part D was about $94.6 billion less than what Medicare's actuaries had initially estimated.[34]

It also improved beneficiaries' adherence to drug regimens. A survey of Medicare beneficiaries taken a year prior to the beginning of Part D examined cost-related medication nonadherence (CRN), which means that cost compelled a beneficiary to either stop taking a drug, take a smaller dose, or skip a dose of a medication to make it last. It found a 29.6 percent rate of CRN among disabled beneficiaries and 12.6 percent among seniors.[35]

A follow-up survey after Part D began in 2006 found significant declines in CRN among the elderly and among those with lower incomes. It also found fewer beneficiaries having to spend less on basic needs like food and heat to afford prescription drugs.[36] Another study found that after Part D began, the usage of drugs to prevent strokes and heart attacks and to lower cholesterol increased significantly among those beneficiaries who had not previously had drug coverage.[37]

But CRN did not drop among all groups. There was no significant decline among the disabled or those with multiple comorbidities—i.e., those who are likely to have the largest drug costs.[38] That was likely the result of the donut hole.

One study found that 41 percent of beneficiaries who, like Donna, had diabetes, hypertension, and high cholesterol reached the donut hole.[39] Another study examined the risk a beneficiary with a particular illness or illnesses had of falling into the donut hole. The average risk for all beneficiaries was about 15.9 percent. Having had a stroke added another 5.6 percentage points to the risk. High cholesterol added 2.6, hypertension 4.3, and diabetes 11.6. In short, Donna's risk of hitting the donut hole was at least 63 percent—and the study didn't include some of her other ailments like osteoporosis and a thyroid condition.[40]

Those beneficiaries who hit the donut hole reduce the amount of medication they take by an average of 14 percent.[41] About 15 percent of those beneficiaries who hit the donut hole stop taking at least one type of drug.[42] Among those who like Donna take Plavix, usage of the drug declines about five percentage points per month as more and more beneficiaries reach the donut hole.[43]

As of yet, no one has conducted a study looking at the health outcomes of beneficiaries who stopped taking prescription drugs once they reached the donut hole. But one doesn't need a study to know that stopping medications for serious illnesses can be dangerous.

At an April 2003 hearing before the House Energy and Commerce Committee, Bruce Vladek, former head of CMS, warned Congress that a donut hole would harm the people most in need of coverage:

> I understand all the fiscal constraints and the tradeoffs, but the fact of the matter is that if you look at prescription drug expenditures by Medicare beneficiaries they occur across a wide range of income distribution in many different parts of the country, for people in many different kinds of circumstances, and the more sophisticated and the more elaborate we get in our design of caps, and "collars," and "donuts," and "donut holes" and what else one might call it, the more folks who are going to find the benefit a hollow promise that is of very little value to them, and the fewer of those with the greatest needs we are going to effectively cover.[44]

If that warning wasn't enough, there was plenty of research conducted prior to 2003 that Congress could have consulted suggesting that the sickest would be most likely to fall into the donut and that those in the donut hole would respond by discontinuing their medication:

- Those with more chronic conditions had much higher spending on prescription drugs. They were also more likely to be elderly.[45]

- Prior to Part D, seniors with some type of drug coverage were six percent to 17 percent more likely to treat health conditions with prescription drugs than those seniors with Medicare alone.[46] Among low-income seniors, those without coverage were two to three times more likely to forego medication.[47]

- Medicare+Choice and Medigap policies were a source of drug coverage for some seniors before Part D. Many of these plans put dollar limits on the amount of drug coverage enrollees could receive annually. After the dollar limit was reached, enrollees would have to pay out-of-pocket for their drugs. Once the gap was reached, enrollees were nearly 24 percent more likely to reduce the amount of medication they were using and 16 percent discontinued using at least one prescription drug.[48]

- Higher drug costs also lead to more adverse health outcomes. One study of those 70 and older in the U.S. found that those who restricted their medication use due to cost had higher rates of angina, non-fatal heart attacks, and strokes.[49] A study of Quebec, Canada, found that when the government imposed higher cost sharing on the drug coverage for low-income people and seniors, use of medication declined among those populations. That led to higher rates of emergency room visits.[50]

- In the early 1980s, some state governments tried to control costs in their Medicaid programs by limiting the number of prescriptions a beneficiary could have to three per month. A study that examined low-income seniors on Medicaid in New Hampshire found those seniors had higher rates of hospitalization and nursing home stays after the three-prescription limit was put in place.[51] A study examining mental-health patients yielded similar results.[52]

Donut Holes and Elections

Given that the donut hole would harm the most vulnerable of Medicare beneficiaries, why did Congress choose such a design to hold down costs?

Surely there were other designs. One possibility might have been expanding the deductible to, say, between $500-$700. Insurers would not have been allowed to waive it, but it could have been lowered for lower-income recipients like Donna. The savings that would have been generated by a larger deductible could have been used to reduce the size of the donut hole. Yet, as Table 4 shows, that option was never seriously considered as the Part D legislation moved through Congress.

Table 4: Out-of-Pocket Costs in Different Versions of Medicare Part D			
Legislation	Deductible	Cost Sharing*	Donut Hole
HR 4945 (House Way & Means Committee)	$250	$575	$2,975
HR 4945 (House Energy & Commerce Committee)	$250	$650	$2,800
S 1 (Senate Finance Committee)	$275	$1,194	$2,369
HR 1 (House Floor)	$250	$350	$2,900
S 1 (Senate Floor)	$275	$2,113	$1,313
FINAL BILL	$250	$500	$2,850
*Cost sharing after the deductible and before the donut hole is reached.			
Source: Congress.Gov			

Rather, the debate appeared to center around the size of the cost sharing and the donut hole. Table 4 suggests that Republicans never really considered pushing the deductible up to, say, $500 to reduce the size of the donut hole.

Speaker Hastert later gave a hint as to why Republicans didn't make the deductible larger.

"We really wanted to get people in the program, and most people could afford $250," he said.[53]

It was by no means only Republicans worried about getting a lot of beneficiaries into the program. When Senate Democrats were designing their plan in 2001, they worried about the cost of the monthly premium. The *New York Times* reported:

[L]awmakers worry that many people will simply decline to sign up for new drug benefits if they think the premiums are too high. Senator Bob Graham of Florida, the principal author of the Democratic plan, said the prospect of $53 premiums was causing "concern across the board." Democratic senators from rural states, including Max Baucus of Montana, said that many of their elderly constituents could not afford such expensive monthly payments, even with generous subsidies for the lowest-income people....Democrats are now trying to lower the premium, perhaps to $30 or $35 a month, even though that might mean raising the amount that beneficiaries would have to pay out of their own pockets for each purchase of medicine.[54]

As noted above, both Clinton and Gore released plans that had large out-of-pocket gaps for beneficiaries. In explaining the gap in Clinton's plan, a *New York Times* article reported that "[Clinton] Administration officials said the design of the President's prescription drug proposal had been heavily influenced by politics. Mr. Clinton, they said, wanted to provide some tangible benefit to a large number of people, rather than helping a small number with high drug expenses."[55]

What many Democrat and Republican lawmakers shared in common was that they wanted to provide the biggest benefit possible to the largest number of seniors. Seniors, of course, vote at rates higher than most other groups. For the sake of politicians' health, it became crucial to design a benefit that kept most seniors pleased. A higher deductible did not seem to fit the bill.

Trading a smaller deductible for a larger donut hole turned out to be a pretty good way to keep most seniors reasonably pleased. A survey conducted in October 2007 found that about 83 percent of seniors with a Part D plan were either very satisfied or somewhat satisfied with their drug coverage.[56]

At the same time, the number of beneficiaries who might be upset with Part D's donut hole turned out to be quite small. Initial estimates found that only about 12 percent to 16 percent of seniors fell into the donut hole each year, and an even smaller four percent to seven percent went all the way through the donut hole.[57]

Those estimates would prove high. When ObamaCare began closing the donut hole in 2010, the Obama Administration trumpeted the number of seniors who were seeing their drug costs reduced even though they entered the donut hole. In 2010, about 8.5 percent of beneficiaries—roughly 4 million—reached the donut hole.[58] In 2012, it was even lower, about 6.8 percent or 3.5 million beneficiaries.[59]

Thus, very few seniors were going to get hit with huge drug costs. As a result, members of Congress didn't have to worry about loads of voters angry about insufficient Medicare drug benefits showing up at the polls.

Extra Help

The donut hole might have persisted indefinitely had it not been for ObamaCare. Passing such a massive bill meant that Congressional Democrats and the Obama Administration would need to build a broad coalition of interest groups in support of it. Two groups crucial to that effort were pharmaceutical companies and the AARP.

Closing the donut hole was one policy that kept the two groups on board the ObamaCare effort. Pharmaceutical companies might make up to an extra $30 billion in sales between 2010 and 2020 as the donut hole closed.[60] The AARP supported the idea because it supports most legislation that provides more benefits to seniors.

Thus, it seems, Republicans miscalculated. A politically acceptable method of keeping down the cost of Part D for taxpayers later turned out to be an important tool in passing ObamaCare—a law which almost all Congressional Republicans opposed. Yet, it is probably unfair to charge them with a lack of foresight. After all, almost no one had heard of Barack Obama in 2003.

The closing of the donut hole helped Donna, initially. Yet, the donut hole became redundant for her when she left Petro at the end of 2011.

"Petro, which was a family-oriented company, sold out to another company that was anything but," she said. "It was disgusting. They treated their employees poorly. A lot of older employees saw the writing on the wall and left. I put up with it for about a year, until I'd just had enough."

With the loss of income, she now qualifies for more assistance with her prescription drugs.

"After I retired, I found 'Extra Help' when I was looking through the Medicare booklet" she said.

Extra Help is a federal program that helps seniors like Donna who make less than $13,440 annually with their prescription drug costs.

"Thanks to programs like that I now pay very little for my drugs," she said. "That has helped tremendously."

5. Too Small, Too Sick, Too Transient

Clay Bell grew up in the Detroit area. He lived in the Motor City suburb of Ferndale, about four blocks north of Eight Mile.

The photos hanging in the living room show a very active Clay.

"That was back in my day," Clay said in his weakened voice. "That was all of the fun stuff."

Taken during the 1980s and 1990s, some photos show him nimbly handling snow skis. In another, he's riding motorcycles with friends and has a big smile on his face. Another shows him on a jet ski, making a hard left turn, his hands clutching the handle bars.

By 2011, his hands were immobile, placed in splints to keep them from contorting should they suffer spasms.

Clay's troubles began in January 1999. An electrician by trade, he was on a job using a ladder. He was about 14 feet up when he fell off. As he got up from the ground, he had trouble moving his right leg.

The physicians that he saw initially thought that he had suffered a back injury and gave him an epidural for the pain.

Yet, Clay did not improve. He started using a cane to walk around. He began seeing other physicians in the hope one would give him a diagnosis that would allow him to receive workman's compensation.

Finally, in 2001, one of the physicians gave him a fuller work-up and referred him to a neurologist. After examining Clay, the neurologist ordered an MRI scan that revealed Clay had Multiple Sclerosis (MS). It was primary progressive MS, the worst kind. About 10 percent of MS sufferers have primary progressive.

"I hit the lottery," Clay joked.

MS is a neurological disorder that erodes the protective insulation in the nerves surrounding the brain and spinal cord. As the disease progresses, it becomes increasingly difficult for nerve cells in the brain and the spinal cord to communicate with each other. This can lead to fatigue and numbness and to more serious symptoms such as muscle spasticity, tremors, impaired mobility, chronic pain, and swallowing disorders. Approximately 250,000 to 400,000 people in the United States have some form of MS.

There are different types of MS. Clay's kind, primary-progressive MS, results in a gradual accumulation of neurological problems and loss of bodily functions. The vast majority of sufferers experience relapsing-remitting MS, in which the patient has occasional flare-ups of MS symptoms followed by periods of recovery. Other patients develop secondary-progressive MS. This begins as relapsing-remitting MS but eventually devolves into primary-progressive in which there are no recovery periods.

Some pharmaceuticals are effective in treating MS but most treat only relapsing-remitting MS. For someone like Clay, they are useless.

Fortunately, Clay has a lot of support. He got married in 2001 to Karen, who makes a good income at an auto dealership.

"My wife helps me through thick and thin," Clay said.

Another huge help is his longtime friend, Joe Kopytek. Kopytek, a retired machinist, lives just a few miles from Clay. He comes over most days to help Clay out of bed, into the shower and then into the recliner in which Clay spends most of his time.

"Clay had to be hospitalized recently," Joe said. "He had low oxygen and a fever. His eyes were glassy. It looked like pneumonia."

It was Clay's third bout with pneumonia since developing MS. During his second bout, his physicians said that he wouldn't survive.

"But I did," Clay said with a bit of pride in his voice. "I'm not going to let MS beat me."

This last time, Clay was in the hospital for six days.

"Someone was there with him around the clock," Joe said. "Clay has a phobia of being left alone in the hospital. During one stay, he was left alone for about four to five hours and had problems."

When discussing his disease, Clay often wavers between defiance and resignation.

"MS tries to beat me, but I will beat it," he said. "I will be back."

A few minutes later, though, he said, "It's a very draining disease. I try not to let it win but so far it has."

For someone like Clay who is suffering from primary-progressive, only physical therapy combined with occupational therapy is effective. (Physical therapy usually focuses on improving balance, walking, and movement, in addition to the relief of pain. Occupational therapy focuses more on helping patients regain skills that help them manage the tasks of their daily lives, such as bathing or using silverware.)

But this course of treatment cannot cure primary-progressive MS. Rather, the two therapeutic approaches can delay the decline by helping the patient compensate for his loss of various functions. They can improve movement and help relieve pain, improving the MS patient's independence and quality of life.

Clay received physical therapy until Medicare terminated it in 2009. Clay first went on Medicare in early 2004, two years after he was approved for Social Security Disability Insurance. His wife's insurance helped him get through the two-year waiting period.

He began receiving physical therapy at the Rehabilitation Institute of Michigan in 2004. By that time, it had become increasingly difficult for him to move his legs and he often had to use a walker to get around. A therapeutic pool became an important part of Clay's therapy.

"It became harder and harder for Clay to move his joints," Joe explained. "The weightlessness of the pool makes the resistance on his joints much less."

The physical therapists would put Clay on a table before he entered the pool to help him stretch and warm up. Once in the pool, Clay was able to stand up and walk.

"He was able to do that in the pool even after he'd lost most of the use of his legs and had to use a wheelchair," said Joe. "It was good for helping him keep his muscle tone."

Clay also received occupational therapy, which included using electrodes to manipulate his hand muscles, hand stretching, and exercises such as holding a pen and squeezing a ball.

In physical, occupational, and speech therapies, the therapist gives the patient an initial evaluation to determine how much ability he has to move his body or speak. For Clay, both physical and occupational therapies continued as long as he showed some improvement in his ability to move when compared to his initial evaluation.

But therapy can only do so much because primary-progressive MS is a degenerative disease. Clay would eventually lose movement in his body, and, in the long run, the best therapy could do was slow his decline.

For someone like Clay, though, slowing the decline was crucial. It could mean being able to live more comfortably for a few extra years.

"The physical therapy made his quality of life much better," said Joe. "Now, without it, he's lost a lot of muscle tone. Because of that, he can't sit in a car as long or in his wheelchair as long."

Although by 2008 Clay had to use a wheelchair, he still had some use of his legs. He also had a great deal of movement in his arms and could grasp things with his hands.

In early 2008, his therapists stopped his physical therapy for the first time.

"We went in for a visit, and the people at the Rehab Institute told us Medicare wouldn't pay for any more," Joe said. "They told us Clay wasn't showing any improvement."

"They axed me out of that," Clay said. "I was bummed out."

Joe and Clay did their best to compensate. Joe would stretch out Clay's legs and arms. They also looked for pools nearby so that Clay could continue his therapy on his own. But it was difficult.

"I tried taking Clay to the YMCA and the Jewish Community Pool," Joe explained. "But the water had to be 90 degrees. If the water was too cold, Clay could tighten right up, and he wouldn't be able to walk. We had a hard time finding the right pool."

In early 2009, Clay visited his neurologist again. His neurologist wrote him another prescription for more physical and occupational therapy at the Rehabilitation Institute of Michigan.

As Clay and Joe remember it, about nine months lapsed between Clay's final physical therapy session in 2008 and his return to physical therapy in 2009.

"I deteriorated quite a bit during that time," Clay recalled.

He lost whatever dexterity remained in his hands. He could no longer walk at all and he was losing the ability to move his arms.

Unfortunately, Clay's therapy didn't last long in 2009. He showed no ability to regain any of the dexterity in his hands, so the therapists at the Rehabilitation Institute stopped the occupational therapy after about three weeks.

His physical therapy continued for about another five to six weeks before the therapists stopped that too.

"I was pissed," Clay said, his usually weak voice rising slightly in volume. "I felt like a number they just threw away. They're supposed to help people. I saw a lot of people who'd had strokes [at the Rehab Center]. They'd just release them and say there was nothing else they could do for them. And then it was my turn. I thought these people were there to help me. Instead, they turned on me."

Clay stopped for a moment. When he continued his voice had softened.

"I know it's not their fault. But I just felt somebody could help me. Therapy may have prolonged my movement."

Therapy Has Evolved, Medicare Hasn't

Clay was a victim of "Medicare undertreatment." Medicare undertreatment occurs when a beneficiary does not receive vital medical care because: (*i*) Medicare's rules and regulations prohibit it or (*ii*) the care needed does not fall under the list of treatments Medicare pays for; or (*iii*) Medicare's price controls result in insufficient payment for the treatment, which discourages health care practitioners from providing it.

It seems inevitable that a program as enormous as Medicare would fail to properly treat at least some patients. But Medicare undertreatment is seldom accidental or the result of some "fluke." It happens, in part, because government rules and regulations tend to calcify, unable to keep up with changes in treatment. Therapy is one such area.

Medicare first began paying for therapy in 1968. The Centers for Medicare and Medicaid Services (CMS) have instituted various guidelines under which patients qualify for therapy. Those guidelines allow a patient therapy if it is "reasonable and necessary." One of the conditions for being reasonable and necessary is that there "must be an expectation that the patient's condition will improve significantly in a reasonable (and generally predictable) period of time."[1] This is what has become known as the "improvement standard"—a patient must show that the therapy is causing his injury or illness to improve. If the patient stops showing improvement or, like Clay, has an illness that will not improve, Medicare stops paying for therapy.

It's not clear exactly when CMS adopted the improvement standard. The earliest reference to it appears in a 1987 Government Accountability Office (GAO) report: "Medicare covers outpatient rehabilitation services, such as physical and speech therapy, only when the services can be reasonably expected, within a predictable time, to significantly improve a bodily function impaired by illness or injury."[2]

Even as recently as the late 1980s, an improvement standard for therapy likely made sense. Most patients who received therapy underwent it for an injury, say, to a knee or hand. The rationale for therapy was that it was might succeed in improving the function of the injured body part, possibly restoring it to its pre-injury state.

But, over time, medical professionals often find that a treatment intended for a particular illness has multiple uses. Therapy is no exception.

In the last 20 years or so, physicians and other medical providers have found multiple uses for therapy. According to a review of the medical literature, no therapy treatment has yet proven effective in stopping MS but some treatments have proven useful in treating the symptoms.[3] For example, a recent article showed therapy can slow primary-progressive MS's progression by minimizing problems that result from decreased mobility or by compensating for a loss of function.[4] A "meta-analysis" of the effect of occupational therapy on MS patients found that occupational therapy was generally effective in improving muscle strength, range of motion, walking and daily tasks like bathing and dressing.[5] Another study of MS patients found that extensive therapy helped them maintain their activity level.[6]

Other studies have shown that therapy benefits patients suffering from Alzheimer's disease. Alzheimer's patients in a walking program showed improvement in activities of daily living and a slower decline in mental activities.[7] Another article showed improvements in balance and a slowing of cognitive decline using physiotherapy, occupational therapy, and physical education.[8] Various types of speech therapy also improve health outcomes for dementia patients.[9]

The results of such studies offer hope, but many of the benefits listed above do not necessarily satisfy the improvement standard. Improving muscle strength or the ability to carry out daily activities might qualify. But things like "slowing the progression," "treating the symptoms," and "slowing cognitive decline," probably would not.

Clay's condition didn't satisfy the improvement standard. Nor did Clay qualify under the other part of the guidelines that allowed therapy to be used when it was "necessary for the establishment of a safe and effective maintenance program required in connection with a specific disease state."[10] A more likely candidate for a maintenance program would be someone who had a knee replacement and needed physical therapy to help him regain his ability to walk. However, once his therapy was completed he might need a daily exercise program to remain ambulatory. Medicare will pay for therapists to show patients what exercises they should do to maintain the abilities they've regained in therapy. For Clay, sadly, an exercise program was of no help since there was no longer any body movement to maintain.

Plateaus Are for Geology, Not Therapy

One isn't surprised to learn that James Reiss belongs to the Teamsters Union. Physically, he fits the stereotype with a stocky build, square jaw, slightly bulbous nose, and short, dark hair.

He also has a no-nonsense demeanor. But it's there that the stereotype ends. James also has a great deal of compassion and patience. That's much to the benefit of his wife, Dolores, who suffers from dementia.

Dementia is a disease affecting the elderly. It occurs because of the gradual death of brain cells in the cerebral cortex, the area of the brain believed to be responsible for memory, action, thoughts and personality. Patients with dementia often have impaired memory, speech, and ability to plan. The most common cause of dementia, of course, is Alzheimer's disease, which accounts for half to three-fourths of dementia cases.

Dolores was diagnosed with dementia in 2003 after James took her to a neurologist. What prompted the visit was Dolores's hairdresser commenting to James about her growing lapses in memory.

For someone who has suffered with dementia for that long, Dolores is in remarkably good shape. For this she largely has James to thank because he keeps her in a routine. Since exercise is supposed to be beneficial for such patients, he makes sure that he takes regular walks with Dolores. For a decade, he has been taking her once a year to vacation at Disney World. Each time, he makes sure they stay in the same hotel room. Although her memory is impaired, she recognizes many parts of Disney World once they arrive.

James also has a good sense of humor. When asked what it is like living with someone who has dementia he replied, "Well, we've been married over 50 years, and the first 30 were worse than the last 20!"

Dolores laughs at that, although it's not clear if she understands James or is laughing because everyone else in the room is laughing too. She has a habit of repeating the last word or expression that someone else makes. She does it over 20 times in the space of an hour.

Indeed, Dolores's speech impairment is the most noticeable symptom of her illness. She struggles to put her thoughts into words and forming sentences is often very difficult.

Speech therapy can be very beneficial for dementia patients, as it exercises the speech centers of the brain. When Dolores goes to speech therapy, she shows considerable improvement. Unfortunately, she does not go all year-round. And when she is not in speech therapy, her abilities decline. Her habit of repeating another person's words is a sign that it is a time of year when she is not going to speech therapy.

In a subsequent interview, at a time when she is in speech therapy, she barely repeats other people's words at all. Instead, she will actually try to engage in the conversation.

"She gets pretty vocal as she has more therapy," said James. "Her speech therapist said that she gets more involved in what you're talking about the longer her therapy goes on."

Even when she is in therapy Dolores struggles to form complete sentences but at least she can put some words together.

"Need, need [unintelligible], more?" she asked her guest as she points to his coffee cup. "More [unintelligible] you?"

She was clearly grasping for a word. She tried again and succeeded. "Co ... coffee, you, more?"

She is much more able to understand a word like "coffee" when she is in therapy. "Anything over four letters, it's iffy when she's not in therapy," James said. "You can tell her words like 'go' or 'stop' and she'll get it. But when she's not in therapy, her ability to grasp more complex words declines."

The longer she is out of therapy, the more likely she'll have a thought in her mind but will not be able to say the words. Apparently, Dolores finds this very frustrating at times. Yet, her normally sweet and jovial demeanor can make it difficult for someone not familiar with her to discern when exactly Dolores feels frustrated.

"I'm here every day, so I'm used it," said James. "I can tell when she's having a hard time forming a word. Sometimes I know right away what she wants. We have a routine and if it is a particular time of day, I know she'll want to go for a walk or maybe she wants ice cream. Other times though, it gets difficult. The doctor says that she knows what she wants to say in her brain, but she can't bring it out."

When she gets frustrated, James brings out a large book of pictures that he has compiled over the years based on the things that Dolores has tried to say.

"We then go through the pictures and she'll point to what she is trying to say," said James. "Then I know what she's trying to say, and I can practically put the sentence together."

The fixed amount Medicare pays for speech therapy (more on that below) is sufficient to cover 20 visits to Dolores's speech therapist. In consultation with the speech therapist and the neurologist, James has decided that the schedule that works best for Dolores is for her to attend her first 12 sessions from January to March. She then stops until late September. She then has another four to five visits with the speech therapist until James takes her on their annual week-long trip to Disney World in November. After they return, Dolores goes to the remainder of her visits.

Both her neurologist and speech therapist would prefer that she attend speech therapy almost every week.

"The problem is that the therapist, in her report, has to show that Dolores is improving," James said. "If she gets to an even keel, then Medicare won't pay for it."

In other words, Dolores often improves in speech therapy to the point where she reaches a plateau. Once she reaches that plateau she is no longer "improving" and so her therapy must be stopped under Medicare's improvement standard.

Dolores usually reaches that plateau near the end of March. Not long after she stops, her speech abilities begin to decline.

"After she declines, then we go back and the speech therapist and our neurologist will reevaluate her," said James. "They'll then determine that she qualifies for more therapy."

In short, once Dolores's speech abilities decline, there is room for her to improve again. It would probably be better for Dolores if she could go almost every week to therapy so that her speech abilities would be the same year round. But Medicare does not make exceptions for maintaining a plateau.

Making Exceptions

If Dolores could get therapy year-round, she would almost certainly exceed what is known as the therapy cap, a limit that Medicare imposes on therapy payments. Technically, Medicare has two therapy caps: one for physical and speech therapy combined, and another for occupational therapy. As of 2015, the caps are set at a limit of $1,940 each.

There is an "exceptions process" which allows a patient to exceed the allowable limit. To qualify, the patient's therapist must file a report that satisfactorily explains to Medicare why the patient needs more therapy. Both the therapy caps and the exceptions process have been at the center of much political wrangling since the late 1990s.

Therapy caps came about because of legislation Congress passed in 1987 aimed at improving nursing homes. The legislation required all nursing homes participating in Medicare or Medicaid to conduct a full medical assessment on all their patients to determine which services were needed to improve their condition. The nursing homes then had to provide those services, including therapy. While Medicare would only pay for a brief stay in a nursing home, it would continue paying for a patient's therapy long after the nursing home stay.

The result was an explosion in charges to Medicare for therapy. Between 1990—the year the nursing home reforms went into effect—and 1996, Medicare spending for therapy grew at almost twice the rate of Medicare spending overall.[11] A GAO report found that the number of outpatient rehabilitation facilities participating in Medicare grew 60 percent in the four years after the change took effect.[12] It also found that Medicare was supposed to pay for only the "reasonable cost" of therapy, but that "the standard of 'reasonableness' for these services is so vague that there is almost no limit on the type and amount of costs that Medicare will reimburse."[13]

Congress first tried to get Medicare's therapy costs under control when it imposed caps on therapy as part of the Balanced Budget Act of 1997. It set the caps at $1,500, and permitted them to increase each year at a special rate of inflation known at the Medicare Economic Index. The therapy caps went into effect in 1999, but after that Congress suspended them from 2000 to 2002. The caps were in effect for part of 2003, but at the end of the year Congress again suspended them until the beginning of 2006.

One reason Congress suspended the caps is that lawmakers received numerous complaints from therapy providers about patients who needed more therapy than the reimbursement rules allowed. They got an earful from the groups that represent therapists in Washington, D.C., including the American Physical Therapy Association, the American Occupational Therapy Association, and the American Speech-Language Hearing Association. As later research would show, hundreds of thousands of patients would not receive adequate therapy if the caps were enforced. Enforcing the caps would also cost therapists hundreds of millions in Medicare reimbursements. The three major therapy organizations kept pressure on Congress to suspend the caps.

A second reason was that the Department of Health and Human Services (HHS) had been unable to develop a better system of paying for therapy as the Balanced Budget Act of 1997 required. HHS was supposed to develop a "needs-based" system that would take into account the amount of therapy a patient needed based on his health.

In late 2005, the GAO released another report noting that HHS had "made little progress toward such a system."[14] The GAO hinted that HHS faced an extremely complicated task. For example, HHS didn't have the tools to determine if certain diseases were more likely to require therapy beyond the caps. Data CMS had collected did not show "any particular conditions or diseases as more likely than others to be associated with payments exceeding the therapy caps."[15] The GAO also noted that most studies it examined did "not define the amount or mix of therapy services needed for Medicare beneficiaries with specific conditions or diseases" because "of the complexity of the patient factors involved."[16]

Since HHS was not able to develop a needs-based system, in 2006 Congress passed legislation requiring the CMS to develop an "exceptions process" for when therapists could exceed the therapy cap. Initially, CMS issued guidelines that were quite restrictive, listing specific instances when the therapy cap could be exceeded.[17] But the major therapy organizations objected, and CMS eventually revised the exceptions process, making it considerably easier for therapists to exceed the cap. Congress has never made the process permanent, instead renewing it on a year-to-year basis. For all this hassle, though, Congress has not been able to reduce the amount Medicare pays for therapy. Medicare expenditures for therapy grew an average of 10.1 percent annually between 1998 and 2008, while the number of beneficiaries receiving therapy grew only 2.9 percent annually.[18]

The guidelines for the exceptions process only reinforce the improvement standard. They state that "covered and medically necessary services"[19] qualify for exceptions to the cap. Again, though, therapy under Medicare's rules is considered "medically necessary" if there is "an expectation that the patient's condition will improve."[20]

The guidelines allow a patient to exceed the cap but only when more therapy is needed to achieve the patient's "prior functional status or maximum expected functional status within a reasonable amount of time."[21] The guidelines also state that "the condition or complexity that caused treatment to exceed the caps must be related to the therapy goals and must either be the condition that is being treated or a complexity that directly and significantly impacts the rate of recovery of the condition being treated such that it is appropriate to exceed the caps."[22]

Concepts such as "achieving prior functional status" and "rate of recovery" clearly imply improvement. There is nothing in the exceptions process that allows for exceeding the cap to help a patient slow the decline of a degenerative condition or to maintain a plateau.

A recent article in the *Journal of Poverty Law and Policy* noted exactly who is most likely to suffer because of the improvement standard:

> The impact on beneficiaries with chronic conditions is staggering. As the health of beneficiaries deteriorates, their need for nursing services and physical, occupational, and speech therapies increases. The skilled care denied them under the improvement standard is critical to slow the progression of the disease and to maintain functional ability. Yet these are precisely the people who are most likely to have their coverage terminated.[23]

The article argues that since the improvement standard is based on guidelines and is not found in the actual laws or regulations regarding Medicare, it is a phony standard. It could be easily corrected, the article contends, by CMS or by an executive order from the President. But, it notes that neither of those is likely, so the best course of action is litigation in the courts. Indeed, the Center for Medicare Advocacy filed a lawsuit hoping to settle the matter in federal court.[24]

Members of Congress could have modified the improvement standard so that people like Clay and Dolores would be eligible for additional therapy. The limited evidence that we have suggests that the reason

Congress didn't is that the improvement standard harmed only a relatively small number of Medicare beneficiaries.

There is no research estimating the number of Medicare beneficiaries who have their therapy discontinued due to the improvement standard. However, we can make inferences about the number of people harmed by the improvement standard based on other evidence.

First, CMS commissioned two studies examining the number of patients that were exceeding the therapy caps. In 2002, about 4.4 million Medicare beneficiaries received some form of therapy, and about 635,000, or 14 percent, would have exceeded the therapy cap.[25] If the caps had been enforced, therapists would have lost about $761 million. A later study in 2008 found about 5.1 million Medicare beneficiaries received therapy, and about 826,000, or 15 percent, exceeded the caps. Therapists would have lost $1.1 billion if they had not been permitted to go over the caps.[26]

With that many patients and that much money at stake, therapists surely complained to associations that represent them in Washington, D.C. about the number of patients who were making progress but would not reach their goals if they were not allowed to exceed the therapy cap. The lobbying disclosure forms of the American Physical Therapy Association, the American Occupational Therapy Association and the American Speech-Language Hearing Association show that each group spent hundred of thousands of dollars annually to lobby Congress, and that they try to influence Congress to either remove the therapy cap or to extend the exceptions process.

However, those forms show no lobbying for the purpose of changing the improvement standard. Imagine, though, that the improvement standard was affecting the same number of patients and costing therapists a similar amount of money as in the reports mentioned above. In that case, it is almost certain that the professional therapy associations would lobby to change the improvement standard.

In short, the major therapy associations did not push to modify the improvements standard. Rather, relief would have to come through litigation.

Uncoordinated

Coordination of care is another area of Medicare undertreatment.

In practice, what coordination of care means is that a health care provider, usually a primary care physician, monitors a patient's care so that his various treatments complement and do not conflict with each other. Properly coordinated care ensures that a patient sees the right providers (often physicians who are specialists) for his ailments; that each provider involved in the care is aware of what the other providers are doing to treat the patient; and that he is taking the proper medications and not taking ones that can produce harmful interactions. It also involves educating the patient on what he needs to do to properly care for his illness(es) and periodic checking up on the patient to ensure that he is taking his medications and keeping his appointments with physicians or other health care providers.[27]

A fairly extensive review of medical literature demonstrates the benefits of coordinating care. Patients with congestive heart failure who received coordinated care after leaving the hospital had lower readmission rates and improved mortality.[28] Diabetes patients receiving coordinated care had fewer problems controlling their blood sugar levels.[29] Care coordination helps patients having hip and knee replacement surgery recover with less pain and improves their functioning after the operation.[30] Other research finds that patients who are hospitalized for an illness are less likely to be readmitted if their care is coordinated following discharge.[31] Patients with multiple chronic conditions, known as "comorbidities" in the medical literature, were not only less likely to be re-hospitalized with the condition that put them in the hospital to begin with, they were also less likely to be hospitalized for any of their other illnesses if their care was coordinated.[32]

Unfortunately, Medicare beneficiaries often fare poorly in areas where better health outcomes depend on coordinated care.

Two areas with a troubling lack of care coordination include pharmaceutical use and cancer. Pharmaceutical use among patients age 65 and older who were at increased risk for death or functional decline found low rates (50 percent or less) of educating patients about their medications and monitoring patient use of medication.[33] A study of Medicare beneficiaries who had survived colorectal cancer found they had lower rates of follow-up care for heart conditions and diabetes than did non-cancer patients. The study stated that oncologists "may not be aware when their patients expect them to fulfill a primary care role" of coordinating care.[34]

Stroke is an area in which lack of care coordination has very serious consequences for Medicare beneficiaries. One study found that among patients hospitalized for a stroke, over half were re-hospitalized within a year,[35] while another study found more than 85 percent would be re-hospitalized over the next five years.[36]

Re-hospitalization has been a problem for Medicare beneficiaries for decades. In 1984 the *New England Journal of Medicine* reported that 19 percent of Medicare beneficiaries were readmitted to a hospital within 30 days of their initial admission.[37] A quarter century later, the same journal reported a nearly identical 30-day readmission rate of 19.6 percent. That article noted that a lack of follow-up visits, an integral part of care coordination, was a likely culprit: Billing records showed that 50.2 percent of the patients had no follow-up visit with a physician between initial discharge and re-hospitalization.[38]

Avoiding re-hospitalizations often means coordinating care for people with chronic conditions. As two prominent health care researchers put it:

> Our analysis of Medicare claims data suggests that the average Medicare beneficiary with one or more chronic conditions is seen by eight different physicians during a year; this indicates that the potential scope of the problem is quite large. The need for coordination of care and integrated information systems becomes especially important when a person has multiple chronic illnesses (for example, heart disease, asthma, and depression), each of which might

require treatment by a different specialist. In these cases, each clinician may be unaware of the exact treatments being delivered by the others.[39]

The authors estimated that about 20 million patients with chronic conditions received contradictory information from health care providers annually. Eighteen million were given different diagnoses for the same condition, and 17 million only discovered potential interactions among prescription drugs they were taking when they visited the pharmacist.

So why do Medicare beneficiaries fare so poorly in areas that can be much improved with greater coordination of care? The simple reason is Medicare doesn't pay providers to coordinate care.

The physicians most likely to coordinate care are primary care physicians. Consider the description CMS provides of a Medicare payment for an hour-long visit between a primary care physician and a new patient: "Office or other outpatient visit for the evaluation and management of a new patient, which require these 3 key components: A comprehensive history; a comprehensive examination; medical decision making of high complexity."[40] Coordination of care is not included. Thus, any physician who provides it is, in effect, providing it free of charge.

Hospitals are not paid to coordinate care either. When a patient is admitted to a hospital, Medicare pays for treating the illness that the patient was admitted for and any follow-up care the hospital may need to provide within 30 days of the patient being discharged from the hospital. After that, Medicare won't pay the hospital again unless the patient is readmitted. That provides hospitals a perverse incentive to avoid coordinating care since doing so helps prevent readmissions.

One reason Medicare doesn't pay for coordination of care is that Congress has never changed Medicare from a system that is largely an acute care system to one that is also a chronic care system. Acute care treats a patient for a brief period of time for a short but severe illness like a heart attack. Chronic care involves treating patients who have long-term conditions, such as a diabetes or heart disease. When Congress created

Medicare in 1965, medicine could treat acute illnesses but was very limited in what it could do for chronic conditions. In the decades since, medicine has made huge strides in treating chronic conditions. But Medicare, like most other government programs, adapts to changing conditions at a glacial pace if at all.

There is one part of Medicare that does use coordinated care to achieve better results. It's Medicare Advantage, the program in which beneficiaries receive their benefits through private health insurers. Medicare Advantage plans that are part of the Alliance of Community Health Plans, an organization that focuses on improving the delivery of health care, have a much better record of preventing re-hospitalizations and keeping patients out of the hospital in the first place than traditional Medicare.[41] They achieved these results by using coordinated care such as educating patients and families about the effects of certain drugs and the importance of proper nutrition and making certain patients had a follow-up visit with a physician after being discharged from the hospital. This is the same Medicare Advantage program that ObamaCare is supposed to cut $145 billion from between 2012 and 2017.

Unfortunately, the study on the Alliance of Community Health Plans, written just before the debate over ObamaCare, reached the wrong conclusion:

> In health care reform legislation, Congress has the chance to structure Medicare payment incentives and encourage system reforms that foster coordinated care and continuous patient engagement. By focusing on quality and delivery system reforms, Congress can promote the positive outcomes described [in the study].[42]

No, Congress can't. A company operating in the private sector relatively free from government regulations, like Alliance of Community Health Plans, has the flexibility to innovate, to try certain techniques and keep the ones that work and adjust or abandon the ones that don't. By contrast, lengthy, intricate regulations usually govern Medicare programs.

If following the regulations does not achieve improved outcomes for patients, providers in the programs do not have the flexibility to discard the regulations and try something else. If providers don't follow the regulations, they will not get paid. That is an important reason why Medicare coordinated-care demonstration projects, on average, rarely achieve good results.[43]

Are You in the Hospital?

Marion Dixon was 75 years old when she was admitted to a hospital in late 2003. After spending three days there, she was transferred to a skilled nursing facility. She assumed that Medicare would pay for both her hospital and skilled nursing facility stays. She was only half right.

CMS refused to pay for her stay in the skilled nursing facility. CMS claimed she had *not* spent the three days in the hospital that Medicare requires before paying for a stay in a skilled nursing facility.

In November 2004, Dixon filed suit against CMS with two other plaintiffs who were in a similar situation. However, the District Court of Connecticut sided with CMS.[44] The case was appealed, but the Second Circuit Court also agreed with CMS.[45] In the end, Dixon was stuck with a bill for over $11,000 for her skilled nursing home stay.

The courts sided with CMS because two of the days Dixon was in the hospital she was under "observation status." Under observation status, the hospital monitors a patient for a certain period of time until a physician determines that the patient can return home or has to be admitted as an "inpatient." Medicare does not consider a patient under observation status to be an inpatient—indeed, Medicare pays separate fees for observation status and inpatients status. Dixon ended up with a hefty bill because Medicare will only pay for skilled nursing facility care if a patient has spent *three days in the hospital as an inpatient.* Days spent in observation status do not count.

For reasons that are not fully understood, hospital use of observation status has been increasing. From 2001-2009, its use doubled.[46] The biggest increase came in recent years with a 25 percent jump from 2007-2009.[47]

About 3.5 percent of Medicare beneficiaries are put on observational status annually. An Inspector General report found that beneficiaries who received skilled nursing facility care and were not reimbursed by Medicare incurred an average of $10,503 in charges.[48] A recent story in the *New York Times* revealed a Medicare patient who incurred $35,000 in charges from her stay in a skilled nursing facility.[49]

One reason for the increase in the use of observational status may be that it seems to be better for patients' health. Research suggests that observation units often provide high-quality care and are generally safer for patients.[50] The same literature also shows the practice may be more efficient for hospitals.

The most likely cause of the growth of observational status is Medicare began paying for it in 2002. It initially paid for observation status for three types of diagnoses: chest pain, congestive heart failure, and asthma. In 2008, it began paying for observational status for any diagnosis.

By 2010, the growing trend in observational status caught the attention of CMS. A number of CMS officials held a conference call with medical providers. The officials were concerned that some patients admitted under observation status stayed more than two days. They said that CMS "has been clear through its guidance documents that we don't expect observation care to last more than 24 or 48 hours."[51]

CMS would have more reason to be concerned due to ObamaCare. One portion of ObamaCare tried to reduce the number of hospital readmissions among Medicare beneficiaries by penalizing hospitals that had too many readmissions. CMS defined a readmission as one that took place within thirty days of the initial admission. However, under CMS rules, a patient wasn't initially admitted unless he was admitted as an inpatient. Obviously, this would give hospitals incentive to keep patients even longer under observation status.

To avoid this, CMS instituted the "two-midnight rule." Under this rule Medicare would consider someone admitted to the hospital to be an inpatient when a "physician expects the beneficiary to require care that crosses two midnights and admits the beneficiary based upon that expectation."[52] That made it far more difficult for a hospital to keep a patient more than two days without admitting him or her as an inpatient.

However, what if a patient needed inpatient care in a hospital but would not need to stay two days? In such instances, CMS had now substituted its judgment for the judgment of physicians who dealt directly with patients. For Frank Alfisi, it would prove deadly.

Frank grew up in New York City. He had raised four children with his wife, Phyllis. By 2013, he was retired. The chemotherapy from a bout with cancer a few years earlier had caused his kidneys to fail. Three times a week he would go to dialysis.

One morning in mid-November 2013, he woke up nauseous and vomiting. Thinking he had the stomach flu, he decided to stay home and rest. He missed his scheduled dialysis for that day.

Frank woke up the next day feeling worse and, seeking help, called his daughter, Amy DiFrancesca. As Jeffery Lord explained in his account in the *American Spectator*:

> Amy instructed her Dad to quickly push his life alert button. Knowing the soon-to-arrive ambulance would take him to St. Joseph's Hospital in Bethpage, Long Island, Amy called ahead. "I called ahead to the ER and told them the last time he was dialyzed was 3 ½ days ago. I also gave them all the pertinent info; meds he's taking, his medical conditions, Doctor info, etc."[53]

Frank needed dialysis, but under Medicare's rules, he couldn't receive it at a hospital unless he was an inpatient. Yet dialysis only takes a few hours and thus provides no justification for a physician to admit such a patient for two days in the hospital.

Soon, the toxins in Frank's body had built up dangerously high, causing his blood pressure to increase. After about 10 hours in the hospital,

Frank's increased blood pressure caused him to have a seizure. A few hours later he had a second seizure.

At this point Frank was in such bad shape one of his physicians was able to justify having him admitted to the hospital as an inpatient. Finally, he was able to receive dialysis. Frank briefly recovered, but the damage was done. He was now wheelchair bound, needed portable oxygen, and had lost much of his sight.

Frank's quality of life had deteriorated to the point that he lost the will to live and decided to move into a hospice. He never made it, dying on January 14, 2014 in the hospital.

Chances are other patients may have suffered a similar fate. According to Amy:

> When my sister-in-law, an ER nurse in Upstate NY, found out about this, she said similar situations have happened where she works. Patients who should be admitted for a day are discharged because they don't fit the criteria to be admitted for two or more days. She said it's not a secret and while we, the public, may be unaware of this, it's well known by doctors and nurses.[54]

Unfortunately, while Frank's case may not be isolated, it probably is rare, possibly too rare for much political pressure to be brought on Congress to make changes in the two-midnight rule. Amy has contacted her Senators, Charles Schumer and Kirsten Gillibrand, and her Representative, Peter King, about her father's plight. She has not heard back from any of them.[55]

Too Small, Too Sick, Too Transient

The reason Congress has not addressed the issues of the improvement standard, coordination of care or the three-day inpatient rule for skilled nursing facility care is that the groups affected by Medicare's policy failures in these areas are too small, too sick, and too transient to be an effective political force. In the case of the two-midnight rule, the reason for Congressional inaction is more likely that it is still very new. CMS only finalized the rule in August 2013. But given how few people seem likely to suffer from it, the political forces for changing it are probably small as well.

Patients with primary progressive MS were some of the most likely to run afoul of the improvement standard. Of the roughly 250,000 to 400,000 Americans suffering from MS, primary-progressive accounts for 10 to 15 percent of those, or 25,000 to 60,000. Even if their physical limitations didn't present serious obstacles to political organization, their numbers at most average about 137 per congressional district and 1,200 per state—not even a blip on the radar of House or Senate elections.

There are far more Alzheimer's patients, an estimated 5.4 million in the U.S. Exactly how many of them ran afoul of the improvement standard is not known, but if it was even one-fifth, they might have the numbers to influence Congress. But, of course, Alzheimer's patients also suffer from mental impairment. People who suffer from confusion, memory loss, and attention and language difficulties, sadly, aren't going to be a political force to be reckoned with.

The beneficiaries who are most in need of coordinated care are usually some of the sickest beneficiaries with many comorbidities. Patients that ill are not likely to do what needs to be done to pressure Congress. Consider stroke patients.

Roughly 795,000 people suffer a stroke annually in the U.S., but not all of those result in serious impairment. Estimates put those severely impaired by a stroke at about one-third, or almost 265,000. Since this happens annually, over time it might amount to enough numbers to be a viable political force. But those with severe impairment suffer from brain damage, obviously a huge impediment to effective political organizing.

Even if they had the capability to engage in political activity, many of these patients won't survive long enough to wage the often lengthy political battles needed to achieve policy changes. Stroke is the fourth leading cause of death in the U.S. Alzheimer's is the sixth and diabetes is the seventh.[56] Heart disease is the leading cause of death and, depending on the study, those with chronic heart failure survive an average of 2.5 to 4 years after a heart attack.[57]

And, finally, becoming politically active may be the furthest thing from such patients' minds. When asked, Clay Bell and Joe Kopytek said they hadn't contacted their representative or senators about Clay losing his therapy treatment.

"I'm not sure why," Joe said, when asked. "With all the things we were dealing with, I guess we just didn't think about it."

James Reiss gave a similar response.

"No, it just never occurred to me to contact them," he said. "I suppose I should."

Fortunately, the Reiss's may get relief. In late 2012, the HHS jettisoned the improvement standard in the face of the Center for Medicare Advocacy's lawsuit. Apparently, attorneys at HHS realized that since the improvement standard was not based on law or regulation, HHS would probably lose in court. Instead, HHS settled and agreed to re-write the standards so that Medicare coverage of therapy "'does not turn on the presence or absence of an individual's potential for improvement,' but is based on the beneficiary's need for skilled care."[58]

The change came too late for Clay Bell. Sadly, he passed away in May 2012 at age 52. Would more therapy have stemmed his decline and given him a longer life? Now we'll never know.

Nor will we probably ever know how many other people with MS or dementia saw their health decline or died prematurely because of the improvement standard. What we can be sure of is the medical community will eventually discover another treatment that can help a group of Medicare beneficiaries that Medicare doesn't pay for. And, if that group is too small and too ill to wield sufficient political clout, chances are slim Medicare will change its payment policy. Given the way Medicare functions, that scenario is almost inevitable.

6. What Is "Waste"?

Selma Hartmann was lying on a hospital bed, her body swollen to twice its normal size. Sadly, it didn't have to happen.

Selma's life was one filled with challenges that she overcame. She lost both her mother and her brother at a very young age. She came down with rheumatoid arthritis early in life.

Nevertheless, she had a positive outlook.

"She loved life, in part because she knew how it could be shortened so quickly," said her daughter Sandra Klos.

Selma worked most of her life and managed to raise three daughters. When she retired, she began volunteering at nursing homes.

"She called herself 'Sel the Party Gal,'" laughed Sandra. "Wherever there were people, that was where she wanted to be."

When she was in her 50s, physicians found cancer in her colon close to her rectum. She had two surgeries. The first removed the cancer, but left adhesions and scar tissue that made bowel movements difficult. The second surgery was a colostomy, in which an incision, called a "stoma," is made in the abdomen and the colon is then sutured to it. A medical device, usually an "ostomy pouch," is then attached on the outside of the stoma to collect fecal material.

By the time she was in her 80s, Selma's arthritis was getting the better of her. Getting around was increasingly difficult, so with Sandra's help she moved into a nursing home.

In February 2002, blood was found in her feces. Selma's physician suggested she see a gastroenterologist because the blood could signal the return of her colon cancer.

She saw a gastroenterologist who recommended a colonoscopy.

In a colonoscopy, a camera-equipped device known as a colonoscope is inserted through the patient's rectum into the colon. This allows the physician to see the colon on a television screen. A pump in the colonoscope allows the physician to inject air into the colon, a process known as insufflation. This expands the colon, making it easier to detect cancer and pre-cancerous growths called polyps.

On February 18, 2002, Sue, one of Selma's other daughters, accompanied her to DePaul Hospital in St. Louis for the colonoscopy. Selma was brought to the endoscopy suite and given a mild sedative.

The colonoscopy had difficulties from the start. A hernia near Selma's stoma made it difficult to maneuver the colonoscope into the colon. Eventually, the physician switched to a pediatric colonoscope, normally used on children. Since it was smaller, the physician hoped it would be easier to place it in her colon. However, the physician was unable to maneuver the device to view the upper portion of the colon and Sandra believes he overcompensated by using too much insufflation during the procedure.

After the procedure, a nurse let Sue know that she could visit her mom. Sue found Selma moaning in pain and her body swelling up.

Hysterical, Sue ran to a phone to call Sandra.

"My sister called and told me that mom was about as big as house," Sandra said. "She thought that she'd had an allergic reaction to the sedation."

Sandra called her husband, Robert, who worked very close to the hospital. She asked him to go to the hospital to find out exactly what was going on and to support her sister.

It took Sandra a while to get to the hospital because in recent months she had developed breathing difficulties. Hearing her sister in hysterics triggered a breathing attack, and she had to wait until she got it under control.

When she finally arrived at the hospital, she was shocked at her mother's condition.

"She weighed about 130 pounds and she looked like she was over 250," she said.

Sandra had spent many years working as a physician assistant and knew medical terminology. Confronting the gastroenterologist, she asked, "Did you perforate her?"

A perforation refers to a small puncture in the colon caused during a colonoscopy. Although relatively rare, it can cause air to leak from the colon into the rest of the body. Bacteria from the colon spreads to the rest of the body, causing an infection that can lead to inflammation of the lining that covers many of the internal organs, a potentially deadly condition known as peritonitis.

The gastroenterologist replied, "Well, I'm 99.9 percent sure that I didn't do anything." He agreed to send Selma for a CAT scan to determine what went wrong.

He ordered a CAT scan "with contrast." That meant Selma would have to drink a dye so that the organs in her abdomen would be highlighted during the scan.

"The nurse brings a great big bottle of contrast and said, 'Ok, she has to drink that,'" Sandra said. "And I said to the nurse, 'Gosh, why don't you overwhelm her?' So I took the bottle of contrast and gave it to my mom little by little in a cup. And just as I had managed to get her to drink most of it, she spewed it up."

It took about three hours to get Selma the CAT scan.

After Selma was returned to her room, more hours passed before a general surgeon visited them.

He asked who was in charge of Selma. Sandra and Sue replied that they were.

"Well, the CAT scan is terrible," the general surgeon said. "There is air everywhere in her. I can do surgery on her, but she'll either die on the operating table or she'll die in the hospital. She'll never survive. What do you want to do?"

Sue fainted.

"I thought, well, I don't want to lose her on the table, I want to be able to talk to her," Sandra said. "She was able to talk a little bit. It hurt her, because her whole face was swollen. Even her eyes—they were swollen shut and they stayed that way until she died."

Although Sandra had at first said no to an operation, she and her husband then hemmed and hawed about what to do. The surgeon got testy and impatient, finally saying, "We'll put a central line in her and start giving her antibiotics.'"

"I guess that gave me some hope that my mom might survive," said Sandra. "I don't know, at that point I guess I was just dreaming."

Sandra, her husband and Sue stayed the night with Selma. The next morning, Sandra ran into the general surgeon outside in the hall.

"Is it still okay to do surgery on my mother?" she asked.

"Oh no, it's too late," he replied.

Sandra went back into her mother's room.

About an hour later, the general surgeon came into the room. He was doing rounds with some medical students.

"Is she still on a central line?" the surgeon asked. When Sandra said yes, the surgeon replied, "How long are we going to play this game?"

"Well, he was the one who suggested the central line," Sandra recalled, anger welling in her voice. "You throw somebody a straw like that, they're going to grasp it, and I did. He was the one who suggested the antibiotics, now he was calling it a game."

The central line was removed. After that, Selma asked Sandra if she should have the surgery. Sandra had to tell her that it was too late. Silence ensued, until Sandra asked her mom if she wanted her dentures put in, which were sitting on a bedside table.

"Oh, yeah, yeah," Selma replied.

Selma then requested that some of her music be brought to the room. Her grandson, Sandra's son, went to her nursing home and retrieved her tape recorder and some tapes.

"These were all childhood songs she'd grown up with and taught to us," Sandra said. "So we sang along to the music, and she sang with us."

About two days after entering the hospital for a colonoscopy, Selma Hartmann passed away.

An autopsy later revealed Selma had suffered far worse than a perforation. Apparently, the physician blew so much air into Selma that the upper portion of her colon had what are known as "serosal tears." Sandra described the difference between a perforation and serosal tears as the difference between a small hole in a car tire and an actual blowout.

Two other aspects make her death all the more tragic. First, the autopsy revealed that Selma did not have any tumors or polyps in her colon. Sandra would later learn that her mother experienced diarrhea for a few days in February, something that could have caused the blood to be in her feces.

Second was Selma's age. She was 88, which leads to the question, why would she be having a colonoscopy in the first place? Even if the physicians had found cancer in her colon, what could they have done? At that age, she was unlikely to survive surgery or chemotherapy. Performing the colonoscopy was wasteful and forgoing it would have saved Selma's life.

Medicare and Colonoscopy

Medicare produces much waste or, as it is called in health-policy circles, "overuse." There are two basic reasons for this. First, Medicare is a third-party payer system, which means that it—and not the patient—pays the physician for the services used by the patient. In most other areas of our economy, the consumer pays the provider directly. To save money, the consumer often limits how much he purchases. Under Medicare, a patient doesn't save any money if he uses less, so he has much less incentive to restrict how much care he receives.

The second reason is that Medicare uses a system of price controls. Rather than let buyers and sellers determine prices, the bureaucrats at Medicare set them at what they think is the correct price. They are almost always wrong. Medicare pays too little for some services, which creates shortages that can keep people from getting the services they need, and it pays too much for other services, which encourages physicians and hospitals to provide too many of them.

Colonoscopies appear to be one of the services for which Medicare pays too much.

Prior to 1998, Medicare paid for colonoscopies on a very limited basis. Starting in 1998, Congress required Medicare to pay for colonoscopies for high-risk individuals, such as those with a family history of colon cancer.

Jay Monahan's death from colon cancer in 1998 precipitated Medicare's expanded coverage of colonoscopies. A legal commentator for NBC, Monahan was married to Katie Couric, then co-host of the *Today Show*. The death of her husband propelled Couric on a colon cancer awareness campaign. As part of it, she underwent a colonoscopy shown on *Today* in March 2000. Within weeks, stories ran in local newspapers about physicians and hospitals overwhelmed with requests for colonoscopies. Indeed, a statistical analysis found that Couric's colonoscopy led to a temporary jump in the number of colonoscopies performed in the U.S.[1]

After that, Washington began to feel the pressure to expand Medicare coverage of colonoscopies. By fall 2000, Congress had proposed the "Medicare Benefits and Improvement Act," which would permit Medicare to pay for a colonoscopy for each beneficiary once every 10 years, regardless of risk, beginning July 2001. President Bill Clinton initially opposed the bill, but in October 2000 he joined Couric at a rally against colon cancer. This public appearance made his opposition to a bill including Medicare coverage of colonoscopies less tenable. The bill was incorporated in budget legislation and signed into law in December 2000.

106

The number of colonoscopies Medicare paid for increased dramatically. From January 1998 to June 2001, when Medicare paid only for colonoscopies for beneficiaries at high risk, an average of 889 out of every 100,000 beneficiaries had a colonoscopy per quarter. That more than doubled, to an average of 1,919, every quarter from July 2001 to December 2002.[2]

The three most common colonoscopies Medicare pays for are a diagnostic colonoscopy, a colonoscopy with a biopsy and a colonoscopy with a polypectomy. Medicare paid over $632 million for those three procedures in 2000, the last full year that Medicare paid only for colonoscopies for high-risk patients.[3] In 2002, the first full year after the policy change, Medicare paid over $785 million for those procedures, an increase of 24 percent.[4] By 2009, that figure rose to $882 million, an increase of almost 40 percent from 2000.[5] That increase could not be accounted for by a rise in Medicare enrollment, which rose only about 15.4 percent over that time. The increase strongly suggests that Medicare pays well above the market price for colonoscopies.

Did the increase in colonoscopies result in improved health for Medicare beneficiaries or greater waste of health care? Well, probably both.

An analysis that compared the period when Medicare paid only for colonoscopies for high-risk patients to the period immediately following the policy change (July 2001-December 2002) found that early detection of polyps in the upper portion of the colon rose from 22 percent to 24 percent.[6] From 2000 to 2009, deaths from colon cancer among those age 65 and older declined from 43,616 to 38,120, a drop of over 16 percent.[7] Of course, many factors probably contributed to that drop, but it's likely that Medicare's coverage expansion was one of them.

Yet with the improvement in colon health also came overuse of colonoscopies. A study in the *Archives of Internal Medicine* examined beneficiaries who had a colonoscopy and then had another one within the next seven years. It found that over 42 percent of those beneficiaries had *negative* colonoscopies the first time—that is, there was nothing in their first colonoscopies that would warrant a follow-up colonoscopy within seven years. It also found a sizeable number of repeat colonoscopies among beneficiaries for whom removing a polyp would likely do very little if anything to extend their lives, such as those who were at least 80 years old and/or quite ill.[8]

Fortunately, the rate of complications and deaths from the procedure is very small. A 35-year study ending in 2001 found the highest risk of a perforation was about 0.73 percent and the highest risk of death was about 0.03 percent.[9] However, if Medicare overpays for colonoscopies, then more Medicare beneficiaries are encouraged to have the procedure and are subjected to those risks.

In the last few years, the effectiveness of the colonoscopy has undergone a re-thinking, initiated by the same physician who aggressively pushed its use in the late 1980s. In 1988, Dr. Alfred Nuegut co-authored an article arguing for the widespread use of the colonoscopy.[10] At the time, the procedure for seeing the colon was known as a sigmoidoscopy, a scope that was only able to view the distal, or lower part, of the colon. When the colonoscopy came along, the "thought was if looking at one part of the colon is good, looking at the whole colon must be better," said one physician.[11]

In a recent article Dr. Neugut and co-author Dr. Benjamin Lebwohl wrote that:

> Despite the increased adverse effect profile of colonoscopy, including higher perforation rate, need for sedation, time and bother commitment of the patient (who must adhere to an arduous bowel preparation and miss a day of work), and increased cost, the presumed mortality benefit of colonoscopy has been used as a justification to outweigh these negatives.

> Thus, it is disconcerting to recognize that even today limited evidence demonstrates reduced mortality for those who undergo colonoscopy vs sigmoidoscopy.[12]

They note that recent studies have shown colonoscopies only improve the detection of colon cancer or pre-cancerous polyps in the lower colon. Although the research is still preliminary, it is possible that colonoscopies do not improve mortality any more than sigmoidoscopies. *If* a sigmoidoscopy is as effective as a colonoscopy, then Medicare has been paying for a lot of waste. And since a sigmoidoscopy is safer than a colonoscopy, Medicare's payment policy has also been subjecting beneficiaries to needless risk.

No Hard Feelings

Sandra felt as though the hospital and physicians had treated her mom with a lack of compassion. It was the decisive factor that made her take the physician and hospital to court.

"I didn't care that much about the money, but just the way they treated my mom," she said. "I just wanted my mom to have her day in court, her rights protected and to let other people know about this so it wouldn't happen again."

Sandra still has a pretty vivid memory of the court case.

"The doctor we had on our side made a presentation, but I'm not sure how effective it was," she recalls. Apparently, Selma's injury was referred to as a "perforation," not the serosal tears that had actually occurred. Sandra doesn't think that the jury ever knew the full extent of the damage to Selma's upper colon. Her attorney, it seems, never fully emphasized that Selma's colon suffered from serosal tears.

Sandra's attorney argued that the physician had over-insufflated Selma. But in the final summation, the defense attorneys appeared to get the upper hand. They showed the jury a model of a lower colon and argued that any extra air would have settled there. They claimed that the autopsy showed that the lower colon had expanded by only about one-quarter of an inch, not enough to suggest excessive insufflation.

"I remember thinking, 'Why would the air settle there?'" Sandra said. "All of the air went up into her body."

But the defense got to go last in the summation so there was no way for the plaintiffs to refute it. Apparently it did enough to confuse the jury.

Ultimately, the jury voted 9-3 in favor of the defense. (In a civil trial in Missouri, only nine of twelve jurors must agree to reach a verdict.)

"I later asked one of the jurors if my mother's age had had anything to do with their decision," Sandra said. "He said no, that they just couldn't decide if the death was due to the perforation or the insufflation." Legally, perforation is considered a risk of colonoscopy and usually not actionable in court.

While Sandra was deeply disappointed by the jury's verdict, she didn't seem defeated.

"I decided early on that whatever my peers decide, I would accept."

At the end she showed extraordinary grace. "Afterwards, I went up to the doctor who gave my mother the colonoscopy, shook his hand and said, 'No hard feelings.'"

Dartmouth

While there is waste in Medicare, exactly how much waste is there? Where is it most likely to be found? And what can be done to reduce it? One group that claims to have found some of the answers is the Dartmouth Atlas.

The Dartmouth Atlas is a major project run out of Dartmouth College that uses Medicare data to examine wide variations in the amount of medical treatment across the nation. One of its most significant claims is that patients in regions that spend more on health care often don't have better health outcomes (and sometimes have worse outcomes) than patients in regions that spend less.

While the Dartmouth Atlas now covers the entire nation, its origins are in one of the smallest states, Vermont. In 1967, John E. "Jack"

Wennberg was hired at the University of Vermont as the director of a Medicare program for regional planning. Wennberg, a graduate of the McGill University Faculty of Medicine who interned at Johns Hopkins University, would use the money from a government grant to determine medical need in the state. Along with a statistician named Alan Gittelsohn, Wennberg managed to get the 16 hospitals in the state to computerize their data on medical treatment. They hoped that the data would reveal where medical resources could be better targeted.

What they found stunned them. The use of certain medical procedures varied widely even in a small state like Vermont. For example, in one area of the state only seven percent of children had had a tonsillectomy, while 75 miles away about 70 percent of children had had their tonsils removed. They also found wide variations among regions for hysterectomies, appendectomies, and mastectomies.

Wennberg and Gittelsohn tried to come up with explanations for the variations. One possibility was that patients in some areas demanded more treatment than those in other areas. That parents in one area of Vermont would demand tonsillectomies for their children at a rate nearly 10 times higher than parents in another area, though, didn't seem likely.

They also considered the possibility that people in some regions were sicker than those in other regions. The problem with that explanation is that Vermont is fairly homogenous. It was highly improbable that children in one area of the state were 10 times sicker than children in another.

The explanation they settled on was that physicians caused the variation in medical care. Physicians had different practice patterns. Some favored using surgery more than others, regardless of whether there was evidence that surgery was necessary.

This perspective made them quite unpopular among most of the medical community.

Yet Wennberg was undeterred. He next turned his attention to Maine, where again he and his fellow researchers found wide variations in tonsillectomies, hysterectomies, hernia repair, and other surgeries.[13] In 1979, Wennberg was hired by the head of the medical school at Dartmouth who recognized the importance of his work. He and a group of researchers who had, over the years, joined him at Dartmouth worked on the Clinton health care plan in the early 1990s. Although that reform effort fell apart, the work Wennberg and his colleagues conducted became the Dartmouth Atlas.

Eventually, Wennberg and his fellow researchers coined the term "supply-sensitive care." It means that the supply of medical care in a region is heavily influenced by the attitudes of physicians in that region and the supply of medical resources they have at their disposal. As Wennberg would later write,

> The theories that drove individual physician's decisions also varied. As we would eventually discover, individual practice styles appeared to be determined in part by specific ideological factors, enthusiasms for a particular diagnostic tool or treatment such as tonsillectomy, and in part by the sheer supply or availability of medical resources. In other words, physicians who practiced in a region of the state where hospital beds were in abundant supply tended to hospitalize their patients more often than their colleagues in regions where beds were less available.[14]

To better examine the variation in medical care across the United States, the researchers at the Dartmouth Atlas focused on Medicare spending and divided the nation into 306 "hospital referral regions" (HRRs). An HRR contains a population of at least 120,000, is geographically contiguous, and must contain at least one hospital where patients are referred for major cardiovascular procedures and one hospital where they are referred for major neurological procedures.[15]

To determine how much of the variation in Medicare spending was caused by patient demand and what was the result of supply-sensitive care, the Dartmouth Atlas examined Medicare data on what HRRs spent on end-of-life care. More precisely, they examined how much was spent on chronically ill patients in the last six months of life because such patients are usually quite ill regardless of which area of the country they live in.

Thus, differences in the amount spent on end-of-life care could not be attributed to factors associated with patient demand.

An examination of Medicare data from the mid-1990s found that on average, HRRs in the lowest-spending quintile spent about $9,074 on Medicare patients in the last six months of life, while in the highest-spending quintile HRRs spent $14,644, a difference of 61 percent. Supply-sensitive care appeared to account for the wide variation in end-of-life spending. HRRs in the highest-spending quintile had, on average, 31 percent more physicians and over one third more hospital beds than HRRs in the lowest-spending quintile.[16] They also found wide variations in Medicare spending not only on end-of-life care[17] but also on chronic conditions such as cancer, congestive heart failure and chronic obstructive pulmonary disease.[18]

The higher Medicare spending in some areas did not result in better health outcomes. Dartmouth researchers found that patients who had suffered hip fractures, heart attacks or colon cancer in the higher-spending HRRs had no better survival rates than those in the lower-spending HRRs.[19] A study of heart attack survival from 1996-2002 found that survival rates were no better in hospitals that increased spending during that period.[20]

Other research suggested that increased Medicare spending could cause harm. An examination of Medicare spending at the state level found that people in higher-spending states had lower quality health outcomes than people in states with lower spending.[21] Dartmouth researchers also suggested that, in areas with higher spending, patients were often exposed to greater risk because they were more likely to be treated for ailments that needed little to no treatment.[22]

It wasn't until shortly after 2000 that the Dartmouth Atlas came to prominence. It did so for three reasons. The first was a series of articles that Wennberg and his colleagues Elliot Fisher and Jonathan Skinner published between 2001 and 2003 that grabbed the attention of health care policy experts. In the first, they presented research showing that because of wide variations in treatment across the United States, "nearly 20 percent of total Medicare expenditures … appears to provide no benefit in terms of survival, nor is it likely that this extra spending improves the quality of life."[23] (They would later increase the estimate of overuse to 30 percent.[24])

In early 2002, they published an article in *Health Affairs* that repeated the arguments about wide regional variations in Medicare spending. However, unlike most academic articles, this one couched the findings in rhetoric that was unforgettable: "The difference in lifetime Medicare spending between a typical sixty-five-year-old in Miami and one in Minneapolis is more than $50,000, equivalent to a new Lexus GS 400 with all the trimmings."[25] In the following years, that line would be repeated countless times in articles, blog posts and interviews about health care in the U.S.

Elliot Fisher and some other colleagues followed that up in 2003 with two articles in the prestigious *Annals of Internal Medicine* examining Medicare spending on end-of-life care. They found that Medicare patients in the highest-spending regions received over 60 percent more care than those in the lowest-spending regions in the last five years of life. Yet patients in the high-spending regions did not have better health outcomes, nor were they any more satisfied with the quality of their care than those in the lowest-spending regions.[26] The message was clear: there was a great deal of waste in the Medicare system.

The second reason the Dartmouth Atlas came to prominence was the 2007 book, *Overtreated: Why Too Much Medicine Is Making Us Sicker And Poorer*. Its author, Shannon Brownlee, brought to life many instances of overtreatment, from psychotropic drugs to heart surgery. The most captivating part of *Overtreated* was its explanation of the Dartmouth Atlas. Brownlee took its research and theory of supply-sensitive care and put it in language more accessible to a larger audience.

The final reason was that the Dartmouth Atlas's research became politically useful. President Obama's point man on the health care overhaul was his chief of the Office and Management and Budget, Peter Orszag. Orszag often touted the work of Wennberg and his colleagues when promoting ObamaCare:

"Researchers [at the Dartmouth Atlas] have estimated that nearly 30 percent of Medicare's costs could be saved without negatively affecting health outcomes if spending in high- and medium-cost areas could be reduced to the level in low-cost areas—and those estimates could probably be extrapolated to the health care system as a whole."[27]

For Orszag, the Dartmouth Atlas must have seemed like a dream come true. Finding waste in the Medicare system was relatively easy—just look at the high-spending regions. Furthermore, by eliminating that waste, the federal government could cut spending without inconveniencing Medicare patients. If some of that waste in Medicare could be diverted to help fund the health insurance and Medicaid expansions in ObamaCare, all the better!

It also meant that for Orszag and his ilk, transforming the health care system would be *relatively* easy. If physicians are largely responsible for the waste, then government only has to control a relatively small group of people to make changes. Granted, there are just under one million physicians, and it is by no means an easy feat for government bureaucrats to control that many people. But it is easier to control them than the nearly 50 million Medicare beneficiaries. The Dartmouth Atlas supplied Orszag with the theory he needed to justify government controlling the behavior of physicians.

As we shall see, Orszag should have been far more circumspect before the ideas derived from Dartmouth Atlas were ever put into public policy. Subsequent research suggests that there are major holes in the Dartmouth Atlas theories. Yet for someone on a mission like Orszag, circumspection is not a common quality. Orszag would succeed in putting provisions in ObamaCare based on the Dartmouth Atlas, provisions that could prove harmful to many Medicare beneficiaries.

ACOs

One way that the Dartmouth Atlas influenced ObamaCare was by supplying the framework to overhaul the way care is delivered to Medicare recipients. Wennberg claims that "high spending levels and poor outcomes may be the consequence of a *third* factor—poor organizations and system coordination failure, which we know are endemic in our health care system."[28]

This led other Dartmouth Atlas researchers, such as Elliot Fisher and Jonathan Skinner, to argue that what was needed was a "reform proposal for Medicare designed to foster the development of accountable care organizations (ACOs)." ACOs would, "if broadly implemented ... offer a feasible path toward achieving higher-quality, more efficient care that meets the interests of payers, patients, and providers."[29]

ACOs were subsequently included in ObamaCare. CMS released regulations on participating in Medicare as an ACO in 2011, and in 2012 over 100 ACOs began operating for Medicare patients.

An ACO is, in the jargon of health care policy wonks, a "model" of health care delivery. Under the ACO model, groups of health care providers—including physicians, nurses, hospitals and others—will take responsibility for the care of at least 5,000 Medicare patients. If an ACO improves the health of its patients while also saving on costs, the providers will get to share in the savings. In theory, this will incentivize the providers in the ACO to work together to coordinate patient care.

Like a health maintenance organization (HMO), a patient's care in an ACO will be centered around a primary care physician who will take care of a patient's basic health care needs and refer him to the care of other physicians in the ACO when needed. Unlike an HMO, patients are not restricted to seeing only the physicians within the ACO. A patient can choose to go outside the ACO anytime he wishes.

Much ink has been spilled debating whether ACOs will succeed at improving the quality of care while reducing costs.[30] Chances are, as with any model of health care delivery, some will succeed while many will fail. The only reason this has to be a concern for Medicare beneficiaries is that the aim of ObamaCare is to put most, if not all, of the beneficiaries into ACOs.

Nancy-Ann DeParle, one of the architects of ObamaCare, wrote that reforms like ACOs "will unleash forces that favor integration across the continuum of care ... Consequently, the health care system will evolve into 1 of 2 forms: organized around hospitals or organized around physicians groups." She continues that:

> Physicians who embrace these changes and opportunities are likely to deliver the greatest benefits to their patients, the health system, and themselves. Physician practices that accept the challenge will be rewarded in the future payment system. Once we accomplish this transformation, the U.S. system will be more reliable, will be more accessible, and will offer high-quality and higher-value care.[31]

Medicare beneficiaries will find themselves joining ACOs via their physicians. Presumably so many physicians will join ACOs that beneficiaries will have a hard time finding a physician that is not a member of one. As one critic put it, patients "will be getting these mysterious letters from their hospitals and doctors saying, 'Gee, you might be in an ACO and here's what it means.'"[32]

The early results are mixed. Medicare's biggest ACO project is called the Medicare Shared Savings Program. As of 2013, 220 ACOs had enrolled in the program. CMS released data on the savings generated by these ACOs program in September 2014 that was underwhelming. Just over half of ACOs achieved any savings. Of those, only 52, less than one-fourth, saved enough to actually share the savings with Medicare.[33]

The amount saved was small as well. Between the ACOs in the Shared Saving Program and the ACOs in another program called Pioneer, the saving generated by ACOs in 2013 was $372 million. About 4.1 million Medicare beneficiaries were enrolled in those ACOs. If the $372 million in savings is generated for 4.1 million beneficiaries, then a rough calculation shows that $4.7 billion in savings would be generated if all 52.3 million Medicare beneficiaries were in an ACO. That's about one percent of Medicare's total budget.[34]

No data was released on whether ACOs in the Medicare Shared Savings Program improved the health of the Medicare beneficiaries who were enrolled, patients in ACOs in the Pioneer program did show some improvement.[35] But beneficiaries may end up suffering because ACOs are usually relatively large organizations that employ many physicians. A recent study found that physician practices with 10 or more physicians had 33 percent more preventable hospital admission than did practices with only one or two physicians.[36]

Medicare beneficiaries are too diverse to push all or most of them into one health care delivery model with any reasonable expectation of success. At one extreme are Medicare beneficiaries with multiple chronic conditions; at the other, beneficiaries with virtually no health problems. In between is a whole range of beneficiaries with varying degrees of illness. There is such a wide diversity of health care needs and preferences among the millions of Medicare beneficiaries that no one model can serve them all. A wide variety of health care delivery models are needed, and beneficiaries must be able to choose among those models to find the care that best meets their individual needs and wants. Unfortunately, the Dartmouth Atlas has helped move Medicare in the opposite direction.

IPAB

Another cost-containment measure in ObamaCare that was influenced by the Dartmouth Atlas is the Independent Payment Advisory Board (IPAB). IPAB is a commission comprised of 15 people appointed by the president and confirmed by the Senate, who will wield enormous power over Medicare spending. It will submit proposals to Congress to cut Medicare spending when that spending is projected to exceed a specific threshold. Its proposals automatically become law, unless Congress overturns them with a two-thirds vote of both chambers. When it does so, Congress is required to produce a proposal of its own that cuts Medicare by the same amount as the IPAB proposal.

Not surprisingly, Wennberg has praised IPAB: "This entity will have broad authority to develop proposals for new reimbursement strategies, which will be implemented if Medicare grows in excess of amounts specified in the legislation."[37] Since one of IPAB's duties is to target sources of excess cost growth, naturally, the Dartmouth Atlas' work on Medicare can help. According to Wennberg, "Data about the rates of growth in utilization and spending, and the patterns of variation among regions and hospitals, could help the board carry out this task, and through its decisions, it could begin to limit spending according to the degree of overuse by specific providers in high-use regions."[38]

Peter Orszag considers the IPAB to be the most crucial measure for reducing Medicare costs contained in ObamaCare:

> Perhaps most important, the legislation creates an Independent Payment Advisory Board, a panel of independent medical experts who will look for more ways to improve Medicare's cost-effectiveness. Under the law, any policy that the board issues takes effect unless legislation to block it is passed by Congress and signed by the president. This way, inertia works in favor of cost containment rather than against it.[39]

One reason IPAB is so important, according to Orszag, is that it is an example of how to solve the nation's needs by becoming less democratic. Politically we have become a polarized nation, Orszag contends, and that polarization now infects Congress, making it increasingly difficult to enact much needed policy. To solve this problem, "we need to minimize the harm from legislative inertia by relying more on automatic policies and depoliticized commissions for certain policy decisions. In other words, radical as it sounds, we need to counter the gridlock of our political institutions by making them a bit less democratic." He acknowledges that such a solution will "reduce the power of elected officials and therefore make our government somewhat less accountable to voters," but it is necessary to end the "polarized, gridlocked government [that] is doing real harm to our country." IPAB is perhaps "the most dramatic example of this idea."[40]

Indeed, looking at the structure of IPAB, it's hard not to come to the conclusion that the first goal when designing it was to make it wholly unaccountable and that reducing Medicare expenditures was almost an afterthought. Consider:

- Members of IPAB are to be appointed to no more than two six-year terms. However, a member can continue to serve after the expiration of his term until his successor has taken office. If the president doesn't nominate a successor then, presumably, the member can serve indefinitely.[41]

- IPAB may act as long as a majority of its members are present. Although IPAB is supposed to have 15 members, if only nine have been appointed, then only five would be needed to conduct business. Proposals can be approved by a majority of members present; so if five are present, three members will be able to make decisions over vast areas of Medicare. Hypothetically, if there is only one member of IPAB, he would have complete control over decisions.[42]

- If IPAB fails to submit a proposal to Congress, then the authority to make the proposal falls to the Secretary of Health and Human Services. Hypothetically, the president could refuse to appoint anyone to IPAB, thereby vesting all of IPAB's power in the Secretary.[43]

- ObamaCare explicitly states that an IPAB "proposal shall not include any recommendation to ration health care." However, the law never defines "rationing." Price, of course, is one way in which goods are rationed. After 2019, IPAB has the power to reduce the price of Medicare services to the point that physicians and hospitals will no longer provide them.[44]

- Congress may only repeal IPAB by proposing a resolution in 2017 by February 1 of that year. Congress must then pass the resolution by a three-fifths vote by August 15, 2017. Then the president must sign it. Otherwise, Congress can never repeal IPAB.[45] This is almost certainly unconstitutional. Nevertheless, it shows how far Orszag wanted to go to "reduce the power of elected officials."

- Does IPAB have the power to tax? ObamaCare explicitly forbids IPAB from raising revenue under sections 1818, 1818A or 1839 of the Social Security Act. One study argues that IPAB may have the power to tax as long as the tax it increases is not covered under those parts of the Social Security Act. If IPAB were to include a tax increase in one of its proposals and Congress did not overturn the proposal, it's not clear who would be able to put a stop to it.[46]

Shielding IPAB from accountability would make it easier to reduce Medicare spending by reducing reimbursement for treatments it deems ineffective. As the experiences of a similar organization in the United Kingdom show, this can have life-and-death consequences.

Under Britain's National Health Service, an agency known as the National Institute for Health and Care Excellence (NICE) determines whether new treatments are cost-effective. If it does not approve a treatment, then the National Health Service will not pay for it.

One pharmaceutical that NICE has rejected more than once is Avastin, a drug that can prolong the life of those with advanced cancer. But for patients with late-stage colon or ovarian cancer, NICE did not deem the extra few months of life patients could gain from taking Avastin as worth the cost.[47] NICE has also rejected drugs used to treat lupus, liver cancer, breast cancer, leukemia, and late-stage kidney cancer.[48] A 2010 report by the Rare Cancers Forum found that about 20,000 people could have benefitted from cancer drugs that they could not receive because the drugs were either denied by NICE or were delayed in the decision-making process.[49] It is not known how many of them died prematurely.

One of the more sadly ironic instances of NICE policies on drugs involved Alice Mahon, a former Member of Parliament and ardent supporter of the National Health Service. She suffered from macular degeneration in her left eye, a disease that causes blindness. The drug Lucentis can treat the disease, but it must be taken soon after diagnosis. Mahon was unable to get the drug because NICE had yet to approve it at the time of her diagnosis in 2006.[50] She initially threatened to take her case to court, but dropped it after she lost the sight in her left eye and her physicians informed her Lucentis could no longer help her.[51] NICE did not approve Lucentis until 2013. How many Britons went blind in the meantime is not known.

It would be tempting to dismiss this as peculiar to Britain, whose health care system is in increasingly poor shape. Yet a recent paper suggests that cuts to Medicare may have already harmed beneficiaries. The Balanced Budget Act of 1997 cut Medicare reimbursements for hospitals. A recent paper examining California hospitals found that the survival rates from heart attacks slowed in the hospitals that experienced the largest cuts.[52] To the extent that IPAB makes cuts like these, the harm it causes will prove deadly.

The biggest problem with IPAB is that the incentives its members face are not likely to lead to good decisions. For starters, IPAB may have a hard time attracting top-flight people. Many of the "experts" in medicine and academia may already earn salaries higher than the $165,000 that members of IPAB will be paid. As one health care expert stated, "it would be difficult to find 15 people willing to go through the confirmation process and 'abandon everything else for six years' for a civil servant's salary."[53]

If that is true, then IPAB is likely to attract people who view it as a big step up the career ladder. Many of those in medical and academic circles will consider it prestigious to have served on IPAB. It will be even more status enhancing for IPAB members if they concoct plans to make substantial changes to Medicare. Thus, it is very likely that serving on IPAB will enable its members to go on to more highly regarded institutions with higher compensation when they return to the private sector.

While there is tremendous upside for participation on IPAB, what is the downside? Specifically, what cost will IPAB members pay if they make a decision that results in harm for patients? Very little. The most they might suffer is public criticism and having to resign before their term is up—assuming, of course, that the consequences of their decisions become apparent before their term expires. Given how long it can sometimes take for policy decisions to be linked directly to bad consequences, IPAB members may be long gone from the board before the results of their work are known.

With that set of incentives, what are the chances that IPAB's decisions will result in good outcomes? Indeed, given the reasonable assumption that people make better decisions when they have to pay the cost for being wrong, IPAB is little more than a recipe for disaster.

The people who will pay that cost will be physicians and patients. Physicians will likely see a loss of income and the agony of seeing their patients suffer. Naturally, patients will pay the most, suffering greater pain and possibly the ultimate cost, premature death.

People who pay the cost for making a wrong decision should be the ones with ultimate authority over that decision. The further the decision is removed from the person paying the cost for being wrong, the more the chances increase that the wrong decision will be made. The end result will be that patients will suffer, while the decision-makers escape largely unscathed.

Do Physicians Really Cause Most Of The Waste?

It is Florida where one begins to finds holes in the Dartmouth Atlas' theory of supply-sensitive care. A 2003 *New York Times* article described how seniors in Boca Raton used physician visits as "a social activity":

> Many have 8, 10, or 12 specialists and visit one or more of them most days of the week. They bring their spouses and plan their days around their appointments, going out to eat or shopping while they are in the area. They know what they want; they choose specialists for every body part. And every visit, every procedure is covered by Medicare.[54]

Seven years later, the *Times* followed up with another article on Boca Raton and found the same phenomenon. It recounted the story of Dr. Robert Colton, an internist, whose Medicare patients constantly demanded tests and treatments that he was certain were unnecessary. When asked what he did, Colton replied, "I do the damn test. There is no incentive for me, Rob Colton, to reduce overutilization. If the person wants it, what are you going to do, say no?"[55]

The articles show that Medicare beneficiaries were initiating the demand for health care, not physicians. Granted, the articles amounted to anecdotal evidence, not the sophisticated research of the Dartmouth Atlas. Nevertheless, they suggested that Wennberg and his colleagues might be missing important factors that would explain the wide variations in Medicare spending.

There is, however, far more rigorous research that challenges the Dartmouth Atlas. After examining the differences in Medicare spending by state, Dr. Richard Cooper concluded that the differences were driven by different population demographics. Specifically, states with higher amounts of Medicare spending had poorer, and hence less healthy, populations than areas with lower Medicare spending.[56] Researchers associated with the Dartmouth Atlas claimed that Cooper used empirical methods that were inadequate.[57] However, more recent research using more sophisticated methods has come to a similar conclusion.[58]

Another shortcoming of research associated with the Dartmouth Atlas is that it does not sufficiently account for the severity of patients' illnesses. If so, then areas with higher Medicare spending could, in fact, be treating sicker patients. Studies that take into account the comorbidities that patients have and whether a patient suffers a complication while in the hospital (such patients are usually sicker than patients who do not suffer a complication) come up with different results than the Dartmouth Atlas.

For example, a study of patients undergoing vascular or orthopedic surgery found that those patients that were treated in higher-spending hospitals had lower mortality rates and a better chance of surviving a complication.[59] A study of six California hospitals examining Medicare patients who had suffered heart failure found that patients in the higher-spending hospitals had a lower mortality rate over the next six months.[60] A study of Pennsylvania hospitals showed that Medicare patients with a high probability of dying upon entering the hospital had a higher survival rate if they were treated in hospitals with higher levels of end-of-life treatment.[61]

An article in *The New England Journal of Medicine* studied Medicare patients across the U.S. between 2000 and 2002, taking into account both the patients' initial health status in 2000 and any health changes that occurred between 2000 and 2002. The authors found that accounting for those health factors explained about 29 percent of the difference between the HRRs with the highest and lowest Medicare spending.[62] Finally, Professor Robert Kaestner and Dr. Jeffery Silber examined Medicare patients who either underwent vascular, orthopedic or general surgery, or who suffered a heart attack, congestive heart failure, stroke or gastrointestinal bleeding between 2000 and 2005. With the exception of the heart attack patients, a 10 percent increase in Medicare spending was associated with a 3.1 to 11.3 percent decline in 30-day mortality. Kaestner and Silber warn:

[O]ur results suggest that even though it may be cost-effective to eliminate some portion of inpatient spending, this reduction would come at a considerable cost for survival, at least for inpatients ... Based on our results, the narrowest interpretation of the "flat-of-the-curve" hypothesis—that health care spending could be reduced by 20 to 30 percent without adverse health effects—may be seriously misleading.[63]

Greg Scandlen thinks that the Dartmouth Atlas has a habit of overlooking other important factors that can explain the variation in Medicare spending. Scandlen, a long-time health care policy analyst and advocate for consumer-driven care, says, "They are locked into this very limited understanding of what drives patients and what drives medical care."[64]

Consider some of the geographical comparisons of medical care made by Dartmouth researchers. Wennberg writes that, "In 2007, patients in Manhattan spent, on average, 20.6 days in the hospital during their last six months of life, almost four times more than patients in Ogden, Utah, where the average was 5.2 days."[65] An article by other Dartmouth researchers noted "Medicare [spending] in 1996 was $8,414 per enrollee in the Miami, Florida, region compared with $3,341 in the Minneapolis, Minnesota, region."[66]

Scandlen, however, sees other factors other than physician preferences at work in areas with higher use of medical care:

Something that as far as I know Wennberg never considered was that the elderly in Miami are generally transplants from somewhere else. They've left their families behind. They've left their support systems behind—their participation in, say, the Lions Club or their church. And so they move to Miami and they've got no personal network and few friends around to support them if they get sick. So there is not the kind of 'at home' care-giving of an informal kind that the people in Minneapolis would be getting. Nobody moves to Minneapolis when they turn 65 to retire ... I think it is also true in the end-of-life studies that compared New York City to Ogden, Utah. What's different about those two cities? There is plenty. People in New York may live in a third-floor walk-up, and it's really hard for them to go out and get meals and do grocery shopping. There are real crime problems in New York City. No wonder they want to stay in the hospital—they don't have anywhere else to go. But in Ogden, Utah, the elderly are probably living in a one-story ranch house. They have their kids and grandkids who can come over and check on them. There are personal qualities that have much more to do with medical decisions and outcomes than are accounted for in the Dartmouth Atlas.[67]

A study that appeared in *Health Services Research* attempted to account for some of the social factors that Scandlen mentions. First, it found that factors related to patient demand accounted for far more Medicare spending than did ones related to physician demand. It also examined whether a Medicare beneficiary moved to another state or census division during the period of the study. Such moves, the authors argued, could be associated with factors such as wanting to be closer to family members or a desire to obtain specialty care not available locally. Moving to another state was associated with an increase of $1,365 in Medicare costs, and moving to another census division was associated with an increase of just under $2,000.[68] While this only scratches the surface of the effect that family and other support networks have on the cost of medical care, it implies that those effects can be substantial and could explain a significant amount of the variation in Medicare spending.

So is the Dartmouth Atlas wrong? Most likely, it is incomplete. It has identified patterns in Medicare spending that need to be explained, and it has probably also identified where at least some of the waste in Medicare is located. Even the studies contradicting the Dartmouth Atlas cannot account for all of the differences in Medicare spending between high-spending and low-spending regions. Some of the higher spending that remains unexplained could very well constitute waste.

However, Dartmouth's tendency to put the onus largely on physicians is misplaced. Demand for health care can be driven just as much by patients as physicians. Simply controlling the behavior of physicians cannot reduce waste in Medicare.

What Is "Waste"?

During the debate over ObamaCare, terms like "waste" and "overuse" were thrown around repeatedly but seldom defined. This meant that discussions of waste, a very complex problem, were often superficial.

In *Overtreated,* Shannon Brownlee defined waste as "care that does nothing to improve our health."[69] Yet it is often difficult to determine exactly when health care does nothing to improve our health. Indeed, waste seems to be one of those terms that is easy to discuss in the abstract but difficult to recognize in the real world.

Let's take another look at colonoscopies. Surely, many of the colonoscopies performed after Medicare changed its policy in 2001 were ones that did nothing to improve the health of Medicare beneficiaries. But which ones? It would be tempting to say that it is those colonoscopies that found no tumors or polyps, but it is not that easy. Look at the following three scenarios and decide which ones you think are wasteful:

1. John has a colonoscopy that shows his colon is completely healthy. He was anxious about colon cancer, but now he has some peace of mind.

2. Jane has a mother who suffered from colon cancer. According to American Cancer Society guidelines, that puts Jane at a higher risk to suffer from colon cancer too. She receives a colonoscopy that reveals a healthy colon.

3. Jim has a colonoscopy that finds one polyp in his colon. He has it removed via polypectomy. Yet the polyp is less than 2mm in length. Much research on the matter (although not all such research) suggests that polyps that size are not likely to lead to colon cancer.

So, which of these is wasteful? The answer is all of them and none of them. Many people would argue that at least the first one is wasteful. But think of the relief that comes with knowing that you don't have cancer or some other disease. For at least some people, merely achieving that peace of mind is worth the cost of a colonoscopy or other medical test.

Chances are that fewer people would find the use of a colonoscopy in examples two and three wasteful. They would argue that being high-risk or having a small polyp is worth the cost of a colonoscopy—better safe than sorry. Yet, even in those higher-risk scenarios, there are some people for whom a couple hundred dollars for a colonoscopy is not worth paying when compared to the relatively small risk of cancer.

One of the unfortunate consequences of the 2009-2010 debate over reforming the U.S. health care system is that elites like Orszag trivialized the notion of waste. To listen to his ilk, experts could eliminate waste with relative ease by focusing on the areas with higher Medicare spending. More likely, waste is spread throughout the system, in both areas with high Medicare spending, low Medicare spending and the areas in-between. Selma Hartmann's colonoscopy was both wasteful and harmful, but the hospital at which it took place, DePaul, is below the national average on Medicare spending.[70]

Orszag and others overlooked factors that make determining waste very difficult. One such factor is that waste is a highly subjective concept—one person's waste is another person's vital procedure. In the first scenario above, many people might consider achieving peace of mind wasteful, but others would consider it an improvement in health. It is impossible for any group of "experts" to know in each individual case if a particular treatment is wasteful because individuals have different values, concerns and goals regarding health care.

Another factor making it difficult to determine waste is that it is often not possible to know if a procedure is wasteful before it is performed. Notice that in all of the above scenarios, it is impossible to tell if the colonoscopy is wasteful until it is finished.

Of course, by considering factors such as the patient's age, whether his parents had colon cancer and so on, it is possible to hazard a rough guess as to the likelihood that a colonoscopy will be wasteful. But that only tells a patient the probability that a colonoscopy will be worth the cost. It can't be known *with certainty* if a colonoscopy will be wasteful prior to having it performed. Indeed, with many medical procedures it is impossible to know if the procedure is wasteful until after the fact, and not even Orszag, IPAB or the Dartmouth Atlas can change that.

Ultimately, whether a procedure is wasteful should not be left up to "independent" boards that have no stake in the result. Rather, the decision of whether a treatment is wasteful should lie with the patient, who has the greatest interest—avoiding pain and death—in the outcome. To facilitate this, we must switch to a Medicare system that gives beneficiaries the money to pay for their own care directly.

7. THE NEXT EXODUS

In late 2009, the highly respected Mayo Clinic grabbed national headlines when it announced that one of its primary care centers was no longer accepting Medicare. Henceforth, Medicare patients visiting its family clinic in Glendale, Arizona would have to pay cash. In 2008, Mayo lost $120 million on Medicare patients at all of its Arizona facilities. At the Glendale clinic, Medicare had covered only about half of the clinic's expenses for treating the elderly.[1]

When physicians limit their exposure to Medicare by either dropping out of the program or restricting the number of Medicare patients they treat, it seldom receives any press coverage beyond local media, if it receives any coverage at all. Nevertheless, physicians' reluctance to accept Medicare patients is a growing problem. The epicenter appears to be Texas. "Texas Doctors Fleeing Medicare in Droves," blared a *Houston Chronicle* headline. Data compiled by the newspaper found that Texas physicians were dumping Medicare at a rate of about 100 to 200 per year.[2] In 2010, a Texas Medical Association survey found that 18 percent of the state's physicians were restricting the number of Medicare patients they treated, while 16 percent were no longer seeing new Medicare patients.[3]

Nationally, the number of physicians who still participate in Medicare is unclear. As of 2008 only 58 percent of physicians were willing to see all new Medicare patients, while fully 13.7 percent were no longer willing to see any new Medicare patients, a survey by the Center for Studying Health System Change survey found.[4] A 2011 National Ambulatory Medical Care Survey found that about 17 percent of physicians were restricting the number of Medicare patients they treat, while a 2012 Physicians Foundation survey found that 52 percent of physicians had limited the number of Medicare patients they were willing to see or were planning to do so.[5]

The evidence suggests the primary reason why physicians are fleeing Medicare is that it doesn't pay enough. Over one-third of physicians surveyed by the Physicians Foundation in 2008 said Medicare payments did not cover costs.[6] A 2010 American Medical Association (AMA) survey found that 85 percent of physicians capping the number of Medicare patients they treated cited Medicare's stingy payments as a reason.[7] According to the Center for Studying Health System Change, about 62 percent of physicians cited inadequate Medicare reimbursements as either a very important or a moderately important reason why they refused to accept new Medicare patients.[8]

Yet Medicare's inadequate payment structure does not repel all physicians equally. Among primary care physicians, who tend to be the physicians who have first contact with a patient, the trend is considerably worse. An AMA survey that found 17 percent of *all* physicians were limiting the number of Medicare patients they saw, also found that 31 percent of primary care physicians were doing so.[9] Because Medicare tends to compensate "specialists"—physicians who focus on one area of medicine—better than primary care physicians, it is no surprise that specialists aren't limiting their exposure to Medicare to the same extent as primary care physicians. According to the Center for Studying Health Change, the percentage of primary care physicians who were no longer seeing Medicare patients was about double that of specialists.[10]

Texas showed the same pattern. In 2011, the Texas Medical Association found that only about five percent of specialists had stopped taking Medicare as a form of payment, while over 13 percent of primary care physicians had stopped.[11]

One of those primary care physicians is Dr. Juliette Madrigal-Dersch.

Texas Flower

Dr. Juliette Madrigal-Dersch's office is in Marble Falls, Texas, not far from Austin. On the wall in one of the patient rooms there hangs a picture frame. It contains a white canvass with a black bead in the middle. Underneath the bead are words that Dr. Madrigal's daughter, Helena, said to her when she was three years old: "Mommy, I might have accidentally put something in my nose I think."

It's indicative of the friendly, relaxed atmosphere that Dr. Madrigal has created in her office.

Spunky and energetic, it's easy to see why patients flock to Dr. Madrigal. A note left behind by one of her patients reads, "Thanks for weighing my opinion into your decisions." But praise her for having a good "bedside manner," and she responds, "I think it's because I have such great patients."

"Yes, that's Dr. Madrigal," laughs her assistant, Bruce. "She will not take a compliment."

It's the first day of school in Texas in 2011, so the traffic in her office this Monday is light. One of the few patients there is a woman, "Pamela,"** who is in her mid-60s.

It's obvious Dr. Madrigal knows her well as she enters the examination room. She gives her a big hug, followed by an upbeat "How have you been doing?"

Pamela gives a weak smile and replies, "So-so."

Less than two years ago Pamela had a sarcoma removed from her arm. She'll soon be heading back to the hospital to have the meniscus in her knee repaired. But those aren't the reasons she's paid a visit to Dr. Madrigal.

** The names of the patients in this chapter have been changed to protect their privacy.

"My emotions," she explains to Dr. Madrigal. "I feel good very early in the day, but very lousy in the afternoon. It makes it hard for me to do any work."

Dr. Madrigal asks her a series of questions, all the while typing answers into her laptop.

After Dr. Madrigal is finished with the questions, she explains, "Your body often treats physical and emotional stress the same. With the cancer and now the knee, these are not letting your stress hormones go back to normal."

After some discussion, Dr. Madrigal suggests that Pamela try Zoloft, an anti-depressant.

Pamela is also often congested from her allergies, something Dr. Madrigal thinks could be a concern going into the patient's upcoming knee surgery.

"Whenever the flow is slow, the bugs can grow. If you're really congested going into surgery, and they put a tube down your throat, it increases the chances of a really bad sinus infection or even pneumonia," Dr. Madrigal explains.

Dr. Madrigal tells Pamela that she wants to see her just before she goes in for surgery to check her allergies. Pamela assures her that she will make an appointment.

As Pamela gets up to leave, Dr. Madrigal gives her another warm embrace.

On her way out, Pamela takes out her checkbook and pays the receptionist. She does have insurance, but it's useless in Dr. Madrigal's office.

"When I started my private practice in 2001, I looked at how much I would get paid from insurance, and it wasn't worth it," Dr. Madrigal explained. "I decided to do a cash-only practice. I expected my practice to be in the black in about two years, but I was in the black in about three months."

She disliked the restrictions that come along with private insurance. "They limit you," she said. "They decide what tests a patient can have, what medications they can take, and I didn't want any part of that."

If you want to see Dr. Madrigal, it will cost $75 if your office visit is a simple one and $150 if it is more complicated. However, if you had been an elderly patient when she started her practice, your Medicare card would have paid for your visit.

"As a doctor, you're actually 'born' into the Medicare contract," she said.

Until recently, once a medical student received his medical degree, he automatically received a Medicare provider number. The regulations were changed a few years ago so that new physicians now have to sign up to be part of Medicare. But when Dr. Madrigal first became a physician, she became part of Medicare whether she wanted to or not.

By 2006, she wanted out.

"To leave Medicare, you actually have to do quite a bit of paperwork," she said. She turned to the Association of American Physicians and Surgeons (AAPS), an interest group that in recent years has helped physicians exit Medicare. The AAPS recommends that the physician first tell her Medicare patients that she is leaving Medicare. Second, the physician must file an affidavit stating that while she is opting out of Medicare she "will provide services to Medicare beneficiaries only through private contracts," and "will not submit a claim to Medicare for any service furnished to a Medicare beneficiary during the opt out period."[12] The affidavit must be sent to all of the private companies that handle Medicare claims in the physician's state.

The physician must then fill out a separate contract with each of her Medicare patients, stating that the patient understands that the physician has opted out of Medicare. It states that the patient must accept "full responsibility for payment of the physician's charge for all services furnished by the physician." The patient must also understand "that Medicare payment will not be made for any items or services furnished by the physician that would have otherwise been covered by Medicare if there was no private contract and a proper Medicare claim had been submitted."[13] The patient must sign this contract in order to continue to be treated by the physician.

Although she dropped out of Medicare, Dr. Madrigal's hassles with the government haven't ended. The "opt-out" period only lasts for two years, so Dr. Madrigal must re-file up-to-date affidavits biennially. She must make sure that her Medicare patients sign new contracts every two years as well.

Her reasons for leaving Medicare were similar to the reasons why she never took private insurance.

"There are things in Medicare that are hard to order," she said. "For example, Medicare won't pay for a bone-density scan on a patient to check for osteoporosis unless the patient either has very specific risk factors or already has a diagnosis of osteoporosis."

The risk factors Medicare considers for osteoporosis are things like steroid usage or the patient takes a drug that causes osteoporosis as a side effect.

"The normal risk factors most doctors would use are advanced age, a small frame, family history or history of a fracture," she said. "But that's not what Medicare uses. So, if you have a little 80-year-old lady who is all bent over and looks like her bones could break at any moment, you can't order a bone-density scan on her, unless she already has a diagnosis for osteoporosis. But you can't get that diagnosis without the bone-density scan. It's a frustrating catch-22."

Another reason she dropped Medicare was that it made her feel less than honest. Medicare has very specific regulations and codes that must be met if a physician wants to order a specific test. The problem is that many patients don't verbalize their symptoms in ways that easily match Medicare's regulations and codes.

"For example, my Mexican-American patients talk about their pains in a very personified way," said Dr. Madrigal. "They won't specifically say, 'I have a throbbing pain in my head that is worse when I cough.' They'll tell me, 'It feels like there is a devil in me and it's trying to explode.' Obviously, I can't code that. So, if I take Medicare, I have to make the patient say something that can fit the code. I didn't feel comfortable trying to make people say something that would make it legal.

"Otherwise, to make it fit into a code, I have to come up with my interpretation of what the patient is suffering from. The risk is that if the government ever audits me, the auditor could disagree with my interpretation, which could mean I'd be charged with fraud. That was not worth the risk."

Before she opted out of Medicare, she had about 200 Medicare patients. After dropping Medicare, she initially lost 50 of those patients, although about 40 of them eventually returned to her practice. Despite the fact that any Medicare patient coming to her practice must sign a contract and pay cash, her total number of patients who are covered by Medicare has increased to about 250 now.

"I think the reason is that word has gotten out that I can spend more time with my patients," she said. "I also think there is some perception that you get what you pay for."

In spite of the various problems, Dr. Madrigal might have continued with Medicare if it had paid her enough to care for her patients.

"But it was not covering my costs," she said. "I was losing about $5 to $10 per visit when I saw a Medicare patient. All of the hassles and I'm losing money? In the end, it wasn't worth it."

Dropping Medicare has led to other very positive results for Dr. Madrigal and her patients.

"I make about the same money I made when I took Medicare, but without the billing and paperwork costs of Medicare, I can now afford to treat some of my patients for free," she said.

"I don't charge patients over 90 years old. If you make it that far you are home free," she laughs. "I don't charge an established patient who has cancer. And while they are undergoing treatment, I won't charge their family members to see me either. And the other ones I don't charge are the ones whose cases are so complicated that it would break my heart to see them go somewhere else."

Setting Prices, Soviet Style

There are many reasons why Medicare pay for primary care physicians is considerably worse than for specialists, but three are of signal importance. The first is the process Medicare uses to update its payment system.

In 1992 the Center for Medicare and Medicaid Services (CMS) adopted a system of price controls for paying physicians known as the Resource Based Relative Value System (RBRVS). This system assigns a numerical value called a "relative value unit" (RVU) to medical services and procedures. There are three basic RVUs. The first is known as a Work RVU that is based on the amount of work, effort, resources and stress that goes into providing a service or procedure. The second is known as the PE RVU that is based on the costs of the practice expenses—employee wages, supplies, rent, etc.—required to provide the service or procedure. The third is the MP RVU that is based on the cost of malpractice insurance related to the service or procedure.

Through a rather complicated process, RVUs were assigned for all of the 7,500 services and procedures that Medicare pays for. To get the price of any particular procedure, the three types of RVUs are added together and then multiplied by a dollar amount known as a conversion factor. To ensure that physicians would wield influence over how they were paid by Medicare, the AMA established the Relative Value Scale Update Committee (RUC) in 1991. It is an advisory board composed of representatives from most of the physician specialty societies, such as American Academy of Family Physicians, American Association of Neurological Surgeons, the American College of Cardiology, and so on.

The RUC meets three times annually. In most years it makes recommendations to CMS on new procedures and services that Medicare should pay for and on others that need to be revised. Under federal law, every five years CMS must conduct a comprehensive review of RVUs to identify which procedures and services are overvalued and which are undervalued. The RUC plays a large role in the five-year review as well. Overall, the RUC wields significant influence over what Medicare pays for procedures and services. CMS has accepted somewhere between 88 and 94 percent of RUC recommendations on RVUs since the early 1990s.[14]

However, the composition of the RUC results in a payment system that is biased against primary care physicians. There are 31 members on the RUC, 25 of whom are appointed by the various physician specialty societies. Yet only five are primary care physicians. The other 20 are specialists.

Under federal law, revisions to RVUs cannot result in Medicare payments to physicians that add more than $20 million to the annual Medicare budget. This means physicians are dividing up a fixed Medicare pie. Of course, doling out the pie in Washington is seldom done cooperatively. This makes the RBRVS a political pork barrel for physicians and their interest groups, and the RUC is the battleground. Like most political fights in Washington, it produces winners and losers.

Dr. Neil Brooks, who served on the RUC as a family physician, claims that the process is "highly political, with battle lines and alliances drawn between specialties. Usually, the battle lines were drawn between primary care physicians and everyone else. The specialists often team up to support each others' proposed increases in Work RVUs."[15] As an article in *Kaiser Health News* noted, "Since specialties are all fighting over slices of the Medicare physician payment pie, and many specialists make the bulk of their profits on procedures, primary care doctors say those specialists avoid increasing the values of the procedure codes that are primary care's bread and butter."[16]

Similar sentiments were expressed by Dr. J. Leonard Lichtenfield and Dr. Tom Felger, who represented primary care physicians on the RUC in 2005. They argued for higher reimbursement rates for office visits because an increase in older patients with complex conditions had made visits more challenging. During debate on the matter, Drs. Lichtenfield and Felger almost walked out as discussions seemed to reach an impasse. "I was willing to leave negotiations," Dr. Lichtenfeld said. "I felt we were being stonewalled for economic reasons."[17]

Primary care's bread and butter largely consists of evaluating and managing the care of patients. The bulk of what Medicare pays primary care physicians consists of 10 different types of patient visits, depending on the severity of the visit and on whether the patient is new or established. A visit with a patient that has a minor ailment and lasts about 10 to 15 minutes is a "Level I" visit. On the other end is a Level V visit which is for a patient with a serious ailment and lasts close to an hour. Medicare pays less for a visit with an established patient than with a new patient, presumably because much of the diagnostic work conducted on the first visit does not have to be repeated on subsequent visits. For example, in Dr. Madrigal's neck of the woods, Medicare pays $43.35 for a Level I visit with a new patient, and $20.16 for a Level I visit with an established patient.[18]

Defenders of the RUC deny that it is biased against primary care physicians, pointing to 1997 and 2007 when Work RVUs for primary care visits were increased. "We recommended higher increases in 1997 than CMS accepted," said Dr. Barbara Levy, then chair of the RUC.[19]

But the preponderance of evidence does not show that the RUC improves pay for primary care physicians. First, a look at the years between 1995 and 2010 that were not five-year reviews shows that the RUC seldom recommends new services or redefines services so that primary care physicians are paid better.[20] Of the 2,280 procedures and services that the RUC recommended as either new or in need of revision, only 115 of them, or barely five percent, were designated for primary care. In short, the RUC does not spend much of its resources looking for ways to improve the pay of primary care physicians.

Second, the increases in the Work RVUs for primary care visits that Dr. Levy touts didn't turn out to be such large increases in the end. In both 1997 and 2007 the RVU increases proposed by the RUC added more than $20 million to the Medicare budget. When that happens, CMS has to institute cost-cutting measures to bring Medicare spending back into balance. In 1997, it cut the PE RVUs for all services and procedures by 8.3 percent.[21] In 2007, it reduced all Work RVUs by 10 percent.[22] That offset some of the gains made in the Work RVUs for primary care visits.

Third, some members of the RUC appear to have a conflict of interest. Dr. Roy Poses, president of the Foundation for Integrity and Responsibility in Medicine, discovered in 2011 that 14 RUC members had financial relationships with various medical companies. He noted:

> It seemed obvious that a committee dominated by a majority of physicians who perform procedures would tend to favor bigger financial incentives for procedures. But now it appears the committee also includes a substantial number of people who work part-time or have ownership interests in companies that also stand to benefit from increasing use of procedures. Procedures drive increased consumption of drugs, supplies and devices, and lead to larger revenue for hospitals and clinics. Thus these financial relationships could reasonably be suspected of even further distorting the committee's decision-making in favor of procedures.[23]

Fourth, there is a broad consensus that many procedures are overvalued by Medicare.[24] When the RUC recommends that Medicare should pay for a new procedure, it sets the RVUs relatively high since a new procedure often requires more work to complete. Yet, over time, physicians find ways to do the procedure more efficiently, what economists call "productivity gains." For example, as physicians gain more experience with a procedure, they can complete it more quickly. Or new technology may also reduce the amount of work required to perform the procedure. As that happens, it should be possible to reduce the Work RVUs for those procedures and redistribute them to primary care services.

Yet that seldom occurs. Of the services and procedures that the RUC made recommendations on in the four five-year reviews, the Work RVUs for 1,046 services and procedures were increased, 1,202 remained the same, and only 209 were reduced.[25] There was no redistribution of Work RVUs from over-valued procedures to primary care visits.

Alas, that is to be expected. The specialty societies on the RUC function as interest groups trying to represent their members. Like almost all interest groups, they go to the federal government to get more money for their members. Finding an interest group that is willing to advocate that its members take a pay cut? You'd have an easier time looking for a Dodo Bird.

In 2011, Dr. Paul Fischer, founder of the Primary Care Center in Augusta, Georgia, and Brian Klepper, a health care analyst, began a movement to replace the RUC. They started a website titled www.replacetheruc.net, and, in a widely touted piece, Klepper, along with Dr. David C. Kibbe, encouraged primary care groups to quit the RUC.[26] By May of 2011, they had gotten the attention of the premier primary care group, the American Academy of Family Physicians (AAFP). Later that year AAFP held serious discussions about the possibility of leaving the RUC.[27] Had the premier organization representing primary care physicians dropped out of the RUC, the reverberations would have been felt not only throughout the medical community but also in Congress, possibly leading to a reassessment of the RUC. In the end, the AAFP decided not to leave the RUC, although, according to one spokeswoman, the leadership of the AAFP would "continue to frequently reassess our involvement."[28]

The lower pay of primary care physicians would not matter much if the expenses of running a primary care practice were considerably lower than for specialists. Lower expenses would, of course, make it easier for primary care physicians to make money on what Medicare pays them. Unfortunately, practice expenses—rent, salaries, supplies, billing costs, etc.—eat up a larger portion of the incomes of primary care physicians than specialists. As Table 7 shows, on average practice expenses eat up over 62 percent of primary care physicians' income versus about 55 percent for specialists.

Table 7: Practice Expenses: Primary Care vs. Specialists		
	Average for Primary Care	Average for Specialists
Total Practice Income	$615,593	$906,105
Total Practice Expenses	$384,397	$496,826
Expenses as Percent of Income	62.4%	54.8%
Source: National Society of Certified Healthcare Business Consultants, 2009		

One of the biggest expenses that any insurance program, including Medicare, will impose on a physician's practice is billing costs—the coding and paperwork that physicians must complete to receive payment. Physicians must spend time on billing, time that is not spent making money by treating patients. It also requires them to hire clerical staff to make certain that the physician does the coding properly. Talk to most primary care physicians and they'll say they find coding and paperwork to be a frustrating, complicated hassle.

ObamaCare Is What?!

Dr. John Slatosky grew up in Idaho, joined the National Guard out of high school, and then used the G.I. Bill to attend Idaho State. He attended medical school at the University of Missouri at Kirksville, graduating in 1996.

"I've always liked rural areas," he said. "I just couldn't see myself as anything but a country doctor."

For some people the word *country* may evoke the term "conservative." While that can be a stereotype, for Dr. Slatosky the term fits. He has little use for government involvement in health care.

In the waiting room of his office is a newspaper story of Torron Eeles, a plumber who lives in England, where most people are covered by the National Health Service. In December 2008, he broke his left upper arm in a fall and needed an operation so that the humerus bone would heal properly. At the time of the article, he had been waiting 10 months for the operation. In the meantime, the humerus had knitted back together, leaving Mr. Eeles's arm grotesquely contorted.[29] Above the article Dr. Slatosky has written, "An example of the Miracles of Government-Run Health Care."

He also is not shy regarding his thoughts on ObamaCare, which he refers to as a "stool sample." When asked why he replied, "It's like Speaker Nancy Pelosi said, 'Congress had to pass the health care bill so you could find out what's in it.'"

He met his wife, Dana, a physician's assistant, while at medical school. Afterwards he moved back to Idaho to open a practice. But making ends meet as a country physician in Idaho was difficult, and his wife had mixed feelings about living there.

"My wife, she just couldn't stand the Idaho winters," he said. "My dad always told me that if momma isn't happy, then no one's happy. So I figured I better find a place for us to live where my wife would be happy."

The obvious choice seemed to be Randleman, North Carolina, where Dana's parents lived. In 1999, he interviewed with a hospital nearby in Liberty, about 90 miles northeast of Charlotte. The hospital made him an offer, and he accepted. After working there for a year and a half, they moved him to an affiliate hospital in Randleman.

"I was a typical physician employed by a hospital," Dr. Slatosky said. "I had all the say so of a janitor. We had no say in scheduling or work hours, and if you needed a day off you had to beg for it."

Looking back, he reflects that in that setting he was unable to provide quality care to his patients.

"Most hospitals lose money on their primary care practices because they are so top-heavy with bureaucracy. But this hospital was trying to make its primary care network profitable, so the physicians had to see about twice as many patients as you would at a normal physician practice.

Hospitals are used to dealing with big charges, of thousands of dollars. But primary care is about small charges. Most of it probably costs $50 to $200.

"But with seeing so many patients, you only get to see them for a short time. And you try to take care of things quickly, and you miss things. If you want quality, you have to take some time with your patients, and patients have to be willing to pay for that."

In 2005, Dr. Slatosky had had enough of working at the hospital and started his own practice in Randleman. He currently has over 5,000 patients, about 10 to 15 percent of whom are on Medicare.

On a Monday in September 2011, Dr. Slatosky is visiting with one of his patients, "Pete," a man in his late 60s who is on Medicare. Pete is complaining of pain in his right knee.

"About two months ago, I knelt down and I felt a sharp pain in my knee," he says. "It's been there, off and on, since. I think I might need an X-ray."

Dr. Slatosky begins talking him out of it. "An X-ray might not show much, and it might be a simple problem."

Dr. Slatosky has Pete lie back on the examining table and begins manipulating the leg. "Do you feel that 'click' in your knee?" he asks. Pete nods.

After asking the patient a few questions, Dr. Slatosky concludes that he most likely has arthritis.

"What we can do is start you on some anti-inflammatory medicine," he says. "If that doesn't help, then we can give you a shot of Kenalog, a steroid, in the knee. If that doesn't work then we can move on to an X-ray or an MRI."

Pete says he'd prefer to try the medication first. He looks uneasy when Dr. Slatosky says the word "shot."

Dr. Slatosky, ever the smart-aleck, says, "Oh, don't worry about getting a shot. It's not bad. I've done it to myself and I'm a sissy."

Pete laughs. He has reason to be cheerful beyond Dr. Slatosky's joke. Dr. Slatosky will still accept payment from Medicare to cover his visits. That's because he became a patient of Dr. Slatosky before the end of 2007, when Dr. Slatosky decided to stop taking any new Medicare patients. From then on, any Medicare patients in the Randleman area who were not already part of Dr. Slatosky's practice would have to go elsewhere.

Dr. Slatosky bids Pete goodbye and heads back to his office. On his way back he explains, "I lose about $10, maybe $15, per patient visit on Medicare. I'm doing better now that I've stopped taking new Medicare patients. If I had a lot of new Medicare patients, I'd be in big trouble."

Once at his office, he starts in on his least favorite part of the job: paperwork.

"I can spend four to five hours a week on paperwork that I don't get paid for," he complains. He explains that he particularly dislikes paperwork involving Medicare:

> The biggest problem with Medicare, anytime someone needs anything, the paperwork to get it done can be astronomical. Let's say you have a patient who needs a nebulizer for their cardio-pulmonary obstructive disorder. They run between $60 and $120. To get that, you have to fill out this big form with all these questions, most of which have nothing to do with a nebulizer. So you have to pick out which questions are pertinent. Then you have to send it to a durable medical equipment supplier who then gets the patient a machine. It can be a seven to 10 day turn around. Well, if the person is struggling with acute asthma or COPD, he doesn't have seven to 10 days. So we purchased six nebulizers and we keep them in the office. That way if someone needs a nebulizer long term, they borrow one of ours until they get one of their own.

But even paperwork required for more routine work adds to his costs. Dr. Slatosky estimates that for every 10 to 15 minutes he spends with a patient, he'll spend a quarter to one-third of that on documentation and coding. In order to get paid, he also has an employee who ensures that he has done the coding correctly. And it adds up, since he will have to do that for every patient he sees who has Medicare or private insurance.

Dolphin Bites

In 2009, a group of researchers published their findings on the costs physicians incur interacting with health insurers.[30] They put the physicians into three categories, primary care physicians, medical specialists, and surgical specialists. Unfortunately, the researchers did not break the data down so that it was possible to determine which expenses were due to Medicare and which were due to other health insurers such as Medicaid or private insurance. Nevertheless, it yielded considerable insight into the costs of claims and billing.

Claims and billing ate up the largest portion, 55 percent, of time physicians' practices spent interacting with health insurers. For primary care practices, it accounted for about 53 percent. Clerical staff spent the largest number of hours on claims and billing, spending an average, per week, of 27.1 hours in primary care practices, 29.8 hours in medical specialists' practices, and 28.7 hours in surgical specialists' practices.

For small, one-to-two physician practices, the annual cost of dealing with health insurers was greater for primary care physicians than medical or surgical specialists. Small primary care practices spent an average of $72,675 interacting with health insurers. Medical specialists spent $70,788 and surgical specialists spent $61,187. The clerical staff, which accounted for the bulk of the hours spent on claims and billing, cost small primary care practices an average of $31,666 annually, while they cost medical specialists $27,595 and surgical specialists $27,977. The data strongly suggests that primary care practices could save substantial time and money by reducing if not eliminating billing expenses.

Billing entails a complicated system of coding. There are two types of codes that physicians must use for billing Medicare, private insurance, or any other insurance provider. The first is Current Procedural Terminology (CPT) codes. These are five digit codes that denote the service or procedure that a physician is providing. For example, the CPT code for a

Level I visit with a new patient is 99201, while for a colonoscopy it is 45378.

The second is International Classification of Disease (ICD) codes. These are a system of diagnostic codes that explain to the insurance provider exactly what the patient is being treated for. Depending on the diagnosis, ICD codes are from three to five digits in length. So, if a physician sees a new patient and he diagnoses him with anemia, he would add the ICD code 280 next to the CPT code 99201. If it is a more serious type of anemia, like Plummer-Vision Syndrome, the ICD code used would be 280.8. At present there are about 18,000 ICD codes.

Billing is a bigger expense for primary care physicians than specialists because primary care physicians have to use a far wider array of ICD codes. Dr. Madrigal explains:

> When you are a primary care physician, you are going to see a much wider variety of illnesses. If you are a specialist you are going to see a much more finite number of illnesses, especially if you are, say, an orthopedic surgeon who does primarily knees, probably 90 percent of all your codes are going to be the same five codes. As opposed to primary care, you never know what's going to walk through the door. You could get something very rare. And now you have to be so specific with the codes. You have to code for "fall from uneven ground," or "fall from tractor."

Coding will get worse in October 2015 when CMS switches from version 9 of the ICD codes to version 10. ICD-10 will expand the number of codes to about 80,000. The codes will run from three to seven digits and will impose heavy costs on physicians. A financial analysis conducted for the AMA found that implementing the new ICD codes would cost a small physician practice between $56,000 and $226,000 and a large practice between $2 million to $8 million.[31] While the ICD-10 was supposed to take effect in 2014, Congress suspended the implementation for a year in part due to the cost.

The other reason Congress suspended ICD-10 is that it has become a laughingstock. Under ICD-9, if a patient has been bitten on the finger by an animal and the finger is bleeding, the physician would probably use 883, the ICD code for an open wound on a finger. Under ICD-10, the physician will have to code based on the animal that did the biting.

The initial bite from a dog is coded W540.XXA while a cat is coded W55.01XA. A bite by a parrot is W61.01XA, and for a macaw it is W61.11XA. If the bite is from some other exotic bird, physicians should use code W61.21XA. There is even a code for getting bitten by a dolphin, W56.01XA. And for the swimmer who didn't take the hint the first time, there is code W56.01XD for getting bitten by a dolphin in a subsequent encounter.[32]

There are ICD codes for where an injury took place, such as in a mobile home, an opera house, or near a lamp post. There are codes for the things that cause injury by striking people, like lightning or by getting hit by a falling object in a passenger ship, sailboat, canoe, or other unspecified water craft.[33] Despite the effort at micromanaging physicians that CMS put into the new ICD codes, it failed to include one for "devil exploding in head."

Dr. Madrigal, of course, doesn't have to worry about that anymore. Indeed, getting rid of the billing costs that go along with Medicare was a huge relief. "I saved on overhead costs by dropping Medicare. I'd probably have to hire two more people if I took Medicare, just to do the billing, to make sure I was coding properly and then resubmitting claims and making sure those claims came back in."

For Dr. Slatosky, it will only mean higher overhead costs as he or one of his employees must spend more time tracking down the appropriate ICD codes in order to get paid by Medicare. It may only be a matter of time before he switches entirely to a direct-pay practice.

"Even though Medicare's rates are some of the lowest, I could charge all of my patients, even those with private insurance, Medicare rates *if* all of my patients paid me out-of pocket," he said. "Without all of the paperwork hassles I have to deal with to get paid, I could spend more time with my patients and have a pretty lucrative practice."

Although some research suggests that ICD-10 will, over the long-run, save the health system money, that research still shows substantial implementation costs for small physician practices in the near term.[34] Nevertheless, Congress plans to let the implementation of ICD-10 proceed in October 2015.

Sustainable Headache

While the RUC and Medicare's billing costs impose a substantial financial burden on primary care physicians, the Sustainable Growth Rate (SGR) may have been the proverbial straw that broke the camel's back. It is no accident that the implementation of the SGR roughly coincides with the increase in physicians limiting their exposure to Medicare. The SGR first took effect in 2002 and has threatened physicians who accept Medicare ever since. According to the Texas Medical Association, 78 percent of Texas physicians were still accepting all new Medicare patients in 2000.[35] By 2011 that had dropped to 67 percent.[36] Nationally, about 10 percent of physicians refused to see new Medicare patients back in 2001.[37] Ten years later it had risen to 17 percent.[38]

Passed by Congress in 1997, the SGR is a formula that is supposed to help control Medicare's costs by limiting payments to physicians. Each year the SGR sets an expenditure target for the amount Medicare spends on physicians' fees. If the amount that Medicare actually spends exceeds the expenditure target, then the following year physicians' fees are supposed to be cut by an amount that brings Medicare spending back into line with expenditure targets.

The SGR was exactly the sort of boneheaded idea one would expect Congress to come up with to control Medicare physicians' fees. It gave physicians incentives to *increase* the amount of fees they charged Medicare. As one former administrator of the CMS said:

The problem is that the SGR neither affects nor is driven by the spending of any individual physician. If anything, individual physicians are provided with an even greater incentive to increase spending, because nothing they do as individuals can affect overall spending, but their fees will be affected by what other physicians do collectively, irrespective of their own behavior.[39]

Any physician foolish enough to do his small part to meet the expenditure targets by reducing the amount of services he provided for his Medicare patients would be penalized twice. First when he received less income from Medicare, and second when the SGR cuts were triggered anyway due to other physicians not reducing the amount of services provided for their Medicare patients.

The year 2001 was the first time that Medicare payments to physicians exceeded the SGR expenditure target, resulting in a 5.4 percent cut in physician fees in March 2002. Interest groups representing physicians did not take the cut lying down. Faced with another cut of 4.4 percent in March 2003, physician groups threatened to hit Congress where it would hurt the most. "Physicians cannot afford to treat Medicare patients under the new rates," said Dr. James C. Martin, president of the American Academy of Family Physicians.[40] The American Medical Association followed up with a survey in January 2003 showing that, if another round of SGR cuts were to take place, then a significant number of physicians would restrict the number of Medicare patients they saw.[41] Apparently members of Congress were less than enthused by the prospect of a lot of senior voters struggling to find physicians who would treat them. Congress suspended the 4.4 percent cut and replaced it with a 1.6 percent increase.

For the next decade this kabuki dance would repeat itself. As the date that the SGR cuts would take effect drew to a close, physician groups would issue warnings about the number of physicians who would have to stop treating Medicare patients. Congress would suspend the cut and usually increase payment rates by one to two percent. This ended up increasing the difference between the SGR expenditure target and what

Medicare was actually spending so that each subsequent proposed cut was larger than the last. By early 2014, Congress had to suspend an SGR cut of over 24 percent.

Although Congress routinely suspended the SGR cuts since 2002, the SGR still had the effect of reducing Medicare payments to physicians. That's because the small one to two percent increases to Medicare's payment rates that Congress usually added when it suspended the SGR cuts were not enough to keep up with inflation. Factor in inflation and physicians were being paid *less* over a decade. Consider the reimbursement for a Level I visit with a new patient. In 2001, before the SGR took effect, Medicare paid $35.19 for that type of visit in the Austin, Texas area. By 2014, Medicare paid $43.35.[42] Yet if reimbursement rates had grown at the rate of inflation during that time, Medicare would have paid $47.34. In effect, physicians in Austin experienced an 8.4 percent reduction in their Medicare rates for that service.

The SGR affects all physicians, primary care and specialists alike. But its impact is hardest felt by primary care physicians, since they tend to earn less than specialists. A Texas Medical Association survey in 2011 polled physicians on what their response would be if a looming SGR cut of 29.5 percent went into effect in 2012. It found that 41 percent of primary care physicians had either stopped seeing new Medicare patients or would do so if the cut went into effect, versus 23 percent for medical specialists and 27 percent for surgical specialists.[43]

The SGR also has the pernicious effect of creating uncertainty among physicians. Congress usually waits until right before the SGR cut takes effect before suspending it. On a few occasions Congress suspended it shortly *after* it took effect. Not knowing if they will face reductions in their Medicare payments year after year has been a major factor in causing some physicians to restrict their acceptance of Medicare. The 2010 AMA survey found that, of the 17 percent of physicians who were limiting the number of Medicare patients in their practice, over three-quarters listed the "ongoing threat of future payment cuts makes Medicare an unreliable payer" as a reason.[44]

That is the main reason Dr. Slatosky stopped taking new Medicare patients.

"It was in 2007, when the cut was going to be about 10 percent," he said. "Then Congress came in at the last second and stopped it. But the news stories noted that Congress would have to come in and suspend it again in six months. I pretty much saw the writing on the wall that this was going to be a perpetual mess. You knew Congress was not going to fix it permanently."

Dr. Slatosky decided he wasn't going to keep expanding the number of Medicare patients in his practice while also worrying that every year or so Medicare might cut the amount it paid him to treat them. It was not a decision he made easily.

"It bothered me a lot because now there were going to be Medicare patients who would have the hassle of trying to find another physician in this rural area," he said. "But in the end, it was better to have a physician here seeing some of the Medicare patients in the area than me losing my business and having no physician here at all."

In April 2015, Congress finally passed a bill that repealed the SGR. Whether that will stem the tide of physicians who limit their exposure to Medicare patients remains to be seen. The bill was hailed as bipartisan since both Republicans and Democrats supported it. Indeed, the word "bipartisan" is considered by many inside the Beltway to be one of the highest honors that can be bestowed on a piece of legislation. That's unfortunate, because too often bipartisanship means Republicans and Democrats supporting a bill that is all but certain to produce bad outcomes.

That will likely be the case with the bill repealing the SGR, as it puts in place a new Medicare payment system (dubbed "MIPS") that will encourage physicians to avoid the sickest Medicare patients, a subject examined at greater length in Chapter 8. Suffice it to say, for those physicians who got into medicine to treat sick patients—i.e., almost all physicians—Medicare has just added a new headache to the way it pays them.

Does Primary Care Need Medicare?

In 2008, Dr. Douglas Iliff, a primary care physician, wrote an article with the provocative title, "Does Primary Care Need Medicare?" He complained of Medicare's "reimbursement level that barely covered [his] overhead." Furthermore, after changes made by Congress in the mid-1990s, it was easier for federal prosecutors to go after physicians for Medicare fraud. Dr. Iliff saw federal agents close down a colleague's office and confiscate her billing records. "Although she was found innocent of wrongdoing," Dr. Iliff wrote, "I imagine she had some difficulty getting her reputation back."

That was enough for Dr. Iliff to finally drop Medicare. In the end he lost some Medicare patients but saw his bottom line improve now that he was able to spend more time with patients who had better paying insurance. "It certainly makes you wonder," he concluded, "what would happen if primary care resigned from Medicare?"[45]

Is that really the kind of result we want? If enough primary care physicians leave Medicare, it could eventually result in serious access problems for the program's beneficiaries. It would be especially difficult for those patients unable to pay for services out-of-pocket, most likely the elderly poor and the disabled.

Such an exodus of physicians could also cause considerable harm since the Medicare population is one that may be in the most need of primary care. Patients with multiple illnesses (in medical lingo "comorbidities") are most likely to be found among the elderly and the disabled. Considerable evidence shows that primary care is vital to effectively treating people with comorbidities.[46] Additional research suggests other reasons to keep primary care physicians as part of Medicare, such as primary care's ability to prevent illness and death and reduce costs.[47]

Ultimately, what we should want is a Medicare system that pays primary care physicians without the maddening inconveniences. We should want a way of paying primary care physicians that no longer puts them at the mercy of the RUC, that eliminates most if not all Medicare-related billing costs for primary care and renders unworkable policies like the SGR moot.

The best way to do this is to give Medicare funds to Medicare beneficiaries and let them pay their physicians directly. In effect, each Medicare recipient would be given a type of "medical account" that he or she could use to pay physicians and other health care providers directly. The details of this system are discussed at length in Chapter 10. For now it is sufficient to see how such a system of direct payment would enable physicians to better serve their patients.

Primary care and other physicians who accepted direct payment from Medicare beneficiaries would no longer be at the mercy of Medicare's price control regime. They wouldn't have to worry about the politicking within the RUC or about policies such as the SGR. Their fees would be determined by the supply and demand of the marketplace. They would save money by eliminating billing expenses associated with Medicare. Ultimately, it makes no sense to have billing expenses for primary care physicians. As Dr. Slatosky said, primary care charges are relatively *small charges*. Reducing transaction costs helps when the price for your services ranges from $50 to $200. Primary care physicians already deal with expenses, such as employee salaries, rent and supplies, and the added expense of billing makes it more difficult for them to generate a profit. Getting rid of those expenses would also enable physicians to spend more time with their patients.

The undue burden of billing expenses placed on primary care physicians is an artifact of having a health insurance system in which we expect insurance to pay for everything, even small charges that we should pay for directly. Consider this: In how many areas of our economy do we spend relatively low amounts on goods and services and then expect the provider to bill a third-party payer to get paid? Exactly none, and with good reason. A third-party would just add to the cost of those goods and services, thereby increasing the prices that consumers pay. Paying directly for goods and services is obviously more efficient.

Likewise, patients would see improved quality, affordability and access by paying directly for primary care services. Giving beneficiaries more control over Medicare's resources moves us in that direction.

8. How to Not Be Rewarded for Making Patients Healthier

Medicare has a quality problem.

Despite countless Congressional hearings, studies by government committees, plans and advice from medical professionals and health care policy experts, no one has yet figured out how to make Medicare pay for improving the quality of health care. Worse still, they have yet to figure out how to prevent Medicare from undermining quality, as it often does.

To be fair, quality is a complicated concept, which makes paying for it difficult. Quality often means meeting a standard of excellence, but in health care what are those standards of excellence? Surely, one such standard is providing treatment to the patient that cures or improves his illness. Of course, quality can also refer to a physician who is better than other physicians at treating patients. It may also mean meeting a host of patient preferences such as being friendly and compassionate, listening carefully to the patients' concerns and providing the patient with some peace of mind. In short, quality in health care is far too complicated a concept for government to be a competent purchaser of it.

In the specific case of Medicare, one reason it doesn't improve quality is that it uses a system of price controls. Under price controls, every physician is paid the same amount for the same service regardless of the quality he provides. Physicians who provide excellent quality are paid no more under Medicare than physicians who are mediocre.

Price controls also undermine quality for services and procedures when the amount of the price control is below the market price. In those areas of the market, the price control discourages physicians from providing sufficient care. Often, physicians who try to provide quality service in those areas are penalized with lower income.

A more fundamental reason that Medicare does not improve quality is that government programs are generally not well-suited to paying for quality. It is the nature of government programs that they can usually only pay for one aspect of quality, the aspect that can be measured. Thus, if researchers can develop "quality measures," such as the number of times a physician should prescribe beta-blockers to his heart patients or the proper level of blood sugar for a physician's diabetic patients, Medicare may be able to pay physicians for that. However, even quality measures usually leave out a lot of vital information on quality.

What most government programs cannot pay for is the subjective component of quality. As one health care policy analyst notes, trying to make a third-party payer like Medicare pay for quality "is an immensely difficult task. Quality has multiple dimensions and is often highly subjective, making 'quality care' impossible to define uniformly for diverse populations. Even when it is possible to settle on a reasonable definition of quality, measures can be difficult to translate into financial incentives."[1] The subjectivity of quality is a major problem for Medicare because it must pay for quality for millions of beneficiaries each with their own individual notions of what constitutes quality, notions which often change over time. In short, Medicare is saddled with a near impossible task.

Medicare is ill-equipped to pay for quality, and a physician like Dr. Scott Braddock* knows this all too well.

---

* "Dr. Scott Braddock" is a pseudonym.

How to Make Patients Healthier and Not Be Rewarded for It, Part 1

Dr. Braddock began his career as a practicing physician working in primary care and ended it specializing in endocrinology.

He began the transition in 1999 and by 2001, his practice, located in the Deep South, focused exclusively on diabetes patients.

His practice was not one in which any diabetic could simply make an appointment and then show up. Since he was now a specialist, his patients had to be referred to him by primary care physicians. Without the referral, most insurers would not pay for a patient's visit to Dr. Braddock.

"In a referral business like mine, I'm not seeing the easy-to-treat patients," said Dr. Braddock. "A patient's primary care physician usually didn't say to his patient, "Hey, we see you've got diabetes, your blood sugar is up a little bit, let's send you to Dr. Braddock.

"By the time patients were referred to us they'd typically had diabetes from five-to-twenty years, and they knew it was not under control. And the patient had already suffered one or more complications. They have had lasic surgery because of retinopathy [damage to the retina of the eye], or they've had some sort of serious heart-related problem, or they are seeing the kidney doctor because they already were having kidney problems. They also often suffered from neuropathy [nerve damage to the feet]."

Treating his patients properly required Dr. Braddock to spend a considerable amount of time with them.

"When I saw a patient for the first time, I'd usually apologize in advance for sounding a bit glib," explained Dr. Braddock. "That's because the first thing I'd ask him or her was 'Tell me, why are you here? I know why your doctor sent you here. But I want to know your perspective. Why did you spend the time, money and effort to come here? What is it that you want to accomplish?'"

Typically, the patient would respond by saying he just wanted to feel better, or wanted to get his blood sugar under control, or he didn't want to get up so often during the night to urinate. He might also want to keep his eyesight or kidneys from getting any worse.

"I'd get a response like that and I'd reply, 'Great! I'll do my best to address those,'" said Dr. Braddock. "Then I'd tell the patient, 'Now let me tell you why I'm here. My first goal is that you don't die, and my second goal is that you are not crippled along the way. Everything else is just a detail.'

"Usually that would prompt a deer in the headlights look from the patient. Then I would explain to the patient that it's important from here on out to filter everything though the lens of 'has this treatment that you're doing now or that we're going to do been shown to improve survival or improve outcomes? If it has, by all means we want to do it. If it is neutral but it makes you feel good, that's fine. But if it worsens survival, we have to ask why in heaven's name are we doing it?'"

Unfortunately, it was not uncommon for him to see a patient taking a prescription drug that he shouldn't. He'd often see older women who'd had a stroke and were taking the drug Premarin, a good drug for treating post-menopausal symptoms but one that increased the risk of stroke. He'd also see patients who were taking Norvasc, a drug that treated blood pressure but could also worsen kidney disease.

After going through the drugs the patient was taking, he'd then encourage the patient to tell his "diabetes story."

"I'd ask the patient, 'When did your diabetes start? How was it diagnosed? Were you sick or was it just a routine physical exam? What did your doctor do first to treat you? What did he do next? Ok, what came after that?' I'd also need to find out what 'misadventures' had already occurred. If a patient said he had a bad rash after taking a certain drug, I wouldn't want to repeat that, obviously. And I'd also need to find out what wasn't done in his treatment."

If the patient had eye problems, Dr. Braddock would need to know when the eye problems started, how many times he'd had laser surgery, who his eye doctor was and the last time the patient had seen him.

He'd ask a similar series of questions if the patient also had kidney disease, circulation problem in his legs or neuropathy.

"I'd often ask the patient how he knew he had neuropathy," Dr. Braddock said. "The patient often replied, 'Well, my feet hurt so the doctor told me I had neuropathy.' Then I'd ask, 'Okay, did anyone ever do a nerve conduction study on your feet?' Often the patient would say no. I'd then ask, 'Okay, has anyone done an ultrasound test of your leg arteries to see if there is any blockage?' Again, the patient would often say no."

The extensive questioning could take anywhere from a half hour to an hour. Then the counseling would begin. Dr. Braddock would explain to the patient how the diabetes was affecting him, what prescription drugs he needed to be taking and how to change his diet.

"After that, I'd do a physical exam of the patient," he said. "That would usually take at least another 10 minutes."

Getting the patient to follow his instructions was not only crucial, but also a challenge.

"Whether it's compliance with medicine, dietary instructions, exercise, lifestyle or other issues, it was not only critical that the patient understood what he needed to do but also that he remembered it," he explained. "The problem is that if you only tell somebody something one time, the likelihood they will remember it twenty-four hours from now is very low."

To solve this, Dr. Braddock relied heavily on his nurses. He had one nurse whose job was to take phone calls from patients and answer their questions. When the new patient would return for a follow-up visit (usually within a week), another nurse would accompany him to the examination room, all the while telling the patient what he needed to do to improve his health.

"So now the patient is getting the instructions a second time," Dr. Braddock said. "And then I go into the examination room and I reinforce it a third time. And if the patient still voices any discomfort with the information I provide, I send him to our 'diabetic educator,' and she will spend more time with the patient."

Dr. Braddock also provided his patients with convenience. For patients with neuropathy, Dr. Braddock had the equipment in his office to do nerve conduction tests. His office was also equipped with lab testing, cardio-pulmonary stress testing, and x-rays. "It was one stop shopping," Dr. Braddock said.

Despite receiving such challenging patients, Dr. Braddock achieved remarkable results. When the Blue Cross insurer of his area audited his practice, it found that he achieved the best results for his diabetes patients for any physician in the state.

In 2008, Dr. Braddock joined a study conducted by the University of South Carolina (USC) that surveyed about 125 physician practices on how they treated diabetes patients. There were about 100,000 patients total in the study, and Dr. Braddock notes that, since most of the other practices in the study were primary care offices, they were probably not treating diabetes patients as severe as his.

Despite having sicker patients, Dr. Braddock excelled on many of the measures. For example, one measure was "Hemoglobin A1c," an important measure of blood sugar. For diabetics, the goal is to have a Hemoglobin A1c level lower than seven percent. Nationally, about 40 percent of diabetics have Hemoglobin A1c lower than that level. The median in the USC study was 65 percent—that is, about half of the practices had more than 65 percent of their patients with Hemoglobin A1c level lower than seven percent, and half had less than 65 percent of their patients below that level. From July 2008, when Dr. Braddock joined the study, until June 2010 when he left it, he never had fewer than 69 percent of his patients with Hemoglobin A1c at levels below seven percent. In some months it ran as high as about 75 percent of his patients.

Or consider blood pressure. Ideally a patient should have blood pressure lower than 130 over 80. The national average for diabetics is 35 percent and the median for the study was about 46 percent. Dr. Braddock's worst result was about 54 percent of his patients with blood pressure lower than 130 over 80. His highest mark was 65 percent.

Dr. Braddock managed to improve the health of his nearly 3,000 patients so well that most of them did not have any serious heart problems after they became his patients. Ironically, this did not make Dr. Braddock universally loved within the local medical community. It created tension with the local hospital since fewer patients needing bypass surgery or angioplasty caused revenues to decline in the hospital's cardiovascular department.

He explained that improving the health of these patients meant addressing all of the illnesses associated with diabetes:

> If the goal is to improve survival, just changing how we deal with blood sugar or improving blood sugar is not enough. The studies have not shown that just treating that by itself has a major effect on survival. What has been shown to have an impact on survival and to lower patient costs is a multi-sectorial approach which requires that you simultaneously address blood sugar, blood pressure and cholesterol. I also have to address any prescription drugs they are taking that might be making the problem worse, like clotting drugs. I also have to address tobacco use or anything else that might be causing problems, and I have to do it all at the same time if I want my patients to have better health outcomes.

Despite providing such excellent quality for his patients, Dr. Braddock closed his practice in early 2011.

There were many reasons why he closed his practice, but the primary reason was that he could never consistently make money. In the last three years, he did not earn enough to make a salary. Instead, he made income giving talks for a pharmaceutical company.

Medicare accounted for about 35 percent of Dr. Braddock's revenue. Medicare's price-control system under-valued many of his specialty treatments for diabetes and thereby played a large role in the closing of his practice.

How To Make Patients Healthier And Not Be Rewarded For It, Part 2

The system that Medicare has used since 1992 to pay physicians, the Resource Based Relative Value System (RBRVS), was developed by a Harvard economist named William Hsiao. To create the RBRVS, Hsiao and his research team had physicians rate services and procedures based on the amount of work—defined as the amount of time, mental effort and judgment, technical skill and physician effort, and psychological stress— that went into each service and procedure. For each medical specialty, Hsiao and his team began with a reference service. So, for general surgery, they began with a simple hernia repair and gave it a work rating of 100. Then panels of general surgeons would rate other procedures relative to the value of hernia repair. So if they judged that cancer surgery was four and half times as much work as hernia repair, the cancer surgery would get a rating of 450.[2] Hsiao claimed that the RBRVS would "avoid the price distortions that appear to be inherent"[3] in the system Medicare was then using.

One reason Hsiao wanted to replace the system Medicare was using to pay physicians prior to 1992 was that it was "cumbersome and administratively complex."[4] Given what the RBRVS has become, it's tempting to say foresight was not Hsiao's strong suit.

He did recognize, however, that the RBRVS had limitations. "For one thing, it does not take into account quality of services. At present [1991], it is simply not feasible to differentiate the quality of 500,000 physicians practicing in the United States," he wrote.[5]

Some of Hsiao's critics claimed that the RBRVS's problems were more than just a failure to account for quality. It "will make matters worse," wrote Robert Moffit and Ed Haislmaier of the conservative Heritage Foundation. "The reason: Because the proposed system excludes the market forces of supply and demand in determining the value and price of medical service, it will distort medical prices even further and create shortages of medical care. The result will be a debased quality of care."[6]

One area in which it has made quality worse is in the management of more complicated patients, like the diabetic patients Dr. Braddock attends to. Treating such patients is usually "time-intensive," but Medicare actually pays physicians *less* the more time they spend with their patients.

Ironically, Hsiao noticed this could be a problem with the RBRVS because the values he and his team were generating were based on the average amount of time it took to complete a physician visit. Visits requiring more than average time "would be undervalued. A flexible policy toward supplementing reimbursement for the well-documented and unusually complex case would help to answer this objection."[7]

Hsiao had a poor understanding of how bureaucracies implement policy. They are generally not known for their flexibility. Rather, like most bureaucracies, the Centers for Medicare and Medicaid Services (CMS) used a standardized, one-size-fits-all system when paying for visits. Yet all of the millions of Medicare patients, from the simple to the vastly complex, would have to fit into it.

As noted in the previous chapter, Medicare pays for 10 different types of visits—depending on the severity of the visit and on whether that patient is a new or established patient. Table 8.1 shows how much each visit pays at the national level (before they are adjusted for geographic region) and the number of minutes for those visits that are prescribed by the literature on coding.[8]

Table 8.1: Medicare Pay and Recommended Minutes by Visit Type, 2015				
	New Patient:		Established Patient:	
Visit	Pay	Minutes	Pay	Minutes
Level I	$43.98	10	$20.02	5
Level II	$75.08	20	$43.98	10
Level III	$109.05	30	$72.94	15
Level IV	$165.90	45	$108.34	25
Level V	$208.45	60	$146.84	40
Sources: CMS, Hospice Medicare Director Billing Guide				

On the surface it looks like Medicare pays less for a less severe visit, such as a Level I visit, and more for higher severity visits like Level IV or V. However, that is misleading. A much different picture emerges when the prices Medicare pays for each type of visits are divided by the recommended number of minutes.

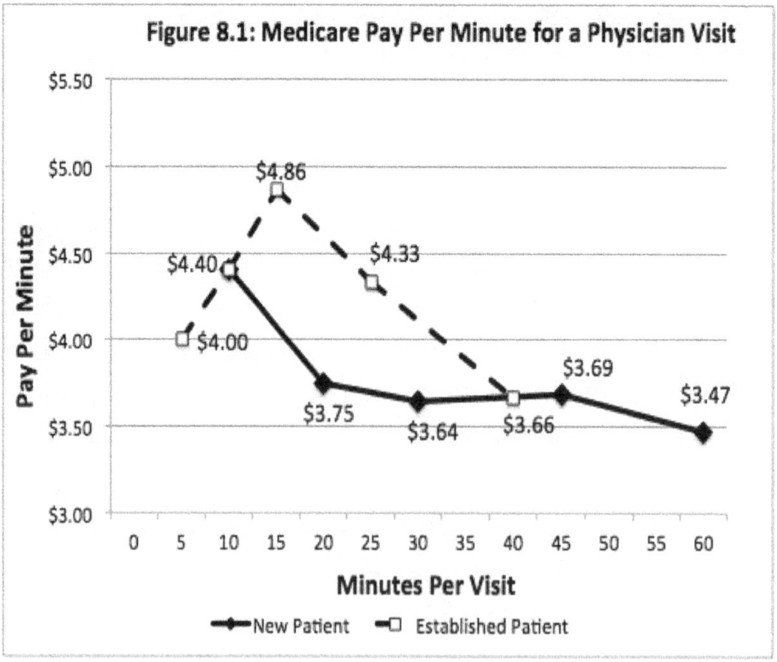

Figure 8.1: Medicare Pay Per Minute for a Physician Visit

As Figure 8.1 demonstrates, physicians, generally, get paid less per minute the longer the visit takes. The way Medicare pays physicians incentivizes them to keep visits as short as possible. Consider two hypothetical physicians each working an eight-hour day, or 480 minutes (And, yes, many physicians work longer than eight hours—this example is *hypothetical*.) Physician A sees 48 established patients in a day each for a 10-minute (Level II) visit. At $4.40 a minute, he grosses about $2,112 per day. Physician B sees 12 established patients in a day each for a 40-minute (Level V) visit. At $3.66 a minute, he grosses about $1,757. Physician A makes about 20 percent more than Physician B. Medicare, in effect, penalizes physicians who try to provide better quality to their patients by spending more time with them.

Of course, as noted above, "quality" is often subjective. For some patients, a quality visit is a short one. We all know people who, for whatever reason, loathe going to the doctor. Their idea of quality is get in, fix the problem and get out.

However, studies that have examined the relationship of quality to length of visit find that most patients prefer longer visits. Two studies have found that patients were generally more satisfied if they felt they had spent more time with the physician than they expected, and were less satisfied if the visit was shorter than what they had expected.[9] Other studies have found that older patients[10] and patients with depression[11] were generally more satisfied with longer visits. Another study not only found that patients were generally more satisfied with longer visits, but also that longer visits enabled physicians to ask more questions and provide more information about the problem and its treatment.[12]

Clearly, patients tend to associate quality with longer visits. Are they getting that quality from their physicians? The evidence is mixed. On the one hand, a Commonwealth Fund survey[13] found that physicians thought they were spending less time with their patients, while a survey by the Center for Studying Health System Change found they were spending slightly more time.[14] Another study found that from 1980-1996, the amount of time internists spent with new patients declined, on average, 12 minutes. The time they spent with established patients declined three minutes on average.[15] On the other hand, studies that have examined data from the National Ambulatory Medical Care Survey have found that, over the last few decades, physicians have spent between two to three minutes more with their patients on average.[16] Critics of those studies, though, claim that the data doesn't distinguish between actual "face time" with patients and other things that can be counted as part of the patient visit such as filling out paperwork.[17]

If physicians are spending more time with patients but face a reimbursement system that pays them less for doing so, we should expect to see physician income decline. There is evidence suggesting that is indeed happening.[18] One possible interpretation is that some physicians, at least, would prefer to spend more time with their patients even if it means sacrificing some income.

That was definitely the case with Dr. Braddock. His commitment to quality often resulted in even less pay per minute from Medicare.

He noted that he'd usually schedule a visit with a new patient at either 11:30 am or 4:30 pm. "Those were the best times to see new patients because they almost always need an hour and a half to confer with," he said.

A visit with a new patient that took that long would always be a Level V visit, for which Medicare pays $208.45. At the recommended number of minutes, 60, it pays $3.47 per minute. By spending 90 minutes with such patients, Dr. Braddock was being paid only $2.32 per minute.

A review of the research on diabetes treatment found that the more comprehensive the intervention, the more likely the patient's health would improve. The intervention included continued education that better enabled patients to recall what they needed to do to improve their condition, including nurses and other personnel in the education process, using computerized records, and getting feedback on the practice from professionals.[19] These were all things that Dr. Braddock was doing.

That sort of care, though, requires spending time with the patient, time that Medicare does not pay for. Medicare inhibits quality for sicker patients by paying physicians inadequately for the time needed to treat such patients. Physicians like Dr. Braddock who try to provide such quality to their patients are faced with going out of business.

The Real Dr. House

Dr. Dariush Saghafi has been consulting with Ted Jensen's two adult daughters, Emily and Amber,[**] when they decide it is time to invite Mr. Jensen into the room. Within minutes, Dr. Saghafi finds himself in a delicate situation.

"I heard you picked up smoking again," Dr. Saghafi asks Mr. Jensen. "Have you been smoking a little bit?"

"Who said that?" Mr. Jensen asks.

"Well, that's what I heard," says Dr. Saghafi.

"You heard wrong," replies Mr. Jensen in a low voice.

"You're not smoking anymore?" Dr. Saghafi asks.

"You heard wrong!" Mr. Jensen says, his voice rising in annoyance.

But Dr. Saghafi won't back down. Mr. Jensen suffers from early-stage Alzheimer's disease and with it a host of other medical problems. Given all of the problems Dr. Saghafi is trying to help Mr. Jensen with, the last thing he wants is for him to take up smoking again.

"Ok, so you're telling me that you are not smoking anymore," says Dr. Saghafi.

"I am not smoking!"

"Ok, that's good," Dr. Saghafi replies.

"Who the hell told you that?" Mr. Jensen demands.

"Well, I heard that you might have been getting some cigarettes," he replies.

Prior to Mr. Jensen coming into the room, Emily told Dr. Saghafi that he had asked for cigarettes a few days earlier. Dr. Sagahfi, an experienced

---

[**] All names of patients and their families in this section have been changed to protect their privacy.

physician, knows he has to keep Emily and Amber's trust in order to properly treat Mr. Jensen. So he goes on dodging Mr. Jensen's question.

Emily, realizing that Dr. Saghafi won't give her up, finally says, "You asked for cigarettes the other night."

"Asking for a cigarette and smoking are two goddam different things!" Mr. Jensen exclaims. "And I don't like to be accused of doing something I'm not doing."

"Fair enough. If you say haven't been smoking, then you haven't been smoking," Dr. Saghafi says.

"I haven't been smoking!" Mr. Jensen repeats.

"How about the Cleveland Indians? You follow them?" asks Dr. Saghafi, trying to get Mr. Jensen's mind onto a different subject.

"No, I don't like baseball."

"Why not?"

"Because, when I was in high school, I didn't play basketball...." Mr. Jensen pauses for a moment. "I didn't play basket...I mean....dammit!"

It's okay," says Dr. Saghafi.

"You can do it," says Amber. "You didn't play baseball."

"We didn't have baseball at my high school," says Mr. Jensen. "We had basketball and football."

The visit has now taken over an hour and it will last another twenty minutes. During the visit, Emily and Amber expressed concern to Dr. Saghafi that their dad becomes more confused and agitated as the day turns to evening. Dr. Saghafi explains that it's a phenomenon known as "sundowning," a common condition among Alzheimer's patients. Dr. Saghafi recommends he try the drug Namenda for it.

Dr. Saghafi also spends time questioning the daughters about the medication Mr. Jensen is taking. Is it working? The dosage changes that were made since the last visit, have they helped? They have an extensive discussion of what medication to try as Mr. Jensen has been having trouble with sleeping and frequency with urination.

He also asks if Mr. Jensen has had any falls since his last visit. His daughter says that he had one when he was trying to get into bed. The paramedics had to be called in to help him get into bed. Fortunately, Mr. Jensen didn't suffer any serious injuries.

Near the end of the visit, Dr. Saghafi tests the reflexes in Mr. Jensen's hands and arms as Mr. Jensen has endured a series of minor strokes. His right side appears a little weaker than the left. Dr. Saghafi then sets up a blood and urine test for Mr. Jensen, and has his office assistant call in the new prescription medications they've decided on.

As Dr. Saghafi finishes up, Mr. Jensen tells his daughters, "I like him. He's one of the few [doctors] I do."

There is good reason for that. For starters, they aren't meeting in Dr. Saghafi's office but in Mr. Jensen's home. Dr. Saghafi, a neurologist, still makes house calls. As far as he knows he is the only neurologist in the state of Ohio to do so.

"A few years after I started my private practice, I decided to do home visits with my patients," Dr. Saghafi explains as he leaves the Jensen's house and gets in his small pickup truck. "Now, about 90 percent of my patient are over age 65 and are at home. Most are on Medicare. For those types of patients, especially those with Alzheimer's or dementia, it's very inconvenient for them to have to find transportation to get to my office.

"One reason I wanted to do home visits was to improve the 'no show rate' in my office. If I had five patients scheduled and only two show up, then I'm not taking much money home. Making home visits eased that problem.

"What I found out, though, is that you gain a lot of information about the patients, especially my geriatric patients, when you visit them in their home. You can see what may be impacting them in their dementia or chronic pain in their home environment. You find out what obstacles they face in complying with their medications. You see what risks they have in falling. Elderly people falling at home constantly—you wonder why? Well, you have throw rugs here, little coffee tables there—all sorts of fall risks for an elderly patient. I can also see how well they are moving around. I can see if they are having trouble getting up from the toilet. Are they having trouble getting into their bed? Ultimately, I can get a bird's eye view of what's going on in their home that's contributing to their health problems."

Dr. Saghafi starts his day at 10 am and tries to end it at 7:30 pm, but it is not uncommon for it to end at around 9:30 pm. And he does it seven days a week.

"Medicare does pay more for a home visit, although not a lot more," Dr. Saghafi explains. "On my best days I can see seven to eight patients. Usually, though, my norm is about three to four patients a day. Compare that to a neurologist who sees 10 or 20 patients a day—a few see thirty a day—in their offices, and they make much more than me."

One of his biggest dislikes of Medicare is that it doesn't pay for phone calls. He guesses he spends four to six hours a week calling patients and their families, along with spending time on the phone with Medicare and other insurance companies seeking approval for treatments.

Dr. Saghafi parks his truck at his next appointment. He walks up to a modest, middle-class house and knocks on the door. No answer.

"Mr. Paulson," Dr. Saghafi shouts. "Mr. Paulson, are you home?"

He knocks again, and he hears someone stirring inside the house.

A tall, elderly, unshaven man, slightly bent over, answers the door.

"Hello, Dr. Saghafi," he said in a gruff voice.

"Hello, Mr. Paulson," he replies.

They go into the living room. Mr. Paulson sits in a chair. Off to the left are various bottles and food wrappers.

"So how have things been going since I last saw you, Mr. Paulson?" Dr. Saghafi asks.

"No major problems, except my back is sore," says Mr. Paulson. "I'm trying to have something set up so it can be looked at, so that we can pursue a surgery that will help me move around."

"You know what my opinion is on you having more surgery on your back?" Dr. Saghafi asks.

"Yeah. Yeah, I know," says Mr. Paulson. "I probably should have taken your advice last time."

"Just let me know before you make a decision on doing anything, if that is the direction you want to go," says Dr. Saghafi.

Dr. Saghafi talks about a condition known as arachnoiditis, an inflammation of the arachnoid, one of the membranes that protects the central nervous system. He explains that multiple surgeries on areas like the back, neck or head can cause arachnoiditis. He writes it down, so that Mr. Paulson will remember it.

"It can result in more scarring, which can lead to more pain," Dr. Saghafi. "Sometimes it can be difficult to tell the difference between the arachnoiditis and back pain. You could fall into this and it can be very hard to treat arachnoiditis. So let me know before you make a final decision."

"Well, I think there's a good chance I'll take your advice and not have more surgery," Mr. Paulson says.

"Good. Would you also take my advice and cut back on your smoking?" Dr. Saghafi asks.

"Yeah, I don't inhale anymore. I'm halfway home," says Mr. Paulson.

Dr. Saghafi shakes his head slightly. "You could run for president. And I'd vote for you."

Mr. Paulson laughs.

"How about your pills for your Parkinson's problem?" Dr. Saghafi asks.

"Well, I'm taking them," he says.

"Do you need a refill?" Dr. Saghafi asks.

"I don't know," he says.

"Well, I'll make sure and have my office check on that," said Dr. Saghafi.

Dr. Saghafi types some notes into his laptop computer, which he brings with him to every house call. He also has a wireless internet card that allows him to access the internet. He types an email to his office assistant about Mr. Paulson's medication.

"But you do have your alarm-clock pill box?" Dr. Saghafi asks as he looks up from his laptop.

Mr. Paulson was having trouble remembering to take his medication on time, so Saghafi encouraged him to buy a pill box that would set off an alarm when he needed to take his medicine.

"I still don't do it right," laughs Mr. Paulson.

"But you are doing much better with it," says Dr. Saghafi.

He looks down at his computer. He's received an email back from his office assistant.

"Okay, the office says that we've ordered a refill for your medication, so we're good on that."

Next Dr. Saghafi asks Mr. Paulson if he has experienced any dizziness or had any trouble walking. Mr. Paulson replies that he hasn't.

"You haven't taken any falls, have you?" Dr. Saghafi asks. Again, Mr. Paulson replies no.

Dr. Saghafi then tests Mr. Paulson's reflexes by having him stretch out his legs one at a time. He then has him spread his arms out and touch his nose with each finger. Finally, he has Mr. Paulson rest his hands on his knees and follow Dr. Saghafi's fingers with his eyes.

Mr. Paulson does well on the tests, but Dr. Saghafi spots something that prompts him to ask, "How does your neck feel?"

"It's been sore, especially in the morning."

Dr. Saghafi touches his neck and asks, "Where does it hurt?"

"At the base, both sides."

"Has it been hurting for a while now?" Dr. Saghafi asks.

"Yes, for a few months," Mr. Paulson replies.

Dr. Saghafi has Mr. Paulson move his head from side to side and then says, "You've got a bit of a tilt to your head."

Mr. Paulson had previously had surgery in his neck to fix degenerative discs.

"Some of that head tilt and some of the soreness in the neck could be due to the degenerative discs in your neck," says Dr. Saghafi. "But it's also common for people with Parkinson's to have that as well. It's sometimes referred to as a torticollis."

He discusses the possibility of getting some Botox injections for Mr. Paulson's neck to relieve the pain.

"Botox is not just to make you beautiful anymore," says Dr. Saghafi. "It can also be used to relieve chronic back pain, instead of you having surgery."

"Okay, let's give it a go," Mr. Paulson says.

"All right, I can get the Botox going for your neck," says Dr. Saghafi. "To get it for your back, that's going to require me getting some added approval." He begins typing notes into his laptop computer.

"Whatever blows up your airbag," Mr. Paulson laughs.

Dr. Saghafi is also worried Mr. Paulson may be in the very early stages of dementia. To test this, he has Mr. Paulson name as many animals as he can in one minute. The goal is to name 15. He could only name 12 during Dr. Saghafi's last visit.

Dr. Saghafi looks at his watch and says, "Go."

"Aardvark, antelope, donkey, cow, chicken, rooster, zebra, hyena, giraffe, rhinoceros, lion, alligator, crocodile....uh...hyena...no I said that...goddam you...um, cow, chicken...no, um, cat, dog, rat, hippopotamus."

"That's a minute," said Dr. Saghafi. "That must have seemed like a long minute, you got frustrated. Let me ask, how often do you practice that?"

"I don't," he replies.

"Well, you need to just about every day. Practice and you'll be able to rattle off 15 without even trying. And then we'll move on to something else..."

"Oh, thanks a lot!" Mr. Paulson interrupts.

"But that's how we keep the ball rolling," Dr. Saghafi says, without skipping a beat. "And we do that and you'll be better able to keep the memory that you have. Last time I was considering putting you on medication for your memory, but today you counted 17, so we can hold off."

Dr. Saghafi has now spent over 45 minutes with Mr. Paulson. Lastly they discuss Mr. Paulson's concerns about his frequent urination, which he claims is up to 30 times a day.

Dr. Saghafi suggests a Prostate Screening Test. He also recommends that they draw blood to test Mr. Paulson's vitamin D level. He types another email into his laptop and asks his office to set up a blood test for Mr. Paulson.

Within a few minutes, Dr. Saghafi has an email back from his office assistant affirming that a blood test is set up for Mr. Paulson the following Monday at a laboratory nearby.

Finally, Dr. Saghafi sets up a return appointment in just over a month.

After he has left Mr. Paulson's house, Dr. Saghafi says, "I wish I could return a bit sooner, within two weeks. The problem is my schedule is so booked up. I'd like to do a phone consultation, if Mr. Paulson was agreeable to that, but Medicare doesn't pay me for that."

PQRS

According to the website Salary Wizard, the median salary for a neurologist is about $230,000.[20] It is reasonable to assume that a physician as good as Dr. Saghafi earns considerably more than that. Thus, it comes as a surprise to learn that, after expenses, he earns about $140,000 annually. That puts him in the bottom 10 percent of neurologists.

Indeed, he'd earn much less if he had to rely solely on Medicare. He also handles disability claims and spends some time each week managing the headache clinic at the local Veterans Administration hospital.

The reason Dr. Saghafi makes much less than the average for neurologists is similar to why Dr. Braddock closed his business. Medicare penalizes Dr. Saghafi for spending more time with his patients. The pay for home visits with established patients follows the same pattern as that of office visits, less pay per minute the longer the physician spends with the patient. Interestingly, home visits with new patients do not follow that pattern; pay can be higher for spending more time with new patients. Of course, those are only a small portion of Dr. Saghafi's visits. Most of his visits are with established patients. (For data on Medicare payment for home visits, see Table 8.2 and Figure 8.2 in the appendix.)

Dr. Saghafi has tried to get extra pay from Medicare for the quality that he provides. He participates in a Medicare program established by Congress in 2006 called the "Physician Quality Reporting System" (PQRS). It is what is sometimes known as a "Pay-for-Performance" (P4P) program. P4P programs provide "financial incentives that encourage physicians and hospitals to provide recommended care" that has proven scientifically effective.[21]

Those physicians and other eligible providers that participate in PQRS receive a bonus. In 2007 and 2008, the bonus was 1.5 percent of a provider's Medicare charges. For 2009 and 2010 it was two percent, for 2011 it was one percent, and for 2012-2014 it will be 0.5 percent.

Despite the bonus, participation has been modest. While about 1.1 million providers were eligible to participate in 2012, only about 31 percent, or 367,000 actually did.[22] The average bonus CMS paid through PQRS in 2012 was $457.[23]

The paperwork requirement, in part, probably explains the lackluster participation. Physicians who wish to participate must report three measures included in the PQRS. On each measure they must report a denominator that includes all of the potential patients that the measure could apply to. Then they must report the numerator that includes the number of patients who either received the recommended treatment or met the standard established under the method but didn't receive the treatment. As of 2012, there were about 164 different quality measures to choose from.

For example, one measure requires physicians to record the number of diabetic patients they have (the denominator) and how many of those patients have Hemoglobin A1c levels above nine percent (the numerator).[24] Another measure requires physicians to record the number of patients they have who have coronary artery disease and have had a heart attack (the denominator) and the number of those patients they prescribe beta-blockers for (the numerator.)[25]

However, they must add more codes to the paperwork for every patient who is part of the measure. So, for the Hemoglobin A1c measure, the physician not only has to include the proper CPT and ICD codes (see Chapter 7 for an explanation of those), he must also include the proper "Data Quality Code." For hemoglobin A1c, he must include code 3046F if the patient's level is nine percent, 3045F it is between seven and nine percent, or 3044F if it is below seven percent. If for some reason the physician does not check the hemoglobin A1c of a patient, he must include an "8P" modifier to indicate that it was not checked.[26]

For the measure of prescribing a beta-blocker to patients with coronary artery disease, a physician must include the Data Quality code 4008F. However, if he does not prescribe a beta-blocker, he must provide documentation for why it was not prescribed. If the reason for not prescribing is a medical reason, the physician must include a "1P" modifier. The physicians must include a "2P" modifier if the reason is the patient declined a beat-blocker, and a "3P" modifier must be included if it is some other reason.[27]

Dr. Saghafi has received bonuses between $1,500 and $3,000 from PQRS, which may not be worth the cost of reporting the measures. "I would say in my case, the bonus probably doesn't cover the cost," said Dr. Saghafi. "It's not just the cost of the paperwork, but it's the time it can take to review these quality measures with the patient."

Medicare, it seems, has found a way of paying physicians for quality while also increasing their costs.

Dr. Saghafi points to another reason why the PQRS may not improve quality. "What I do is I go to the list of [PQRS measures] that the American Academy of Neurology has provided. I look down that list of measures and then figure out which one of these measures I tend to use."

In other words, PQRS isn't paying Dr. Saghafi to improve his quality so much as it is paying him for quality that he already provides. No one knows how many other physicians have responded to the PQRS in the same way Dr. Saghafi has. CMS takes advice about which measures to include in PQRS from many of the interest groups that represent physicians, such as the American Academy of Neurology, the American College of Cardiology, the American Medical Association, etc.[28] Would these groups recommend measures that require their members to do more work or enable them to get paid for the work that they are already doing? To the extent that the answer is the latter, then PQRS isn't doing much to improve quality.

CMS was required by ObamaCare to start making this data public as part of Medicare's "Physician Compare" website in 2013.[29] Supposedly, this will enable Medicare patients to view how their physicians perform on certain quality measures. But it's not clear how useful such information will be for the patient.

Consider the hemoglobin A1c measure. If a physician has only a 60 percent rating on this measure, does this mean that he is a poor physician in that six in 10 of his diabetic patients have Hemoglobin A1c above a recommended level? Or, it could mean that he has very severe diabetics like Dr. Braddock. As Dr. Braddock's practice showed, getting severe diabetics to achieve a healthy Hemoglobin A1c level is a very involved, complicated process.

By contrast, a physician who had a result of 10 percent might not necessarily be a quality physician but one who is trying to "game the system" by avoiding hard-to-treat diabetics. The perverse incentive for physicians to selectively maximize the number of healthy patients, as a means to improving their scores on outcome measures, is a drawback of certain P4P measures.[30]

It's also possible that a physician with such a good score also had generally more cooperative patients. Good health outcomes depend not only on what the physician does, but how much the patient is willing to cooperate by taking his medication regularly, changing his diet, or other behaviors that improve health results. Yet the PQRS by its nature cannot provide data on how cooperative a physician's patients are.

Next consider the measure of prescribing a beta-blocker to patients with coronary artery disease who have previously had a heart attack. On first glance, it would seem that the physician who is prescribing beta-blockers for, say, 99 percent of his heart patients would be doing a better job than the physician who is only prescribing it for 85 percent. However, it's quite possible that the latter physician is doing a better job.

First, beta-blockers can have side effects such as dizziness, which can lead to a fall.[31] For elderly patients, falling can be quite dangerous. The physician prescribing beta-blockers to only 85 percent of his patients may be withholding it from the other 15 percent because they have complained of dizziness.

Another possibility is that the latter physician has more heart patients who are taking multiple medications for other conditions. If prescribing a beta-blocker means a patient will now be taking a fifth, sixth, or seventh drug, it's not clear if the added benefit of the drug will be worth the risk. As an article in the *New England Journal of Medicine* put it, "Is a statin or beta-blocker, for example, as part of an 11-drug regimen, likely to provide greater benefit or greater harm to a 73-year-old whose priority is maximal energy, strength, and alertness today and who is willing to take on an increased risk of myocardial infarction or stroke over the next 5 or 10 years?"[32] Thus, the PQRS could just as likely undermine quality as improve it by causing confusion among Medicare beneficiaries about their physicians.

PQRS necessarily undermines quality by limiting the amount of measures for which it pays a bonus. There are plenty of other types of quality that it doesn't pay for. For example, Dr. Saghafi is providing quality by making a home visit to a patient who has trouble getting to his office. But there is no measure under PQRS that rewards physicians for doing that. Nor does PQRS reward Dr. Saghafi or other physicians who examine the difficulty an elderly patient has moving from the toilet or getting into bed.

Dr. Saghafi notes that PQRS rewards physicians for discussing and reviewing the diagnosis with a patient who has Parkinson's disease. "But that same type of measure does not apply to Alzheimer's or stroke or many other types of neurological diseases. Something like Alzheimer's needs to be reviewed every time you see the patient. There is no way to diagnose Alzheimer's definitively without a brain biopsy. Without that, I need to be reviewing with the patient every time, asking myself, do I have the right diagnosis? PQRS doesn't pay for that." Ultimately, the risk is that physicians are less likely to provide their patients with the quality that PQRS doesn't pay for.

In 2015, Congress absorbed PQRS and some other Medicare quality programs into one program known as the Merit-Based Incentive Payment System (MIPS). Under MIPS, physicians who treat Medicare patients will be evaluated on how well they score on various metrics, receiving an annual score between zero and 100. Each year CMS will choose a "threshold" number. Physicians who score above that will receive a bonus on their Medicare fees. Physicians who score below it will be penalized. The penalties become more severe the lower he scores. The maximum penalties are a four percent cut in 2019, five percent in 2020, seven percent in 2021, and nine percent in 2022. Physicians who score between zero and one-fourth of the threshold will receive the maximum penalty.[33]

Two of the metrics that MIPS will use to grade physicians are how well patients score on quality measures and how many medical resources physicians use to treat patients. If a physician minimizes the use of medical resources while his patients score well on quality measures, he will likely score above that threshold and he will receive a bonus.

While the intent of MIPS may be to improve quality, the incentives it provides physicians will undermine it. MIPS will incentivize physicians to avoid the sickest patients. For physicians, the easiest way to have patients who score well on quality measures and limit the use of resources is to treat patients who are only moderately ill. Patients who have their diabetes or their heart conditions under control will generate better scores on quality measures such a blood sugar level or blood pressure. Keeping such patients healthy will involve fewer resources. These factors will increase the chances that a physician gets a bonus on his Medicare fees.

By contrast, sicker patients will score poorly on quality measures. Treating them will require more resources. A sicker caseload likely means a physician will fall below the MIPS threshold and see his Medicare fees cut. In short, the sickest Medicare patients will have a harder time finding physicians who will treat them thanks to MIPS.[34]

There are many ways to describe a policy that encourages physicians to avoid sicker patients. "Quality improvement" is not one of them. Ironically, MIPS was passed as part of a bill that removed Medicare's Sustainable Growth Rate, another unworkable policy. Leave it to Congress to replace a bad policy with an even worse one.

MIPS's failure will carry on a tradition of Medicare's attempts at improving quality. Since the late 1960s CMS has had the power to conduct "pilot projects" in Medicare, a type of small-scale experiment usually involving a few hospitals or large physician practices. The aim of these projects is not only to improve quality but also to save on costs.

For the most part, Medicare's pilot projects have been an exercise in futility. A review by the Congressional Budget Office found that few of the programs reduced Medicare expenditures or improved quality.[35] These failures are all the more sobering because "in most cases the participants were experienced organizations that were selected in part based on their likelihood of success."[36]

The reason they fail is pilot projects in Medicare boil down to bureaucrats trying to tell physicians and other health care providers how to innovate. As economist John C. Goodman states, the problem with that approach is:

> Successful innovations are produced by entrepreneurs, *challenging* conventional thinking—not by bureaucrats *trying to implement* conventional thinking. There are lots of examples of successful entrepreneurship in healthcare. There are very few examples of successful bureaucracy. Can you think of any other market where the buyers of a product are trying to tell the sellers how to efficiently produce it?[37]

Yet that is exactly what Medicare tries to do with pilot projects, and thanks to ObamaCare, CMS will double down on them. ObamaCare created within CMS a new agency called the Center for Medicare & Medicaid Innovation. This new center states that its mission is to foster "healthcare transformation by finding new ways to pay for and deliver care that can lower costs and improve care."[38] Medicare, it seems, will continue to deliver on quality failure for a long time to come.

Mother Theresas Are Rare

For Dr. Braddock, leaving his practice was difficult.

"I worried that there would be no one there to take my place, to help those patients. I wrestled with it. I still do. Most of all, I think I miss the experience of seeing a patient who was not doing well get better in a relatively finite amount of time," he said.

Dr. Braddock pauses for a moment and draws a deep breath.

"But I don't miss the 16-hour days. And my biggest worry was my wife. She's had and beaten breast cancer three times. But that means the chances are good she'll have it a fourth time. If that time comes and it is the final one for my wife, well, if I stayed in my practice I'd have to decide to keep the business going while Rome was burning at home, or take care of my wife and let the practice die. Now, I can be there for my wife when the time comes."

For Dr. Saghafi, he knows he could make more money if he practiced medicine differently.

"If I was willing to spend less time with my patients, I know I'd earn more," he said. "I've struggled with that for 10 years. But I just can't do it. I can't treat my patients that way. So I spend long hours doing my practice, and the result is that sometimes my family suffers."

Physicians like Drs. Braddock and Saghafi are, in a small sense, like the Mother Theresas of our health care system, willing to make considerable sacrifices, including sacrificing income, to give their patients the best quality treatment they can. And that is precisely the problem. The Mother Theresas of the world are rare. Most physicians are not going to work 12 to 16 hour days, sometimes seven days a week, and sacrifice a good deal of their income to provide quality treatment for their patients. Unfortunately, that is too often the only way to provide quality in a system that penalizes physicians for providing quality health care.

What is needed is a Medicare system that rewards physicians for providing quality. The best way to do this is to get Medicare out of the business of trying to determine quality and, instead, let physicians and patients determine it. First off, we must get rid of Medicare's system of price controls, one of the biggest barriers to achieving quality.

This means that beneficiaries must have more control over Medicare's resources, so that they can pay physicians and other medical providers directly. That will leave physicians and other providers free to innovate, instead of wasting valuable time and administrative costs to make certain that they have properly followed Medicare's regulations and done the coding properly to ensure Medicare reimbursement. Rather, they will be free to experiment with the services that they provide as they try to find the right mix of quality that meets their patients' needs.

Patient preferences for quality are vast and diverse, and the only system that can come close to adequately satisfying them is one that uses prices. More specifically, prices must be allowed to "float," to move up and down in response to patient preference for quality. Some patients are willing to sacrifice quality if it means paying lower prices, while others are willing to pay top dollar to get every last bit of quality possible. In short, prices act as signals to patients, letting them know when quality is likely to be very good, when it is likely to be mediocre and the entire range in between.

Prices also act as a signal to health care providers. If physicians find that they must lower their prices to get patients in the door, it tells them that they may not be doing a good enough job. If they can charge higher prices and patients are willing to pay them, it tells the physicians that they are providing better quality.

Physicians whose innovations provide high quality will be able to charge higher prices and earn larger incomes. Those larger incomes also act as a signal—in this case, a signal to other physicians.

Imagine, for a moment, if both Drs. Braddock and Saghafi earned annual salaries between $300,000 and $400,000. It wouldn't take long before other endocrinologists and neurologists would take notice and want to know how they could earn higher salaries as well. More endocrinologists would study how Dr. Braddock got such stellar results with his difficult to treat diabetic patients. They'd copy his methods—the intense questioning, the education, the follow up, etc. Soon, they'd be providing quality care to their diabetic patients.

Similarly, other neurologists would learn what Dr. Saghafi did that earned him a high salary. How long would it be before many neurologists were doing home visits for their elderly patients who had difficulty making an office visit?

In health care policy circles this is known as "aligning incentives"— encouraging the physician to provide quality care to the patient by properly reimbursing the physicians for it. But most proposals in Medicare to align incentives involve politicians, bureaucrats, panels of physicians, health care policy wonks and other "experts" deciding what quality care is and how a physician should be paid for it. It never seems to occur to them that the best way to align incentives is to let the patient control the money that pays for the care. It's difficult to understand why, since that is the way most of our economy works. The consumer controls the money and the provider must offer him a product or service with sufficient quality to win his business. Otherwise, the consumer will take his money elsewhere.

One can imagine that incentives would very quickly become aligned in Medicare if the beneficiaries controlled the dollars. Once beneficiaries controlled the dollars, physicians would have every incentive to provide the beneficiary with quality treatment.

9. The Big Hospital Lobby

The incision Dr. Thomas Tkach makes into his patient's knee is almost like clockwork. It is Friday morning, and within minutes Dr. Tkach will be doing a knee replacement on a patient who just happens to also be a physician. It is his fifth surgery of the day.

Dr. Tkach is an orthopedic surgeon who practices at the McBride Orthopedic Hospital in Oklahoma City, OK. He has been in private practice for about sixteen years. He is a bit unusual in that he is the type of surgeon who can do 10 or 11 surgeries in a day.

McBride is the sort of hospital that enables Dr. Tkach to do that.

"When I get into the operating room, I don't have to tell my technician which instrument to hand me at what point in the surgery," he said. "He or she has done it so many times they already know. The nurses know exactly what to do."

"He can do about 600 to 800 joint replacements a year," said Todd Wilson, a distributor for implant devices who works closely with McBride Orthopedic Hospital. "Because he's done it so many times, he knows exactly what he's doing is and able to get it done quicker. At other hospitals, a surgeon may perform only a few dozen a year, so it can take them longer to perform a surgery."

McBride is a physician-owned specialty hospital. It is owned by the nineteen physicians who founded it in 2005. The physicians are also part of the "McBride Clinic" which is located in downtown Oklahoma City and has been in existence since 1923. The physicians have their offices at the clinic, where they do most of their consulting with patients.

The lobby of the McBride Orthopedic Hospital is expansive, filled with cushioned chairs and sofas. The walls are cream colored, the doors painted mahogany, and the lighting is soft. On the other side of the inner wall of the lobby is an atrium with green plants and a small, artificial waterfall. Behind the waterfall is a "reflection area" where patients and their family members can go to pray and meditate. The hospital will make accommodations if the patients or family members wish to have clergy with them in the reflection area.

The chair and sofas in the lobby are already about half full by 7:15 am. Mark Galliart's office is just off to the right of the lobby. Galliart is the chief executive officer of McBride.

The building is only one-story, shaped like a "Y". Galliart says that was a deliberate decision on the part of the physicians.

"Our physicians didn't want the elderly patients to have to worry about going to this floor or that floor," he says. "It's pretty easy. You go to one end or the other, and in the middle are the operating rooms."

McBride, he says, has a patient to nurse ratio of 4:1. Patients have their own rooms, and accommodations can be made to let family members spend the night.

Most patients that come to McBride Orthopedic Hospital for surgery have already visited one of the three locations of the McBride Clinic for an appointment with a surgeon. If the surgeon determines that surgery is needed, then it will be scheduled at the McBride Hospital.

McBride also has a small emergency room with four beds.

"On average, patients are seen within fifteen minutes of coming in to our emergency room," Stephanie, a nurse, says. "At most it takes about an hour and a half to get a patient from the emergency room to a hospital bed." How long it takes to get the patient into surgery varies. The shortest amount of time from the emergency room to the operating room, according to Stephanie, is about two hours. In other cases the surgery may be delayed a day or so.

The desire to open McBride Orthopedic Hospital was driven, in part, by the experience the physicians at the McBride Clinic had with the

Surgery Center of Oklahoma, an outpatient facility in which they are also part owners.

"We were very pleased with the product that we got there," said Dr. Tom Janssen, who does a lot of hip and knee replacements. "We found that center was by far and away our preferred place to work. We could get twice as much done. We were far more efficient and the level of care was good. We wanted to have the same experience with our inpatient facility."

Back in the 1990s, the orthopedic surgeons at the McBride Clinic were doing their inpatient work at the Bone and Joint Hospital, which is part of St. Anthony's Hospital. In 2000, a number of new surgeons joined the McBride Clinic.

"Suddenly, Bone and Joint hospital became insufficient," says Dr. David Holden who does a lot of shoulder surgery. He has a large sports medicine practice and is one of the team physicians for the University of Oklahoma. "To expand it was going to be difficult, given the layout of the building. But we really needed more space."

But St. Anthony's management wasn't too keen on the idea, recalls Dr. Mark Pascale, who also has a sports medicine practice and does inpatient surgery on Medicare patients.

"They didn't want to expand," he said. "I suspect it had something to do with the fact that they wanted their beds to always be full rather than have more capacity but sometimes have beds empty."

Dr. Pascale remembers the problems that caused.

"We got to a point where we were doing more surgeries than the hospital had beds for patients to be in. Sometimes we'd have to cancel an elective surgery the week the surgery was supposed to occur because there wouldn't be a bed for the patient to go into after the surgery."

The physicians at the McBride Clinic had to decide if they wanted to continue to pressure St. Anthony's, take their services to another hospital, or start their own hospital.

"We had a meeting two years before we opened McBride Hospital," says Dr. Janssen. "We all sat down and asked, 'How serious are we? Do we want to build our own hospital and take the risk?' We looked around the room and everyone raised his hand."

Another factor that drove the physicians to open McBride Hospital can be summed up in the word "control." They wanted control over how the hospital was run, and they wanted control over the decision-making process. Ultimately, they believed that would give them far greater influence over the quality of care that the patient received.

"We built it because we were afraid that elsewhere we'd be limited in how we could take care of our patients," says Dr. Pascale. "We were afraid that if we got told what to do and where to go we'd be compromising our patients' care. We wanted control over out patients' care."

Dr. Pascale notes that by having a hospital that specializes in orthopedic care, he doesn't have to worry about doing a surgery in an operating room where an infected bowel resection occurred the day before as might be the case in a large general hospital.

"Yes, they clean the rooms, but bacteria are where they are," he says. "The more complicated joint procedures where you've got a lot of metal out in the open and the patient's joints are opened—it takes just one contamination and you've got a big problem on your hands. We don't have those bugs in our hospital because we don't do [bowel resections] there."

The physicians prefer being able to make decisions about how the hospital is run without having to get approval from various vice presidents and committees as they would at a major hospital.

"If we want to get something done, we don't have to ask for permission," says Dr. Jannsen. "We have to agree amongst ourselves, but for the most part we can do that. We are the executive committee."

If the physicians think that procedures need to be changed, they can make those changes relatively quickly.

"We decide we have a problem with a machine, that machine is gone and we get a new one in quick," says Dr. Pascale. "It's not like we have to wait and get approval from the committee and three months later we get the machine we need. You can make decisions and not have to get approval through the corporation like you would at a big hospital."

Dr. Holden thinks one of the biggest differences is in the nursing staff.

"The complaint everybody has at every hospital is nursing care. It's always the main issue," he says. "That's what everybody cares about because that's what the patient sees. Physicians don't have control over that at a large hospital. We do at our hospital."

Dr. Holden was chief-of-staff at McBride Hospital when it first opened, a position that he says was not an enviable one.

"I saw a lot of complaints and it was all about the nursing care. Getting the personnel to the level we wanted was not easy. But because we had control over it we were able to work at it and keep working at it. Now that we've been open these many years, everybody has glowing reports about our nursing care. We can control that, and that's the number one thing that makes a difference in a patient's care."

While McBride Hospital runs smoothly now, getting it open was an enormous undertaking.

"Honestly, I'm sure none of us really fully knew what we were getting into as far as the amount of work that it took to get it going," said Dr. Janssen.

Each of the nineteen physicians had to sign a line of credit worth $2 million with a bank.

"It was a big risk," says Dr. Pascale. "I think there were a lot of guys who lost a lot of sleep worrying about it."

Dr. Tkach was not one of them.

"Was I concerned about it? Not really. That was an investment we made in ourselves. When you invest in yourself, it incentivizes you to work hard. I had no concern that this would not go well."

Dr. Tkach is heading to his next knee replacement surgery. He stops at a large sink just outside the operating room and thoroughly scrubs his hands and arms.

He enters operating room number two at about 9:20 am. The staff is already there. They have prepped the patient, who lies on the operating table. A dressing called "coban" that looks like an ace bandage runs from the middle of the patient's right leg to his ankle. That keeps in place a "stockingnette" that goes from the foot to the middle of the calf.

"That walls off the foot," says Dr. Tkach. "We consider the foot to be dirty. We put the stockingnette on there to keep germs from travelling up the leg and into the surgical wound."

Dr. Tkach and a nurse then wrap a blue, elastic material called an "eschmarch" around the patient's leg. It exsanguinates the leg—that is, it pushes all of the blood out of it. Once that is done, a tourniquet, located near the patient's groin, is inflated.

The scrub technician—the operating room employee whose job it is to make sure the surgeon has the tools he needs—moves three tables filled with orthopedic surgical tools forward so that they form a "C" at the end of the operating table. He stands in the opening of the "C."

At the end of the operating table near the patient's head is a machine with what looks like a vacuum with a hose coming out of it. It is hooked up to a special gown that is wrapped around the patient.

"It's called a 'Bear Hugger'," explains one of the nurses. "It blows warm air on to the patient. If the patient gets cold, it makes the wound healing take longer and increases the chance of infection. It also increases the patient's oxygen demand."

At a few minutes past 9:30 am, Dr. Tkach draws a thick black line down the middle of the patient's right knee. He then makes a long incision down that line. The scrub technician gives Dr. Tkach a "baby retractor" which Tkach uses to pull away the soft tissue from the knee so that the bone is exposed.

The scrub technician then hands Dr. Tkach a drill that he uses to insert pins into the femur and tibia. The pins will stabilize the bones and act as a "guide" to help Dr. Tkach as he saws off portions of the knee bone.

Dr. Tkach hands the drill back to the scrub technician who gives him another drill with a small saw blade on the end of it. Dr. Tkach removes the knee cap—patella—and then begins to saw away at the knee bone, cutting away at the lower part of the femur and the upper part of the tibia. He also saws away the back part of the patella.

Dr. Tkach washes the knee area out with a saline solution. He then inserts the "trial" components of the knee prosthesis. These are components that he will use to test the knee. He bends and extends it several times to make certain that the components fit. If they do not, he will either have to saw off some more bone or get different sized components.

The femoral component is a thin, curved object that is made out of a combination of chrome and cobalt. It will be attached to the bottom of the femur with a special cement.

The tibial component looks like small tray with a wedge underneath. It is also made out of chrome and cobalt. It will be fixed to the top part of the tibia with the cement. However, Dr. Tkach will not need to drill into the bone to make a hole for the wedge. The bone is soft enough that the wedge will go in simply by using a hammer to tap on the top part of the tibial component. On top of the tibial component sits a plastic called polyethylene that will act as the cartilage in the new knee.

Then the patellar component, a small, plastic disc, is attached to the back of the patella with cement. It will be held in place by special grooves that are in the femoral and tibial components.

"The company says these will last 30 years," says Dr. Tkach. "That means probably 15 to 20. Engineers testing these things in a lab is a lot different than the wear and tear from a human leg."

The patient was admitted to McBride at 5:46 am and was in the operating room at 8:44 am. Dr. Tkach finishes up the surgery at about 10:10 am. His physician assistant will suture up the incision.

Upon leaving the operating room, a nurse approaches Dr. Tkach and informs him that he will be in operating room number three next, and then return to number two.

He then heads to the physician lounge to get some coffee and chat briefly with another physician.

Then it is time to call the family of the patient that he just operated on. He lets them know that the surgery went well. After speaking with them, he calls another number and gives dictation—he makes a brief recording of what just happened in the surgery that will go in the patient's chart.

On his way to the next operation, Dr. Tkach reveals his love of hunting.

"I once had a patient who didn't have the money to pay me, but he had a whole bunch of hunting rifles. He asked me if we could settle up that way. I said 'sure!'"

Outside of operating room number three he heads to the sink to scrub down. When he walks in a little before 10:30 am, another crew has the patient all prepared for him.

At 10:33 am he makes an incision on the patient's left leg.

Dr. Tkach and his surgical team work with the same sort of efficiency as with the last patient. He finishes at about 11:05, leaving the physician assistant to suture up the incision.

"One of the benefits of being able to work this efficiently is the patient has the tourniquet on for a shorter period of time," says Dr. Tkach. "The less time the tourniquet is on, the less pain the patient will have after surgery. Also, the less time in the operating room, the less risk of infection."

Then it's off to the physician's lounge, dictation, and a call to the patient's family.

He scrubs up and is off to operating room two a little before 11:30 am to repeat the process.

Owning It

When people think of Medicare, they usually think of the government health insurance program for seniors over age 65. They may even recall that the program also extends to the disabled who are under 65. Few, though, see it as a program that big business and their D.C. lobbyists can use to drive smaller competitors out of business.

But that's a perspective shared by many individuals who work in physician-owned specialty hospitals (PSHs). For years the "Big Hospital Lobby" waged war on PSHs, trying to drive the latter out of business by making it illegal for them to treat Medicare patients, a major revenue source.

With the March 2010 passage of the Patient Protection and Affordable Care Act (a.k.a. "ObamaCare"), the Big Hospital Lobby finally succeeded. ObamaCare prevents any PSHs built after 2010 from treating Medicare patients. Additionally, those PSHs already in existence will no longer be able to expand unless they jump over nearly insurmountable regulatory hurdles.

By limiting the access that PSHs have to Medicare, the big hospitals, which are often bureaucratic, have protected themselves from smaller, quicker competition. In so doing, they have choked off a major source of efficiency and innovation in the health care system and have limited patients' options.

The PSHs that have emerged since the early 1990s tend to specialize in one of three areas: cardiac surgery, orthopedic surgery, and general surgery. Cardiac surgery is, of course, surgery on the heart, such as bypass surgery or angioplasty. Orthopedic surgery involves conditions of the musculoskeletal system and includes surgeries such as hip and knee replacements, spine fusion, and carpal tunnel surgery. Despite its name, general surgery is a specialty that deals with everything between the neck and the waist, with the exception of the cardio-vascular system. It includes many types of cancer, colorectal, and trauma surgeries. Some general surgeons are qualified to perform vascular surgery and occasionally do so. Otherwise, vascular surgery is performed by vascular surgeons.

Physicians who want to start a PSH usually join together as a group, putting up their own money. Often times a group of physicians will partner with a private firm that specializes in opening PSHs. In that case, the physicians and the private firm will each get an ownership share of the

PSH. Each individual physician receives an ownership share based on how much he or she invested in the PSH. Most physicians who invest in a PSH have ownership shares of about two percent, although some shares are as high as 15 percent.[1] At the end of the year, each physician-owner gets a percentage of the profits based on his ownership share.

Regina Herzlinger, a business professor at Harvard who has studied medical specialization in depth, argues that PSHs should be the wave of the future in health care. Many businesses have become specialized, focusing on a few tasks and contracting out other services when needed. This enables businesses to do a few things well, providing better quality and lower prices for consumers.

Herzlinger laments the fact that there are so few PSHs:

> These results are unfortunate: Specialized healthcare facilities, partially owned by entrepreneurial physicians, represent the best hope for a higher-quality and higher-productivity healthcare system. The specialization integrates care that consumers must now struggle to obtain from a system organized by separate providers. Along the way, it reduces costs. And ownership provides an important additional incentive for physicians to provide the best value for the money.[2]

The hospitals that most Americans are accustomed to are what are most appropriately called "general hospitals." They are often large, highly bureaucratic institutions. They tend to practice many types of medicine "under one roof," including primary care, emergency care, many types of surgery, radiation treatment, imaging services, laboratory services, psychiatry, physical therapy, palliative care, diabetes management, maternity care, etc.

Thanks to ObamaCare, patients will have little opportunity to choose between PSHs and general hospitals in the future. To receive payments from Medicare for treating Medicare patients, a hospital must have a "Medicare provider number." For a hospital to receive a Medicare provider number, it must pass an inspection by the U.S. Department of Health and Human Services. ObamaCare prevents any hospital in which

195

physicians are part owners from receiving a Medicare provider number after December 31, 2010. PSHs treat many Medicare patients since the elderly are disproportionately the ones receiving cardiac, orthopedic and cancer surgery. This means that PSHs receive a large portion of their revenue from Medicare. Obviously, physicians won't start new PSHs if a major source of revenue is no longer available.

The new restrictions all but end a major source of innovation in the health care system.

When businesses face new competition—as general hospitals faced from PSHs—they have two basic recourses. They can find ways to lower their prices and improve their products, thereby preventing their competitors from drawing away customers. Or, they can ask politicians to pass laws and regulations that will drive their competition out of business. Since Medicare is such a large portion of all medical payments, the second recourse is the preferred option for those already established in the business of health care. ObamaCare was, in part, the culmination of a decade-long effort by the Big Hospital Lobby—represented by the American Hospital Association and the Federation of American Hospitals—to use Medicare to stop PSHs.

Of course, companies will almost never admit that they are using government to drive their competition out of business. The resulting negative press could undermine the whole effort. Rather, they dress it up in the rhetoric of the "noble purpose." As one supporter of PSHs put it, the Big Hospital Lobby "hides behind their community mission" in order to "stifle competition."[3]

The Big Hospital Lobby advanced three main arguments to make its case that PSHs endangered public welfare. First, it claimed that PSHs impeded the public mission of general hospitals by harming their financial health. The story was that general hospitals relied on more profitable services such as cardiac and orthopedic surgery to "cross-subsidize" less profitable ones such as emergency care. If PSHs took away the more profitable services, then general hospitals would be hindered in their ability to provide crucial health care services to the community.[4]

Second, the Big Hospital Lobby claimed that physician ownership of a hospital was a "conflict of interest." A physician who profited from his ownership of a hospital might refer a patient for surgery, even if the patient didn't need surgery. This would result in not only unnecessary surgeries, but an increase in the total number of surgeries.[5] That would increase costs for Medicare and, ultimately, the taxpayer.

Finally, the Big Hospital Lobby argued that physician-owners would "cherry pick" their patients, referring primarily healthier patients and those with more generous insurance to their PSHs. Healthier patients tend to be less costly, while those with more generous insurance mean higher payments.[6] Both result in higher profits. That would leave general hospitals in an even worse financial condition since they would be stuck with the sicker and thus more costly patients and the ones with low-paying insurance like Medicaid or no insurance at all.

In short, the Big Hospital Lobby argued that PSHs should be stopped because they harmed both patients and the public. Ironically, PSHs had emerged only because Congress had already cut physicians' investment opportunities.

Stark Changes

While there are many factors that led to the rise of PSHs, three seem to be the most important. The first is the growing authority of hospital administrators. During the 1980s and 1990s, hospitals consolidated, leading to more authority for hospital administrators and reduced autonomy for physicians. By and large an independent-minded lot, physicians desired greater control over their practice, something they could achieve when they were part owners of a hospital.

Another factor was the new systems that Medicare established for paying hospitals and physicians in the 1980s and 1990s. Both are systems of price controls that overpay for some types of medical procedures while underpaying for others. Cardiac and orthopedic care are areas where

197

Medicare appears to overpay, given that most PSHs specialize in cardiac and orthopedic surgery. Indeed, one pair of scholars argues that the rise of PSHs is a "market signal" that Medicare is overpaying for certain types of medical procedures.[7] Nevertheless, the introduction of Medicare's price control system inadvertently resulted in new financial opportunities for physicians.

At one time the health care system was teeming with such opportunities for physicians, but Congress circumscribed many of them with laws passed in 1989 and 1993. In the late 1980s, controversy erupted over "physician self-referral," the practice of a physician referring a patient to a medical facility of which the physician is part owner. Around the country, physicians were investing in clinical laboratories and imaging centers. The debate centered on the ethics and costs of such an arrangement. Some theorized that physician-investors would have an incentive to refer patients for unnecessary tests. This would, in turn, result in greater costs for both private insurance and government health care programs. Research conducted at the time, including two studies by the Government Accountability Office[8], found that physicians who were owners of medical facilities referred patients to those facilities for tests at a higher rate than did non-owners.

Congress soon took an interest in clamping down on physician self-referral, since more medical tests meant higher costs for programs like Medicare. The main politician in this effort was then-Representative Fortney "Pete" Stark (D-CA.) In 1972, Stark successfully ran for the House of Representatives from Oakland, California. By the time physician self-referral became an issue in the late 1980s, Stark was the chair of the Health Subcommittee of the Ways and Means Committee, despite having no background in the health care field.

Maybe Stark was chosen because of his empathy for patients, whom he once described as "absolutely irrational, brain dead, sniveling, begging, and fantasizing ills and pains."[9]

Or maybe it was his sympathetic ear for physicians. Referring to physicians' complaints about low Medicare reimbursement, he replied,

"Last time I looked in my district, I didn't see any Porsche dealers going out of business because the doctors are all going broke."[10] This was the man that Congress tasked with protecting patients from physicians who owned medical facilities.

Whose interest was really being served by restricting the ability of physicians to own medical facilities? "There's been no patient uproar over this stuff. Self-referral is a political issue, not a quality or cost issue," said Angus Everton, general counsel for the Medical and Chirurgical Faculty of Maryland, in 1993.[11] In fact, the research conducted on the issue seemed to focus exclusively on the rate at which patients were referred to these facilities, not whether patients were harmed or had complaints. Indeed, patients didn't seem to be complaining much at all.

The people who did bellow were the ones competing against physician-owned laboratories and imagines services. The American Clinical Laboratory Association, which represents non-profit laboratories, and the American Society for Clinical Laboratory Science, which represents lab technicians, supported Stark's efforts. Then there were pathologists, physicians who usually worked in a laboratory they owned, but were not in a position to self-refer patients. Their lobbying organization, the American Society of Clinical Pathologists, said in a statement, "Legislative efforts to prohibit Medicare reimbursement for services performed by an entity in which the referring physician has a direct or indirect financial interest are an appropriate response to this problem."[12]

It was a case of established businesses using government to drive out the upstart competition. At the time, Richard Geier, the executive director for the lobbying group that represents imaging centers, the Quality Imaging Association, was quite frank about this in an interview with *Modern Healthcare*:

"It's good public relations and good business to support any legislation banning self-referrals," he said.

The companies represented by the [Quality Imaging Association] are at a disadvantage when physicians own competing MRI ventures because they lock up referrals and send few patients to the companies' facilities, he said. In addition, if a self-referral ban forces a group of physicians to divest an imaging center, that means less competition for the companies and an opportunity to make an acquisition, although Mr. Geier maintained that his constituency has become less active in the past two years in acquiring imaging centers.[13]

There were surely other ways of dealing with physician self-referral than banning physician ownership of laboratories and imaging centers. Common sense suggests requiring physicians to disclose their ownership interest to patients and giving Medicare and Medicaid patients a financial incentive to think twice about whether they needed a particular test.

But that wouldn't have pleased the groups representing non-physician-owned services since the physician-owned competition would still be in the marketplace. Further, that would have been unacceptable to a politician like Stark who was so much better suited to make decisions about health care than sniveling patients and greedy physicians. So, backed by industry groups, he succeeded in passing what became known as the "Stark Laws." The first part, passed in 1989, banned Medicare from paying for any laboratory services that were the result of physician self-referral. The second part, passed in 1993, extended the ban to other types of services, including imaging and radiology services, physical therapy services and durable medical equipment and supplies. It also applied the ban to another major federal health care program, Medicaid.

The passage of the Stark Laws didn't mean that physicians stopped being independent-minded or entrepreneurial. The new restrictions only meant that laboratories and imaging centers became less attractive options for their efforts. Instead, physicians began focusing on PSHs because of a loophole in the Stark Laws known as the "whole hospital exception." This loophole allowed physicians who were part owners of a whole hospital to self-refer Medicare patients to that hospital. The theory behind this exception was that since hospitals were usually so big, the ownership share that any physician was likely to have would be tiny. With a tiny ownership share, "the financial incentive to self-refer would be insignificant."[14] As Charles Kahn, president of the Federation of American Hospitals, would later complain, "Today's physician-owned model was virtually unknown then. Lawmakers could not anticipate that this exception would spur the proliferation of [PSHs]."[15]

Eliminating Competition

No one knows for certain when the owners or administrators of a general hospital first complained about a PSH. Based on a Lexis/Nexis search, the first time a complaint appeared in print was in June, 1992 in the *San Jose Mercury News*. The term "physician-owned hospital" was not used in the article. Rather, it referred to the small facility in San Jose that five-dozen physicians had invested in as a "boutique" or "luxury" hospital. Nevertheless, the article was a portent of things to come. The hospital was called "The Recovery Inn." Its physician-owners tried to make the hospital more appealing to patients by creating an environment free of the inconveniences of general hospitals and by offering amenities such as small refrigerators in the rooms, pastel carpets, and subtle lighting.

The physician-owners liked controlling the hospital and having more access to prime operating times. The people who ran the general hospitals in the area were less than enthused. They complained that the patients served by The Recovery Inn would be healthier than those at a general hospital and that it would "skim off well-insured patients, whose bills (were) usually inflated to help large hospitals pay for the uninsured." They fretted that if enough of these hospitals were built, some of the general hospitals in the area might have to close. One administrator even hinted that it was not a matter to be decided by patients and physicians, but by politicians. "I don't think, in the long run, it is the best *public policy*. They're going to be able to run that operation at a lower cost than a general hospital like us," said Bob Brueckner, then president of the San Jose Medical Center.[16] (Italics added).

The first time that general hospitals actively tried to quash PSHs occurred in Ohio in 1997. Two years earlier, the state legislature had begun undoing the "certificate-of-need" law, a law that requires a hospital to get the approval of state authorities before it can open its doors. Without the certificate-of-need law, it was much easier to start a PSH in Ohio. By 1997, cardiac surgeons in Dayton were partnering with MedCath, a company that specialized in developing PSHs, to open the Dayton Heart Hospital. This caused great consternation among the general hospital community. Paul Lee, a hospital lobbyist in the state capital of Columbus said that PSHs threatened "the viability of our not-for-profit health care system in Ohio. Almost every hospital, and I've talked to dozens, is concerned about this issue."[17]

By late 1997, the Ohio Hospital Association (OHA), which represented over 180 general hospitals, was calling on the state legislature to impose a two-year moratorium on new hospital construction in the state. "What does this do to existing hospitals if (new players) in effect begin to cherry-pick the bread and butter services of existing hospitals?" said OHA spokeswoman Mary Yost in what would become a common refrain for general hospital apologists.[18] The OHA insisted that this would be merely a temporary moratorium to give established hospitals a chance to adjust to new market competition and a chance for state legislators to look at the issues surrounding PSHs. Yet an OHA board member seemed to let the true motive slip when he said that he would like to see some form of certificate-of-need law return, one that would regulate any new hospital construction or expansion that cost more than $1 million[19]—that is, a law that would make it much more difficult to start a PSH.

The OHA faced opposition from both the Ohio Medical Association, which represented Ohio physicians, and health insurance companies. The insurance companies saw PSHs as a way to lower the price that they paid for health care. Furthermore, the state legislature seemed to be in no mood to revisit the issue of the certificate-of-need law, having worked to repeal it just two years earlier. This time, the general hospitals were unsuccessful in shutting down the competition.

This was only the opening skirmish in a long war that would soon play out on the national stage. The organizations representing general hospitals would spend vast sums over the better part of a decade on research, public relations, and lobbying, with the goal of shutting down PSHs. There were many times when they appeared on the verge of delivering a crushing defeat, only to see the groups representing PSHs narrowly escape.

Unfortunately, a relatively small group like PSHs can seldom resist an immensely powerful political force. General hospitals finally succeeded in landing what may have been the fatal blow against PSHs on March 21, 2010 when ObamaCare became law.

In retrospect, it's amazing that PSHs resisted as long as they did. After all, the American Hospital Association and Federation of American Hospitals are not just large groups, they are behemoths. According to the website Opensecrets.org, the Federation of American Hospitals spent about $23.6 million on lobbying Congress and almost $1.6 million on campaign contributions from 2001-2010. During that same period, the American Hospital Association spent just over $159 million lobbying Congress and $8 million on campaign contributions. By comparison, the lobbying organization for PSHs, Physician Hospitals of America, spent $1.8 million on lobbying and $851,9000 on campaign contributions. MedCath spent $2.7 million and $149,134, respectively, on those items. In money terms, the organizations fighting for PSHs were clearly outgunned.

The American Hospital Association and the Federation of American Hospitals' biggest source of power is the number of potential voters they represent. General hospitals employ just under 5.3 million people in the U.S.,[20] an average of about 105,400 voters per state and 12,100 per Congressional district. When the Big Hospital Lobby speaks, senators and representatives usually listen.

In 2000, Rep. Stark was already signaling that he was eager to fight on behalf of the Big Hospital Lobby. In July, he sent a letter to the Office of the Inspector General at the Department of Health and Human Services asking for an investigation of some of the PSHs that were owned by MedCath.[21] The following year he partnered with Representative Jerry Kleczka of Wisconsin in authoring a bill that would put limits on PSHs. The House of Representatives, though, was controlled by Republicans and Stark was a Democrat. "This is going to be a delicate political strategy," he said of getting his bill passed into law. "My chances as a member of the minority are very slim unless the American Hospital Association takes it on as its cause."[22]

In 2002 the American Hospital Association put together a task force on PSHs after hearing complaints from many of their members around the country. The policy director at the American Hospital Association, Ellen Pryga, complained, "This is not a level playing field for hospitals."[23]

She had a point. Nearly all general hospitals have emergency rooms, and under federal law hospitals with emergency rooms must treat all patients regardless of ability to pay. That means those hospitals must treat patients who are either indigent or are on Medicaid and, because of Medicaid's low reimbursement rates, can't find physicians to treat them elsewhere. Many PSHs did not have emergency rooms and so did not have to treat such patients.

As long as general hospitals had to take indigent and Medicare patients, perhaps it was only fair that PSHs be required to take some of those patients as well. But the Big Hospital Lobby wasn't interested in creating a more level playing field. Rather, it wanted to drive the competition completely out of the game.

This first became evident when the American Hospital Association task force issued its recommendations in late 2002. Chief among them was a proposal to change the Stark Laws so that physicians could no longer use the "whole hospital exception," which would effectively prevent physicians from referring patients to hospitals they owned.[24] Indeed, driving PSHs out of business was *synonymous* with creating a level playing field, as shown by this Federation of American Hospitals press release:

What specialty hospitals call competition is in fact a playing field tilted heavily in their favor. True market competition would ensure a level playing field by *eliminating* conflicts of interest and making only quality of care as the basis of competition for patient referrals.[25] (Italics added).

Eliminating conflicts of interest would mean eliminating physician self-referral since they were one and the same to the American Hospital Association and the Federation of American Hospitals. Of course, doing away with physician self-referral would make it next to impossible for physicians to own hospitals.

In July 2001, Rep. Kleczka had persuaded the chairman of the House Ways and Means Committee, Bill Thomas, to sign a letter requesting the Government Accountability Office (GAO) to study the issue of PSHs. In May 2003, the GAO released its report.[26] The American Hospital Association and Federation of American Hospitals applauded the results. The report showed that PSHs "undercut the ability of hospitals to meet the needs of the broader community by drawing profitable services away from the community hospital," claimed the American Hospital Association.[27] According to the Federation of American Hospitals the report found that PSHs "'cherry pick' healthier patients."[28]

The Big Hospital Lobby would have even more to cheer about later in the year. In November, Congress completed work on the Medicare Prescription Drug, Improvement and Modernization Act. Although the legislation is most famous for creating the prescription drug program in Medicare, it also contained the first big victory for general hospitals over PSHs.

During the negotiations over the bill, Senator John Breaux of Louisiana offered an amendment that would have prevented physicians from referring Medicare or Medicaid patients to hospitals that they owned. Both the American Hospital Association and the Federation of American Hospitals lobbied hard for the amendment. The American Hospital Association flew 100 hospital administrators to Washington to meet with members of Congress and spent $100,000 on advertising.[29] Reportedly, at one point the American Hospital Association threatened to withhold its endorsement of the bill if the amendment was not included.[30]

To get a sense of how important squashing PSHs was to the groups representing general hospitals, it is worthwhile to point out that the House version of the Medicare Prescription Drug Act contained $12 billion in cuts to the hospital portion of Medicare. In the Senate, the chair of the powerful Finance Committee, Senator Charles Grassley of Iowa, was working to remove those cuts. He approached the Federation of American Hospitals to solicit their support. The response that he received left him "shocked." The Federation of American Hospitals told him that $12 billion in cuts were "not the highest priority" for its members. Rather, it "was focusing its efforts on securing language to restrict physician self-referrals to specialty hospitals."[31]

In the end, Physician Hospitals of America and other groups lobbying on behalf of PSHs got lucky. They had a key ally in another Louisiana politician, Representative Billy Tauzin, who was chair of the Energy and Commerce Committee. Its members played a large role in drafting the Medicare Prescription Drug Act. Tauzin, who believed that the increased competition from PSHs was good for the health care system, managed to negotiate a compromise with Breaux. Beginning in 2004, physicians were forbidden from making new investments in PSHs for 18 months while the Center for Medicare and Medicaid Services (CMS) studied the effect of PHSs on general hospitals. (Senators Grassley and Max Baucus, of Montana, would win another six-month moratorium in 2006 while CMS developed a plan for dealing with PSHs.)

Yet it seemed analogous to studying the effect a few drops of water would have on the Great Lakes. In 2003, there were over 4,800 general hospitals in the U.S. There were barely 100 specialty hospitals with another 26 under development. Of those, about 30 percent had no physician ownership. Furthermore, 22 states had no PSHs, and another 18 had no more than two.[32] The threat that PSHs posed to general hospitals seemed puny.

So what had the Big Hospital Lobby so worried? Why was making the extermination of PSHs such a priority? After all the noise that the Big Hospital Lobby had made about the issue, most general hospitals were aware of potential competition from PSHs—and if they weren't, undoubtedly the American Hospital Association and Federation of American Hospitals could alert them. Being forewarned, surely general hospitals could prepare for new competition and find new strategies for dealing with it.

Couldn't they?

Bureaucratic Surgery

Dr. Eric Logan[*] is unhappy with President Barack Obama.

Back in July of 2009, President Obama suggested that surgeons were doing many unnecessary surgeries. "Right now, doctors a lot of times are forced to make decisions based on the fee payment schedule that's out there," President Obama said. "The doctor may look at the reimbursement system and say to himself, 'You know what? I make a lot more money if I take this kid's tonsils out.'"

"I'd love to have him come to the operating room when I'm doing emergency surgery," Dr. Logan grumbles. "He could see exactly how unnecessary these surgeries are."

Dr. Logan, an orthopedic surgeon, works six nights a month on call at First Presbyterian Hospital. As we sit in his office, the conversation shifts to the hospital's inefficiency. A woman in the emergency room (ER) has an abscess in her shin that is causing her a great deal of pain and is not responding to antibiotics. It needs to be removed before the infection spreads. She arrived at the ER at 10 am. It is now about 7:45 pm.

"It takes about two hours to do the tests and so forth to determine if a patient needs surgery," Dr. Logan says. "I got the call around 2 pm that I

---

[*] "Dr. Eric Logan," "First Presbyterian Hospital" and "Dr. Scott" are pseudonyms.

would be doing surgery. But it wasn't until 5 pm that I was told to come in to the hospital."

He picks up the phone and calls one of the nurses he'll be working with this evening. He asks if it is time yet to do the operation. The nurse informs him that the anesthesiologist cannot be found.

"It happens all the time," he says wearily. "The problem is that no one is accountable in the operating room. One part of the hospital is in charge of the surgeons, another is in charge of the nurses, and another is in charge of the anesthesiologists. If you have a problem with someone, you have to go all the way up the chain of command. This lets people get away with not showing up in a timely fashion."

Shortly after 8 pm the anesthesiologist is found. By 8:30 pm the surgery is ready to begin.

A few feet from the operating table sit the tools of an orthopedic surgeon's trade. Two four-by-four tables are filled with drills, screws and pins, making it seem a bit more like auto-shop class than an operating room.

The anesthesiologist gives the patient an anesthetic that renders her unconscious. Since it is only a small portion of the patient's shin that is being operated on, why not give a local anesthetic? The anesthesiologist explains that the area around an infection usually becomes "acidotic." This means that the bodily fluid around the infected area has an increase in acidity that makes local anesthesia less effective.

In the operating room one of the nurses scrubs the patients' shin with an orange liquid known as "Chloraprep," a combination of soap and alcohol.

Dr. Logan pushes on the area around the infection and swabs some of the liquid that comes out. He then draws a small oval around the part of the skin to be removed. He makes an incision in line with the oval and removes the infected portion of skin.

After the skin is removed, Dr. Logan and the resident (a medical student learning to be an orthopedic surgeon) put a tube into the open part of the skin and pump in a disinfectant. Another tube is inserted that sucks the disinfectant out.

"We put a lot of disinfectant in," says Dr. Logan. "We have a saying, 'dilution is the solution to pollution.'" Once that is finished, the resident closes the wound with sutures.

The surgery is finished shortly before 9 pm. The patient has waited nearly eleven hours to have a piece of skin the size of a dime removed from her shin.

"Waiting like this—it isn't good for the patients," Dr. Logan worries. "The longer we wait, the more that swelling can increase, and that can make it harder to operate. It can mean more pain for the patient, increases the risk of infection, and can slow recovery time. Slower recovery time can mean the patient misses more work."

He goes to the waiting room to visit with the patient's family. He lets them know that the operation went well and that she should recover nicely. They seem relieved.

He then walks through a number of corridors. But his walking is almost labored, like something is weighing him down. What it is becomes apparent shortly after he arrives at the doctor's lounge.

"See that nice 55-inch plasma TV?" he smirks. "That was the administration's response to surgeons complaining about the amount of down time between surgeries."

There is a lot of down time in between surgeries at a major hospital. This time it may impact Dr. Logan's family life. His 11-year-old son is playing his first football game at 9 am the next morning. Dr. Logan figures that he might make it by half-time.

Soon he is called in for the next surgery, a man with a hip fracture.

Dr. Logan heads toward the operating room with his labored gait. Then, as he nears the operating room, his pace quickens some and his eyes widen a bit.

He scrubs up and a nurse helps him into a lead vest. X-rays will be used continuously during this operation. All personnel in the operating room must wear a lead vest to prevent the damage from long-term X-ray exposure. The patient doesn't wear one because his exposure will be no longer than the operation.

Dr. Logan puts on two pairs of latex gloves. When doing surgery on bones and joints, a variety of small, sharp objects, such as bone fragments, can tear a glove.

The X-ray machine looks like a big letter C sitting on top of an industrial vacuum cleaner. The X-ray technician is able to rotate it around the patient if necessary. Two cords go from the X-ray machine to a big box. On top of that sit two screens. One shows a top view of the area being operated on, the other displays a side view.

Dr. Logan calls out "picture" every time he wants the X-ray to be updated on the screen. He does this frequently as he drills three pins into the patient's hip. The operation is finished shortly before 10 pm. This patient was luckier than the previous one. He was admitted to the ER around 2 pm.

Dr. Logan heads to the ER to check on his coming workload. A new patient has been admitted from another hospital. He was in a motorcycle accident that snapped his right femur in half. Dr. Logan asks one of the nurses where the patient's X-rays are. She doesn't know. It later turns out that the other hospital sent the patient over without his X-rays.

Dr. Logan must do what he calls a "triage," a process whereby he determines the priority of treating patients based on the severity of the patients' conditions.

"I have a patient waiting with a broken ankle," he says. "Surgery would be best for her, but she will heal just fine with a cast. I'm not going to be able to get through the more serious surgeries I've got if I operate on her."

Dr. Logan meets the patient and her husband and explains to her that they'll be putting a cast on her ankle. She seems relieved.

The difference between a cast and surgery?

"About the same," says Dr. Logan, after he has left the patient. "Although she'll have about two weeks more recovery time with the cast."

The next patient in the operating room is a man in his early 40s who has neglected his diabetes. He also has hypertension and kidney failure. He has had most of both lower legs amputated, and the one portion that he has left below his left knee is now infected. That part of his leg had been surgically drained three weeks ago. At the time, he was urged to go to "extended care" after the operation. He refused. Dr. Logan looks at his chart and notices that he missed a follow up appointment after his last operation.

After the Chloraprep is applied to the man's leg, Dr. Logan draws a big oval on the infected area. He supervises while the resident makes the incision. They put a tube in to drain the infection and they do not close the wound.

Does this patient have even five years left?

"Not at the rate he's going," says Dr. Logan.

After the operation, Dr. Logan tracks down the man's cousin in the waiting room. "He'll have to stay in the hospital because we need to remove the portion of the leg below the left knee," Dr. Logan tells the cousin. "He'll never be able to wear a prosthetic on it, and right now it is nothing more than a breeding ground for infections."

Then it's back to the physician's lounge for some more television before going to the operating room again.

The next patient has fallen off a step ladder. He broke his right ankle and the bone punctured the skin on the inside of the leg.

"Falling off a step ladder is actually a pretty common injury," Dr. Logan says.

After the anesthesiologist puts the patient under, a black foam-rubber block is put under is right leg to elevate it.

The resident begins to make an incision. One can see the bone sticking through the punctured skin. The foot almost dangles off to the right.

The resident makes a second incision on the outside of the ankle. Screws are inserted into the ankle to hold it together.

The resident sutures the incisions in the patient's ankle after the screws are inserted. The patient was admitted to the ER shortly before 9 pm. It is now just after 1 am.

Dr. Logan again finds the patient's family in the waiting room. He lets them know that the operation went well.

He now seems more upbeat. "This night is going a bit quicker than usual. If we don't get hit with a sudden rush of emergency patients in the next few hours, I'll get out of here on time." Which means he'll get to see his son's football game.

After spending some more time in the physicians' lounge, Dr. Logan is called back to the operating room for the patient with the broken right femur. The patient was admitted around 9:30 pm. The surgery begins at 2:45 am.

In decades past, the patient would have spent months in a body cast to heal this sort of injury. Now, a long pin will be drilled into the top of his femur all the way down through the bottom part, fusing the two halves together. Then screws are inserted on each end to secure the pin in place. An additional orthopedic surgeon, "Dr. Scott," is required for this surgery. The camera on the X-ray machine is placed over the patient's right thigh. Dr. Logan and the resident begin the operation by drilling the pin into the top of the femur, while Dr. Scott grabs the patients' right ankle and yanks and twists the leg so that the two halves of the femur will line up. It is difficult as the patient is large—at least 250 pounds—which makes the leg less cooperative. Dr. Logan calls out "picture" countless times so that he can see in the x-ray screen if the pin is being drilled in properly. It's not. As it reaches the bottom of the top half of the femur, it slides off to the side, making it impossible to drill into the lower half. Dr. Scott continues to pull and twist the patient's leg, while Dr. Logan and the resident drill the pin into the femur and then retract it numerous times.

After about half an hour of futility, Dr. Logan decides it would be better to have two physicians pulling and twisting the leg while one physician drills. He and the resident switch places with Dr. Scott, and the

212

tug-of-war continues. It is excruciating to watch. One can't help but send up a thankful prayer for modern anesthetics.

Finally, the two halves line up and the pin is drilled down to the bottom of the femur and then the screws are inserted to keep it in place. It is now 3:50 am.

Was this Dr. Logan's most difficult surgery ever?

"No, not at all," he says.

Was it at least in the top ten?

"Yeah, I think so."

Dr. Logan finds the patient's family sleeping in the waiting room. He wakes them and tells them that the surgery went well and that the man should recover nicely.

As he heads back to the physicians' lounge, he reveals one more hospital inefficiency. It's called the Post-Anesthesia Care Unit (PACU). It's where patients go after they've had surgery. Nurses there monitor the patients until they are either ready to go home, if they've had minor surgery, or ready to be moved to a permanent room in the hospital, if they've had major surgery.

"The hospital limits the ratio in the PACU to one nurse per two patients. If there are 20 patients in the PACU and 10 nurses, then the PACU will refuse to take any more patients until one of the patients in the PACU is moved," says Dr. Logan. "If a patient is in the operating room when the PACU fills up, he must wait until one of the patients in the PACU is moved. So we keep him in the operating room. That means patients waiting for surgery will wait longer." It also costs the hospital more. The operating room costs about $300 an hour to run; the PACU, only $50.

Why doesn't the hospital call in more nurses when the PACU fills up?

He shrugs.

Dr. Logan also works regularly at a local physician-owned orthopedic specialty hospital. (He is not one of the owners). "I can get more done there in twelve hours than I can here in 24," he says.

To be fair, even the most efficient system of emergency surgery would not be as efficient as the scheduled surgeries at a PSH. When the surgeries are scheduled days or even weeks in advance, the staff knows exactly what type of operation they will be doing. That makes it much easier to prepare the necessary equipment.

In emergency or urgent surgery, the staff never knows what type of case is going to come through the door next. If there are three sets of tools to treat a particular injury, but five of those cases come through the emergency room doors, that will result in down time between surgeries. The tools will need to be sterilized between surgeries, a process that can take up to three hours. Furthermore, it may be a type of surgery that the hospital doesn't perform very often, in which case the equipment may have to be brought in from elsewhere.

Dr. Logan also explained it as the difference between "a pop quiz and an exam that you have a few days to study for. You're going to be a lot more organized if you've had time to prepare the material."

But surely the staff at McBride Orthopedic Hospital face similar difficulties when patients come through their emergency room. Yet it's possible for a patient to go from the emergency room to the operating room at McBride in about two hours. What's the difference?

"Our incentives are not aligned at First Presbyterian," says Dr. Logan. Logan gets paid on a patient-by-patient basis. He's responsible for the patients that come in during his shift. He has an incentive to keep the process moving along, so that there is less down time between operations. But the staff who clean the room are paid by the hour. They work an eight to twelve hour shift, and they get paid the same if they do two cases or ten. They have less incentive to work quickly. The anesthesiologists get paid on a hybrid model.

"If everyone got paid on a patient-by-patient basis it would be much more efficient," says Dr. Logan. "And what's frustrating for me is that I go to the emergency room and see the patient in pain and anxiety while he is waiting. And he waits an extra 30 or 45 minutes and does that mean another 100,000 bacteria gets into his wound? It's not good for the patient."

Making changes to this system is a lot like kicking the 800-ton marshmallow. The hospital has many different departments, making it hard to target the people in charge.

"Where I work, the patient goes through the emergency room, the pre-op, the operating room, the post-op, and then to the floor," says Dr. Logan. "Those five areas—each one has its own nurse administrator, each has its different budget. Getting everyone together to make any changes…good luck."

At McBride, if an employee has a problem, he simply goes to the CEO, Mark Galliart.

Clearly, Dr. Logan finds this frustrating, so why doesn't he quit this and work at the specialty hospital full time?

He stops and thinks about it for a few moments. "Well, pride is one reason. I'm one of the few doctors in this town who does what I do. Second, by doing emergency surgery, I'm on the 'frontline' of medicine. That gives me a rush. And, well, what really makes it worth it is I'll see one of my patients come back a few months later and he or she can go to work, take care of their family, and so on. That's very rewarding."

Guardians of Inefficiency

Unfortunately, Dr. Logan's experience is not unique. General hospitals are rife with inefficiency. Consider:

- One study measured the efficiency of transferring patients between different units of a hospital by examining how the process was affected by administrative delays, unavailable beds, unavailable staff, the readiness of units to receive patients and breakdowns in communication. The process was over 87 percent inefficient.[33]

- An article in *Health Services Research* found that hospital "outputs"—patient admissions, outpatient visits, surgeries, and births—could be increased 26 percent by eliminating inefficiency.[34]

- The ability of hospital staff to communicate effectively with one another leaves much to be desired. One study in the *Journal of Healthcare Management* suggests that hospitals waste $12 billion annually on inefficient communication.[35]

- A study examining "hospitalists"—physicians who focus solely on the management of hospital inpatients—found that hospitals that employ them could reduce the average patient length of stay by about 37 percent and average per admission costs by almost 24 percent.[36]

- Inefficiency affects patient mortality. An article in *Health Economics* found that a one-percentage point reduction in a hospital's cost inefficiency was associated with one fewer death per 10,000 patient discharges.[37]

With general hospitals so rife with inefficiency, it's not hard to see why they found PSHs so threatening. In the long run, plodding dinosaurs would be hard pressed against smaller, quicker competitors. To survive, general hospitals would have to do more than merely adapt; they would have to endure an upheaval, drastically changing the way they operated. Better to stop the competition before it proliferated.

The hospital industry had already been through big changes during the decade of the 1990s. Financial pressures resulted in a wave of hospital mergers and consolidations. Hospital markets became more concentrated with more hospitals being owned by fewer companies. This resulted in the number of hospital beds nationwide being reduced 72,000 between 1989-1999.[38]

With more market power, hospitals were able to negotiate better rates from insurance companies. Naturally, the prices hospitals charged increased, as prices usually do when there is less competition.[39] Every 10 percent increase in market concentration among hospitals resulted in a 6.6 percent increase in hospital prices.[40]

By contrast, more competition results in lower prices, something that the people running general hospitals would be less than eager to embrace. And that's exactly what they would get if PSHs proliferated. That prospect was, likely, alarming for the Big Hospital Lobby.

But it needn't have worried. Its fight during the Medicare Prescription Drug Act had attracted the attention of Senators Grassley, a Republican, and Baucus, a Democrat. Both would soon become allies of the Big Hospital Lobby. Since both men were their parties top Senators on the Senate Finance Committee, which has jurisdiction over Medicare in the Senate, the Big Hospital Lobby was assured that the chair of that powerful committee would be a friend for the foreseeable future.

The Big Hospital Lobby probably couldn't have asked for better allies on the Finance Committee. Neither Grassley's state of Iowa nor Baucus' Montana had any PSHs. Thus, the only voters who worked for hospitals in Iowa or Montana that Grassley or Baucus would ever hear from would be those who worked for general hospitals.

In 2005, Grassley and Baucus introduced the Hospital Fair Competition Act that would have closed the whole hospital exception. Although the bill never became law, Grassley and Baucus were clearly singing the Big Hospital Lobby tune. The "bill would level the playing field between specialty hospitals and community hospitals by eliminating incentives in the payment system to cherry-pick the healthiest and most profitable patients," the Senators wrote in a letter urging their colleagues to support the bill.[41]

Within a period of fourteen months, Grassley and Baucus scheduled two hearings on PSHs before the Finance Committee. The first one, in March 2005, was titled "Physician-Owned Specialty Hospitals: In the Interest of Patients or a Conflict of Interest?" The second, in May 2006, was dubbed "Physician-Owned Specialty Hospitals: Profits before Patients?" One of the subjects of the second hearing was an 88-year-old woman who had entered Physicians' Hospital in Portland, a PSH, and died shortly after having back surgery. Physicians' Hospital apparently did not have a physician on site during her crisis and had to call 911 for assistance. Grassley and Baucus had learned of this case a few months before the hearing, and it prompted them to send a letter to the Office of the Inspector General at the Department of Health and Human Services requesting an investigation into the emergency procedures of PSHs. (A few months later, a similar case would occur at a PSH in West Texas).

The two senators and Rep. Stark were distraught at the growing health crisis posed by PSHs.

According to Grassley, "The fundamental problem with physician-owned specialty hospitals is that decision-making is more likely to be driven by financial interest rather than what is best for the patient...You see that in the cherry picking of patients and policies where emergencies are to be dealt with by calling 911 to get to the local community hospital."[42]

"The tragic death of another 'specialty hospital' patient highlights the manner in which physician-owned facilities seem to be eroding the quality of health care in America," said Stark.[43]

"I am deeply saddened and also completely outraged to hear of another death of a patient at a specialty hospital," said Baucus. "Patient safety is my number one priority and I am going to continue to work to make sure that when patients enter a hospital, they can be certain they will receive the care they need."[44]

Had these incidents not involved patient fatalities, the politicians' outrage would have been completely farcical. PSHs had treated thousands upon thousands of patients and Grassley, Baucus and Stark were wringing their hands over two deaths? Thousands of patients die every year at general hospitals due to hospital-acquired infections and medical errors. Yet those deaths did not seem to warrant Finance Committee hearings. When Baucus said that patient safety was his "number one priority," it should have come with the caveat "as long as it doesn't upset the Big Hospital Lobby."

When the Office of the Inspector General released its report on PSHs emergency procedures in January 2008, Baucus and Grassley sounded the alarm. "Specialty hospitals need to do a better job fulfilling the public expectations, and they most certainly need to do a better job protecting the safety of their patients," said Baucus. Grassley warned, "This new report documents the significant and potentially life-threatening shortcomings of physician-owned specialty hospitals when it comes to emergency services."[45] But did it?

The report found that 55 percent of PSHs had an emergency department. Its most troubling finding was that about 7 percent were in violation of the Medicare regulations that a hospital have a nurse on site and a physician on call at all times.[46] However, one thing was curiously absent from the report: any other deaths like those in Oregon and West Texas. Perhaps Grassley called the emergency services of PSHs "potentially life-threatening" because they had yet to live up to their potential.

Further, many PSHs challenged the Inspector General report. The ones the report claimed were in violation of Medicare staffing regulations came "forward with documentation showing that they were properly staffed...during the times in question."[47] A spokesman for the Office of the Inspector General said that it stood by its report. The discrepancies were never resolved.

That didn't stop the Big Hospital Lobby from heralding the report. "The report illustrates yet another reason why Congress needs to take action in the best interests of patients and ban physician self-referral to new limited-service hospitals they own and operate," said American Hospital Association president Rick Pollack.[48]

Financial Health

The American Hospital Association includes the Inspector General report in the chart that is part of its broadside against PSHs, entitled "Self-Referral to Physician-owned Hospitals: What the Research Says." The chart, reproduced below, summarizes all of the research that supposedly supports all of the charges that the Big Hospital Lobby makes against PSHs. At first glance it seems almost damning—until one starts digging a little deeper.

The four case studies by McManis Consulting present the most evidence against PSHs. However, the American Hospital Association paid for these studies. Of course, that does not automatically mean the studies are flawed. It does mean the studies should be treated with an extra dose of skepticism since the American Hospital Association has a vested interest in the studies producing results unflattering to PSHs.

The American Hospital Association chart shows that in all four case studies the opening of PSHs damaged "the financial health of full-service hospitals leading to *cutbacks in services*" [emphasis added]. That's not true. Cutbacks were found only in Oklahoma and Kansas.[49] In South Dakota, the study noted that while the full-service hospitals were facing "difficult choices," the effects had "not fully played out."[50] In Lincoln, Nebraska, researchers found that "quality appears not to have been affected. Both full-service hospitals could point to high quality and patient satisfaction ratings before and after the opening of the limited-service hospitals."[51] The study on Nebraska also claimed that full-service hospital BryanLGH's "ability to continue to fund [its] mental health [program] at present service levels is questionable" because if its loss of revenue.[52] Yet to this day, BryanLGH (now known as Bryan Health) still has a full-service mental health program.

Chart 9.1: AHA Key Findings by Study: Physician-Owned Hospitals	MedPAC	McManis: Black Hils, SD Case Study	McManis: Lincoln, NE Case Study	McManis: Oklahoma City, OK Case Study	McManis: Witchita, KS Case Study	TrendWatch
Physician-owned, limited service hospitals:						
Lessen patient access to emergency and trauma care		✔		✔		✔
Damage the financial health of full service hospitals leading to cutbacks in services	*	✔	✔	✔	✔	✔
Reduce efficiency of full-service hospitals that must maintain stand-by capacity for emergencies even as elective cases are lost		✔	✔	✔	✔	✔
Increase uitlization and costs	✔	✔	✔	✔	✔	✔
Are not more efficient	✔					
Provide no better quality						
Use physician-owners to steer patients	✔	✔	✔	✔	✔	✔
Cherry-pick the most profitable patients by:	✔	✔	✔	✔	✔	✔
-Avoiding low income populations	✔	✔	✔	✔	✔	✔
-Offering the most profitable services	✔	✔	✔	✔	✔	✔
-Serving less sick patients within case types	✔	✔	✔	✔	✔	✔
Provide limited or no emergency services	✔	✔	✔	✔	✔	✔
Raise patient safety concerns with respect to responding to the emergency needs of patients under their care						
Make exceptionally high profits		✔	✔	✔	✔	✔

* Little impact on community hospitals *thus far*

*** Quality reuslt were mixed

[ ] Not specifically addressed in study

Chart 9.1--Continued							
Physician-owned, limited service hospitals:	GAO	Mitchell: Oklahoma City	Mitchell: Arizona	NEJM: Cram et al	CMS	JAMA: Nallamothu et al	Office of the Inspector General
Lessen patient access to emergency and trauma care							
Damage the financial health of full service hospitals leading to cutbacks in services							
Reduce efficiency of full-service hospitals that must maintain stand-by capacity for emergencies even as elective cases are lost							
Increase uitlization and costs		✔	✔			✔	
Are not more efficient							
Provide no better quality				✔	***		✔
Use physician-owners to steer patients		✔	✔	✔	✔		
Cherry-pick the most profitable patients by:	✔	✔	✔	✔	✔		
-Avoiding low income populations	✔		✔				
-Offering the most profitable services		✔	✔				
-Serving less sick patients within case types	✔		✔	✔	✔		
Provide limited or no emergency services	✔				✔		✔
Raise patient safety concerns with respect to responding to the emergency needs of patients under their care							✔
Make exceptionally high profits	✔						

  * Little impact on community hospitals *thus far*
*** Quality reuslt were mixed
   Not specifically addressed in study

It is probably unwise to give much weight to the American Hospital Association's charge that PSHs harm "the financial health of full-service hospitals."[53] It does appear that general hospitals are facing many financial pressures. A survey by the American Hospital Association found that one-third of hospitals were losing money and a Thomson Reuters survey found that half were in the red.[54] But it's doubtful that, thus far, PSHs are the cause of that pressure. Studies by the Medicare Payment Advisory Commission (MedPAC), the Center for Studying Health System Change and the Government Accountability Office (GAO) did not find that general hospitals suffered any long-term financial hardship due to PSHs.[55]

While the McManis studies found that the opening of PSHs lowered the revenues at many of the general hospitals, loss of revenue happens whenever a business faces new competition. It is unreasonable to expect that hospitals would be any different. To stay in business, existing companies must adapt to new competition. A check of the database at the American Hospital Directory shows that many of the hospitals in the case studies did adapt. Of particular note is Wesley Medical Center in Wichita, Kansas which the case study claimed lost $16 million from its heart program from 2001 to 2003 due to PSH competition. Yet in 2013 Wesley had $2.36 billion in net revenue and a net income (revenue minus expenses) of $70.7 million. It was apparently doing well enough to expand the number of beds in the hospital from 469 to 520. Indeed, all 15 general hospitals examined in the four McManis case studies in 2004-2005 are still in existence. Thirteen made a profit in 2013 or 2014, and the two that didn't made profits in the two previous years. Thirteen had increased the number of beds while three decreased them. (See Table 9.2 in the appendix.)

The American Hospital Association also charged PSHs with making exceptionally high profits, although never defined the term "exceptionally high." Many of the PSHs in the case studies did make higher profits than the general hospitals. But that's not remarkable. In many ways, PSHs provide better quality and leave patients more satisfied than general hospitals. When a new competitor that has found a better way to provide a service moves into a market, it will usually make a sizeable profit because its better way of providing the service will attract more customers. The existing competitors will either go out of business or find ways to improve their services and recapture some of those profits. If the latter happens, then over time the profits of the new competitor will decline.

Table 9.1 shows that is exactly what happened to the profits of the PSHs examined in the case studies.

Table 9.1: Profit Rates of PSHs Examined in McManis Case Studies		
Physician-Owned Specialty Hospital	Profit Rate in:	
	2002-2003*	2013
Kansas		
Kansas Heart Hospital	32.0%	0.3%
Galichia Heart Hospital	13.0%	-4.7%
Kansas Surgery and Recovery Center	13.0%	6.8%
Oklahoma		
Northwest Surgery Hospital	21.0%	7.6%
Lakeside Women's Hospital	16.0%	2.2%
Surgical Hospital of Oklahoma	29.0%	3.9%
Oklahoma Spine Hospital	44.0%	7.0%
South Dakota		
Black Hills Surgery Center	40.4%	13.6%
*Time period examined in McManis Case Studies		
Source: McManis Case Studies and American Hospital Directory		

The other study that the American Hospital Association paid for included in the chart is called "TrendWatch." TrendWatch found that physicians at PSHs "cherry pick" the most profitable patients by serving ones that are less sick and referring the sicker ones to general hospitals.[56] The study was conducted by the Lewin Group, a nationally known health care research firm. But, in another study, the Lewin Group found that patients treated at physician-owned cardiac hospitals were, on average, sicker than those at general hospitals.[57] However, that study was funded by MedCath. How to explain the differing results? Perhaps the two studies used different data or were conducted by different researchers at Lewin. Or maybe the results have something to do with who pays the piper.

At least one of the studies shouldn't have been included in the chart due to methodological problems. In the "Mitchell: Arizona" study it isn't clear that the author actually examined physician-owners.[58] She examined PSHs in Phoenix and Tucson but didn't contact the PSHs to find out which physicians were owners. Rather, she assumed that a physician was an owner if he or she treated at least 10 percent of his cases in a PHA. Thus, the physician could have been an owner; or he may have been a non-owner who simply had admitting privileges to the PSH. As another article put it, the "hypothesis that these assumptions reflect actual ownership was never verified."[59]

Two other studies should have been excluded from the chart as well. Both the study in the *New England Journal of Medicine* and the *Journal of the American Medical Association* compared specialty hospitals to traditional hospitals and found that markets with specialty hospitals had higher utilization of medical care.[60] However, the specialty hospitals in the studies included both hospitals that were physician-owned and ones that were not. Thus, whether the higher utilization of medical care was due to the hospitals being specialized or being physician-owned is not something that can be discerned from either study. Indeed, the authors of the *Journal of the American Medical Association* article stated that they "were unable to evaluate the extent to which physician ownership at cardiac hospitals...influences utilization given a lack of publicly available information."[61]

Two inaccuracies appear in the chart under the CMS study. First, the chart claims that the CMS study found that physician-owners were steering their patients toward PSHs and away from general hospitals, and that they cherry picked more profitable patients. But the CMS study actually said that it "did not see clear, consistent patterns of preference for referring to specialty hospitals among physician owners relative to their peers."[62] On the matter of cherry picking, CMS said that it "found only weak evidence that physicians with the greatest financial incentive refer most of their patients to the specialty hospital," and that it was "unable to conclude that referrals were driven primarily based on incentives for financial gain."[63]

Second, the CMS study found that the preponderance of evidence showed that quality in PSHs was better than in general hospitals. CMS examined 42 measures of patient mortality and readmission to the hospital after being discharged. On 29 of those measures PSHs outperformed general hospitals, on seven there was no significant difference, and on only six did general hospitals outperform PSHs. PSHs also performed better than general hospitals on 13 of 14 safety measures.[64] The American Hospital Association chart claims that the CMS study found that the "quality results were mixed"—perhaps in the sense that one or two correct statements alongside dozens of errors is a mixture of fact and fiction.

A study in the journal *Health Affairs*, which the American Hospital Association did not include in the chart, found quality results similar to the ones in the CMS study.[65] PSHs beat out general hospitals on patient mortality, and physician-owned orthopedic hospitals topped general hospitals on patient readmission rates. The only area where general hospitals came out on top was when their readmission rates were compared to physician-owned cardiac hospitals.

Another quality measure in which PSHs outperformed general hospitals was on length of stay. Both MedPAC studies found that, on average, patients were able to go home faster after being treated in a PSH.[66] An examination of the data from the American Hospital Directory showed similar results for the hospitals examined in the McManis case studies.[67]

What most of the research on PSHs has overlooked is the actual patient experience. Fortunately, the CMS study and the one in *Health Affairs* did conduct patient interviews. CMS found that patients admitted to PSHs were generally aware that physicians owned the facility—in some instances the patients had to sign forms that disclosed the ownership arrangement.[68] The *Health Affairs* article found that patients generally felt that physician ownership was a "positive factor." As one patient said, "I think [the physicians] care more because their name's on it…They own it…It's just normal they would put more into it."[69] A comparison of the hospitals in the McManis case studies using data from the American Hospital Directory showed that patients were more likely to give high ratings to PSHs and recommend the PSHs to other patients as compared to general hospitals (see Table 9.3 in the appendix).

Patients found the nursing staffs at PSHs tend to be of higher quality than those at general hospitals. One group of patients who had previous experience in general hospitals found the PSHs' nurses had much greater specialized knowledge and skill than those in general hospitals.[70] Another patient group found PSHs nurses' confidence and knowledge to be helpful in relieving pre-operation anxiety.[71]

Patients also appreciated that PSHs were quieter than general hospitals. PSHs were usually devoid of the overhead announcements and pages typical in general hospitals, and patients in PSHs usually had private rooms. This made the experience more "restful" and, in the patients' minds, made recovery easier. By contrast, patients who had previously been in general hospitals complained about difficulty sleeping because they had to share "rooms with people who were loud, belligerent or required fairly intensive care."[72]

Patients also stated that the PSHs made recovery easier by providing "extra" amenities. For example, most patient rooms were equipped to allow family members to stay the night with the patient. Perhaps one of the most important amenities was the effort physician-owners put into making the patient feel at ease by making their PSHs seem very much *unlike* a traditional hospital. According to CMS:

> Some of the specialty hospitals we visited resembled luxury hotels more than a typical hospital. Lobby entrances and common areas tended to be decorated based on local themes. Muted colors,

comfortable seating, soft lighting and quality artwork were often seen in specialty hospitals. These types of amenities were not found at competing community hospitals. Upscale food was also a common theme in many of the specialty hospitals. In the focus groups we conducted, beneficiaries receiving care at a specialty hospitals had very positive experiences with the hospital environment and expressed appreciation at all the "extras" the hospital provided.[73]

Of course, there are those who couldn't care less that patients prefer the amenities of PSHs. As Stark put it, "If that's what they want, back rubs and silk robes, go to India."[74]

Community benefit, defined as the taxes paid and uncompensated care provided, is another measure on which PSHs excelled, outperforming non-profit general hospitals. While PSHs probably do not provide as much uncompensated care as non-profit hospitals, since they are *for-profit* they pay far more in taxes. As a result, CMS found that the net community benefit of physician-owned orthopedic and surgical hospitals was 7.2 percent of their operating revenue. Physician-owned cardiac hospitals generated community benefits equal to 3.74 percent of their operating revenue. Non-profit general hospitals generated benefits of only .87 percent of their operating revenue.[75] Likewise, the *Health Affairs* article "found that specialty hospitals incurred a greater net community benefit burden than their not-for-profit competitors did."[76]

Cherry Picking

Critics charge PSHs with "cherry picking" the most profitable patients and steering the less profitable ones to general hospitals. They offer two types of evidence to support this assertion.

The first is that PSHs treat fewer patients on Medicaid, the government health care program for the poor. Medicaid is notorious for having low reimbursement rates, and physicians with a single-minded focus on profits would want to avoid Medicaid patients. Evidence from three of the McManis case studies, both MedPAC reports and a GAO report find that PSHs do treat fewer Medicaid patients when compared to general hospitals. It would seem that PSHs eschew Medicaid patients—but it only *seems* that way.

The reason that PSHs don't treat as many Medicaid patients is that they specialize in services that Medicaid patients tend not to use. Medicaid patients are not in as much need of heart or orthopedic surgery than are older patients. General hospitals, on the other hand, do offer obstetric services, something far more likely to be used by young, poor women who are pregnant.

To be fair, it isn't the specialization of PSHs that fully accounts for their lower rate of Medicaid patients. Both MedPAC and the GAO compared PSHs with "peer" hospitals that specialized in similar treatment areas and did find that PSHs treated lower rate of Medicaid patients, although the differences weren't substantial. MedPAC found that Medicaid patients accounted for five percent of revenues at physician-owned surgical and orthopedic hospitals and for nine percent at the peer hospitals.[77] For physician-owned cardiac hospitals, MedPAC found that Medicaid accounted for three percent of their patients and for seven percent of peer hospitals.[78] The numbers were similar in the GAO study, three percent versus six percent.[79]

Yet contrary to the American Hospital Association chart, neither MedPAC nor the GAO stated explicitly that cherry picking caused the difference. MedPAC could only speculate that "specialty hospital decisions such as location, mission, emergency room capability, and physician financial incentives to avoid Medicaid patients may have contributed to the lower Medicaid shares at physician-owned hospitals."[80]

To determine if financial incentives affect physician referral patterns to the detriment of Medicaid patients, a study is needed comparing the number of Medicaid patients referred to PSHs by physician-owners with those physicians who only have admitting privileges to the PSHs. If the latter is greater than the former, then financial incentives are a likely cause of PSHs' lower number of Medicaid patients. If not, the explanation lies elsewhere. Unfortunately, no such study has yet been conducted.

The second type of evidence used to support the claim of cherry picking is the illness severity of the patient. Critics maintain that PSHs admit fewer patients with multiple illnesses or, as the medical literature puts it, "comorbidities," since such patients are more costly to treat. For example, critics charge that a physician-owned cardiac hospital will treat patients with coronary artery disease, but will try to refer patients that have not only coronary artery disease but also diabetes and hypertension to a general hospital.

Yet the evidence is in fact mixed. For example, the 2005 MedPAC report found that on average PSHs did treat less sick (low-severity) patients than general hospitals. But in the 2006 MedPAC study, researchers looked for "an increase in the ratio of highly profitable surgeries to less profitable surgeries" in markets with PSHs under the assumption that such an increase "would indicate that financial incentives may have influenced at least some physicians' behavior."[81] The report concluded that if "specialty hospitals are inducing market-wide shift in the ratio of low-severity to high-severity patients, the magnitude of the shift is too small to be detected with our test of statistical significance."[82]

Likewise, the CMS study yields mixed results. When examining physician referral patterns, it found that in some instances physician-owners referred more of their high-severity patients to their hospitals than did non-owners. But in other cases the non-owners referred more high-severity cases to the physician-owned specialty hospital. It also studied patients being transferred to and from PSHs and admitted to PSHs and general hospitals via emergency departments. In neither of those areas did CMS find that PSHs were systematically treating less sick patients than general hospitals. The Lewin study financed by MedCath found that PSHs treated a higher rate of high-severity patients.

Finally, both the CMS study and a study in *Health Affairs* compared the referral rates of physician-owners with those non-owner physicians who had admitting privileges to the PSHs.[83] If financial incentives were driving cherry picking, then presumably physician-owners would refer higher-severity patients to PSHs at a lower rate than physician non-owners. The results showed no clear pattern. In some cases physician-owners referred more high-severity patients to their PSHs than did non-owners, while in other cases the non-owners referred more high-severity patients to PSHs.

The reason the results on cherry picking are so inconclusive may be that physicians are actually referring their patients to the hospitals best suited to care for them. Studies suggest that general hospitals may be better suited to handle more complex patients. A physician-owned cardiac hospital will have the specialists to treat a patient with heart disease. But if that patient also has hypertension and diabetes, the general hospital will have additional specialists necessary to deal with complications that might arise from those comorbidities. PSHs may improve their ability to treat high-severity patients as time passes and physicians and nurses gain more experience. The Dayton Heart Hospital is a PSH that is partly owned by MedCath. Commenting on Dayton's ability to treat many high-severity patients, CMS noted that because "Dayton Heart Hospital is the second oldest MedCath facility, it may be that, as a specialty facility matures, its service range and ability to treat more severe cases may expand."[84]

Conflict of Interest

Critics of PSHs charge that what is best for physician-owners and what is best for their patients creates a conflict of interest. Even physicians disagree over this.

"I don't think doctors should own hospitals. Period," says. Dr. James Sisk, who practices internal medicine in Oklahoma City. "Obviously, it's a conflict of interest." Dr. Sisk worries that physicians are increasingly unable to make a living at what they should be doing, such as evaluating and managing the patient. He thinks that is why they increasingly turn to endeavors like owning hospitals to make money. His concern, like that of many critics of PSHs, is that since physician-owners share in the profit generated from surgeries, they have an incentive to perform surgery even when the patient may not really need it. "People are going to get surgery they don't need," he says.

But do physician-owners face a financial incentive to refer patients for surgery that is greater than any other physician?

"Even the decision to do surgery, I make money off of that. Any surgery, anywhere, I get a fee for that," counters Dr. Holden of McBride. "I could do unnecessary surgery from day one, if I was that type of person. Just scheduling surgery in the first place is a potential conflict of interest since I get paid for that."

When a patient goes into the hospital for surgery, Medicare pays for a number of different services. First, Medicare Part A pays the hospital a fee to cover the costs associated with providing the operating room, nurses, etc. Then, Medicare Part B pays the physician a separate fee for performing the surgery. Since Medicare Part B pays every surgeon each time he or she performs a surgery, every surgeon has a potential conflict of interest. Thus, critics are wrong to argue that physician-owned hospitals *create* a conflict of interest between the physician and patient. To the extent that such a conflict exists, it is already there due to Medicare's payment system.

At worst, PSHs increase that conflict of interest, but by how much? One researcher points out that if a surgeon performs a bypass surgery, Medicare Part B pays him about $3,622. The hospital gets paid a much larger fee, and the profit on that fee might be as much as $12,000. A physician-owner will get a portion of that profit. However, since the average physician owner has about a two percent ownership share, the average physician owner "would only receive $240 in pre-tax profits, still a fraction of the $3,622 surgeon's fee."[85]

Critics like the American Hospital Association might point to the research supposedly showing that PSHs increase the utilization of surgery as indirect proof that conflict of the interest is greater with physician-owners. Yet the research on utilization doesn't quite say what the American Hospital Association says it does.

The American Hospital Association misleads when it suggests that the MedPAC studies found that PSHs "increase utilization" of surgery. The first MedPAC study found no significant difference in utilization between PSHs and general hospitals. The second MedPAC report did find that areas with cardiac PSHs saw an increase in surgeries, but not areas with orthopedic or surgical PHSs.[86] Research that does not appear in the American Hospital Association chart also yields mixed results. Two recent articles by Jean Mitchell did find an increase in utilization due to PSHs.[87] But an article by Jeffery Stensland and Ariel Winter and another in the *Journal of Bone and Joint Surgery* could find no such increase.[88]

The results on how PSHs affect utilization may be inconsistent because their owners likely choose to locate them in areas where more utilization is needed or where utilization is higher in general. Generally, entrepreneurs are going to try to locate their businesses in areas where there is demand for their products and services. By the same token, physicians would be expected to locate PSHs in areas with a growing population and hence a growing demand for medical care. Thus far, little research has been conducted on a possible link between PSHs and population, although a MedPAC report and a GAO report did find that areas with PSHs had faster population growth than those areas without PSHs.[89]

Inconclusive research on utilization, though, hardly means that physicians who invest in hospitals are not motivated by money. Of course they are. Indeed, many physicians are, at least in part, motivated by financial concerns. Few people endure four years of medical school followed by a grueling residency to live the rest of their lives as monks. Nor would they invest substantial sums of money in a PSH without the hope of achieving long-term monetary reward.

Yet, if physicians were motivated primarily by money, there are more profitable careers, like ones on Wall Street, they could have pursued. Similarly, there are investments other than PSHs that are potentially more profitable. Like most people, physicians have multiple motivations for what they do, money being just one.

One of biggest motivations that drives people to become physicians is a desire to treat patients. That motivation plays a large role in physicians' decisions to become owners of specialty hospitals. A *Health Affairs* article found that controlling the work environment, increasing efficiency, and improving quality were key reasons why physicians owned hospitals.[90] MedPAC found that "the cardiologists and surgeons want to admit their patients, perform their procedures, and have their patients recover with minimal disruption. Physician control, they believe, makes this possible in ways community hospitals cannot match."[91] Physician-owners believed that being owners gave them more control over operating room schedules and staff and helped them avoid down time between surgeries.

Furthermore, making money and providing good care to patients are not mutually exclusive. A good physician should be able to make money by providing good care to his patients.

Dr. Janssen said that money was an issue when he and the eighteen other physicians decided to start McBride Hospital.

"It was a factor," he says. "We feel the success of this hospital is very dependent on the work we do here. We felt like there was a large amount of money being generated by our business and that we would much rather have control over that whether it's in the form of investing it back in the hospital or back in ourselves."

In its chart, the American Hospital Association portrayed physician-owners as motivated by little more than greed. But let's now re-work that chart so that it corrects the inaccuracies by adding research that was not previously included, removing inappropriate research, updating the case studies, and adding some new categories such as patient satisfaction. (See next page.)

When that is done, the chart paints a far different picture of PSHs. PSHs are endeavors in which profits have motivated physicians to improve the quality of health care for their patients. This provides much needed competition for operators of general hospitals who must find ways to improve their facilities.

Chart 9.2: AHA Chart Revised and Updated	MedPAC 2005	MedPac 2006	McManis: SD Case Study	McManis: NE Case Study	McManis: OK Case Study	McManis: KS Case Study	TrendWatch	GAO	Mitchell: Oklahoma City
Physician-owned, limited service hospitals:									
Lessen patient access to emergency and trauma care			✔		✔		✔		
Damage the financial health of full service hospitals leading to cutbacks in services	*	N	N	N	✔	✔	✔	N	
Reduce efficiency of full-service hospitals that must maintain stand-by capacity for emergencies even as elective cases are lost			✔	✔	✔	✔	✔		
Increase uitlization and costs	N	M	✔	✔	✔	✔	✔		✔
Are not more efficient	✔	✔							
Provide no better quality									
Use physician-owners to steer patients	✔		✔	✔	✔	✔	✔		✔
Cherry-pick the most profitable patients by:	U	U	✔	✔	✔	✔	✔		✔
-Avoiding low income populations	✔	✔	✔	✔	✔	✔	✔	✔	
-Offering the most profitable services	✔	✔	✔	✔	✔	✔	✔		✔
-Serving less sick patients within case types	✔	✔	✔	✔	✔	✔	✔	✔	
Provide limited or no emergency services	✔	✔	✔	✔	✔	✔	✔	✔	
Raise patient safety concerns with respect to responding to the emergency needs of patients under their care									
Make exceptionally high profits			✔	✔	✔	✔	✔	✔	
Had lower profit rates in 2014 than 2002-2003			✔	✔	✔	✔			
Provided greater community benefit than general hospitals									
Outperformed general hospitals on:									
-most measures of patient mortality									
-most measures of readmission									
-most measure of patient safety									
Patients had shorter length of stay than at general hospitals	✔	✔	✔	✔	✔	✔			
General hospitals still in existence and made profits 2013-2014			✔	✔	✔	✔			

* Little impact on community hospitals *thus far*
N Study did not find evidence
M Study found mixed evidence

O Study found evidence supporitng oppositie conclusion
U Study unable to come to make a finding
[shaded] Not specifically addressed in study

	Mitchell: 2007	Mitchell: 2010	CMS	Office of the Inspector General	Health Affairs: Greenwald et al	Health Affairs: Stensland & Winter	Lewin: MedCath	Journal of Bone & Joint Surgery	Center for Studying Health System Change
Chart 9.2--Continued									
Physician-owned, limited service hospitals:									
Lessen patient access to emergency and trauma care									
Damage the financial health of full service hospitals leading to cutbacks in services								N	
Reduce efficiency of full-service hospitals that must maintain stand-by capacity for emergencies even as elective cases are lost									
Increase uitlization and costs	✔	✔				N		N	
Are not more efficient									
Provide no better quality				✔					
Use physician-owners to steer patients			U						
Cherry-pick the most profitable patients by:			U						
-Avoiding low income populations									
-Offering the most profitable services									
-Serving less sick patients within case types			M				O		
Provide limited or no emergency services			✔	✔					
Raise patient safety concerns with respect to responding to the emergency needs of patients under their care				✔					
Make exceptionally high profits									
Had lower profit rates in 2014 than 2002-2003									
Provided greater community benefit than general hospitals			✔		✔				
Outperformed general hospitals on:									
-most measures of patient mortality			✔		✔		✔		
-most measures of readmission			✔		✔				
-most measure of patient safety			✔						
Patients had shorter length of stay than at general hospitals			✔				✔		
General hospitals still in existence and made profits 2013-2014									

* Little impact on community hospitals *thus far*
N Study did not find evidence
M Study found mixed evidence

O Study found evidence supporitng oppositie conclusion
U Study unable to come to make a finding
▢ Not specifically addressed in study

While it is doubtful that physician-owners are cherry picking their patients, it is clear that the American Hospital Association is cherry picking the evidence.

Sad Ironies

The goal of the Big Hospital Lobby, though, was never to develop a thorough understanding of the costs and benefits of PHSs. It was about stifling the competition. From late 2007 to early 2009, the Big Hospital Lobby lost three more fights to stop PSHs—two efforts at reauthorizing the State Children's Health Insurance Program and the passage of a "War Supplemental." Each contained some type of restriction on PSHs. But in none of those instances was the Big Hospital Lobby's support crucial to getting those bills passed. When some PSH supporters in Congress objected, the provisions limiting PSHs were jettisoned.

But to pass ObamaCare, President Obama and Congressional Democrats would need most of the key health care players on board— physicians, nurses, pharmaceutical makers, medical equipment companies, the insurance industry and, especially, hospitals. Without the support of groups like the American Hospital Association and the Federation of American Hospitals, passing ObamaCare would have been next to impossible, especially since funding some of the insurance subsidies in ObamaCare would require cuts in the hospital portion of Medicare. The American Hospital Association and the Federation of American Hospitals were not going to go along with that unless they got something in return, such as restrictions on PSHs.

For those PSHs already in existence, the law created a series of bureaucratic hoops to jump through that makes expansion difficult. To expand a PSH, the owners must apply to the Department of Health and Human Services. They can do so only once every two years. They must then wait while members of the community provide input. Further, the PSH must be in a county where population growth is 150 percent of the population growth of the state in the last five years. Inpatient admissions to the PSH must be equal to or greater than the average of such admissions in all hospitals located in the county. The PSH's bed occupancy rate must be greater than the state average. Finally, it must be located in a state where hospital bed capacity is less than the national average. Once a PSH meets all of those conditions, it is prohibited from expanding more than 200 percent.[92]

Those regulations mean that a PSH will expand in only the rarest of circumstances, and they apply even to expansions that were in progress when the law passed. No one seemed to know how much money was lost due to expansions that could no longer go forward.

Physicians and other investors at the Indiana Orthopedic Hospital came close to losing $27 million on a new building with three operating rooms that was only three-quarters of the way finished. "We spent a great deal of time looking at how to restructure it so we could stay within the law," said Dr. John Dietz, an orthopedic surgeon and part owner. "We decided to create a new company through which we could own that building as an ambulatory surgery center." The law does not apply to ambulatory surgery centers.

The Global Rehab and Pine Creek Medical Center in Dallas had to cancel plans for an expansion and for a new 66-bed hospital in Ahwatukee, Arizona. But the physicians there were lucky—not more than $230,000 was lost on either of those since neither was beyond the planning stages. However a physician at the Center, Dr. Hooman Sedighi, said, "We are working at capacity, and if we want to add to capacity, this bill pretty much precludes that. The other thing is the potential job loss — the ones that are under construction or expanding, they would have been hiring additional staff and personnel."[93]

"We were ready to break ground on a multi-million dollar expansion the very next day after the law passed," said McBride CEO Mark Galliart. "As it was, we had only sunk $167,000 into it. We were luckier than some others."[94]

The Big Hospital Lobby wasn't too sympathetic. "They've known that this was in the Senate and House bill, and if they went into new construction they knew that they were taking a risk," the American Hospital Association's Pryga said.[95]

Galliart eventually found an interpretation of the new regulations that enabled McBride Hospital to go ahead with its project to build three new operating rooms. CMS wouldn't permit a PSH to expand its number of beds under ObamaCare, but it did not put restrictions on how those beds were allocated.[96] Galliart simply scuttled three acute-care beds and in their place will put the operating tables that will go in the three new operating rooms.

But Galliart points out there may be an irony in the regulations for the Big Hospital Lobby:

> One of the reasons they wanted this moratorium on growth for physician-owned hospitals was because the doctors cherry picked. Well, what do you think the doctors are going to do now that they can't grow? Now they've pushed us to take the more profitable cases because we can't grow. The only way we can continue to stay afloat is to do the more profitable cases. My costs go up—salaries, the price of medical supplies, everything goes up except the reimbursement. I'm now going to have to start looking at the profitable case and sending the less profitable one to the non-profit hospital. What you've been accusing the doctors of doing, you're forcing them to do because there is no other way to maintain a profit margin. It just cracks me up. Now the hospitals are going to get what they said they didn't want.[97]

An even greater irony arose over two years later. ObamaCare included a Hospital Value Based Purchasing (HVBP) program as part of its changes to Medicare. Under HVBP, hospitals would be rewarded or penalized under Medicare based on quality measures such as patient satisfaction. In late 2012, Medicare released its first set of bonuses under HVBP. Based on the size of the bonuses awarded, nine out of the top 10 and 48 out of the top 100 hospitals as ranked by the HVBP were PSHs. In short, the law that had shut down new PSHs and stymied the expansion of existing ones was now, in effect, saying that they also had the best quality.[98]

Senator Baucus's crucial role in ObamaCare was likely to be a drag on his reelection effort in 2014, so he left Congress in 2013 to become ambassador to China. His seat was won by Republican Steve Daines. Senator Grassley remains in the Senate, but he is now chair of Judiciary Committee. He will probably never head the Finance Committee again, although he remains a member of it.

Representative Stark would experience his own dose of irony in 2012. When Stark first won office in 1972, he ousted incumbent Representative George Paul Miller by emphasizing that Miller had been in Congress too long. "Miller entered the House in 1945...28 years ago," Stark said at the time. In 2012, Stark faced 34-year-old Eric Swalwell. Stark, then a 40-year veteran of Congress, criticized Swalwell for his lack of experience, dismissing him as a "rookie" and "bush leaguer."[99] The irony was apparently lost on Stark but, perhaps, not the voters. Swalwell defeated Stark 52%-48%.

With these obstacles out of the way, it is possible that someday the restrictions on PSHs may be repealed. But, in the meantime, the damage has been done.

For the time being, the new restrictions stop a major source of innovation in the health care system. In other industries, as workers gain experience, they often gain insight into how the industry can be improved. They come up with ideas about how to provide customers with better products and services at lower prices. Becoming an owner of a company gives them the opportunity to put those ideas into practice. So, for example, Henry Ford worked as an engineer at Westinghouse, which built steam engines, before starting the Ford Motor Company; Sam Walton worked at J.C. Penny long before he opened Wal-Mart; and Steve Jobs was an employee at Hewlett-Packard and Atari before he founded Apple Computers, just to name a few.

Likewise, as physicians gain experience in a hospital, they come up with ideas about how to better treat patients. That was a big motivation among the physicians who began McBride Orthopedic Hospital. It would have been difficult, if not impossible, for them to put their ideas into practice without becoming owners. The Stark Laws began the process of stifling that sort of innovation in health care and ObamaCare may have killed it entirely. Whatever benefits patients would have experienced with the opening of new PSHs and the expansion of existing ones between 2010 and the present are lost forever.

The Big Hospital Lobby claimed that it only wanted what was in the interest of the common good. "Eliminating physician self-referral will benefit both patients and communities," said the American Hospital Association's Matthew Fenwick as ObamaCare neared passage. "[I]t saves taxpayers money, ends a serious conflict of interest and, above all, allows full-service community hospitals to provide vital care for all those in need."[100]

Yet, the desires of patients were largely absent from the discussion. While a few articles suggested that PSHs treat patients more effectively, no one ever conducted an extensive examination into the issue. Most of the research examined how PSHs affected general hospitals. As is often the case when medicine meets politics, it was politicians and interest groups who ended up deciding what was best for patients.

"The physicians are the ones who decide where their patients go, not the patients," said the American Hospital Association's Pryga. "It's not a matter of the patient's choice, it's a matter of the physician's choice."[101]

Research suggests that isn't true. As CMS found in its study, physician-owners "are constrained in where they refer patients by several factors" including "patient preference."[102] In fact, the prospect of being hospitalized is when patients are most likely to challenge their physicians by requesting a second opinion.[103]

Ultimately, it is the patient who should decide what type of hospital he or she should use because it is the patient who will be paying the cost if the decision is the wrong one. The patient is the one who will endure an unpleasant recovery in the hospital, experience pain if there are surgical complications, suffer a readmission after being discharged or, ultimately, die. Politicians, the Big Hospital Lobby, physicians, hospital administrators—none of them pay those costs. It is the patient who has the best incentive to make the right decision as to whether a PSH, a general hospital or some other surgical facility is the best place to have surgery.

Unfortunately, powerful political interests can use Medicare to limit the ability of patients to make the health care choices that best suit them.

10. Trade-Offs

Reforming Medicare so that it is less likely to victimize patients means putting Medicare beneficiaries in direct control of Medicare's resources. When beneficiaries control the funds, then they will be able to pursue treatments as they best see fit with much less interference from politicians and bureaucrats.

However, Medicare reform must also save money since the program is, in the long run, fiscally unsustainable. This is of particular importance for the sickest people on Medicare. If Medicare spending is reduced by cutting reimbursements and eliminating benefits, those reductions will fall hardest on those lacking political clout. And, of course, people with little to no political clout are often the sickest. Those who will be in need of the most medical resources will have the most limited access to them.

Looking at the annual Medicare Trustee's report shows how big a financial burden Medicare poses. Each year the Medicare Trustees estimate the program's shortfall over the next 75 years. They express the shortfall as a "present value" which means the amount of money we would have to invest in an interest-bearing account to cover the shortfall over the next 75 years. In the 2014 Medicare Trustees report, the estimated shortfall was $28.5 trillion.[1] Twenty-eight trillion is a huge, largely meaningless number except for budget experts and astronomers. To turn it into a number that non-mathematicians can fathom, divide it by the population of the United States, which is about 319 million. This yields over $89,300. That's the amount every individual in the U.S.—man, woman and child— would have to pour into Medicare this year to cover its long-term shortfall.

Since that isn't going to happen, any reform of Medicare must reduce its costs in addition to putting beneficiaries in charge of Medicare's resources.

Ryan-Wyden

Representative Paul Ryan, chairman of the House Ways & Means Committee, and Senator Ron Wyden have put forward the best-known Medicare reform in recent years. Under their plan, Medicare beneficiaries would be given a "premium support" for the purchase of a private health insurance plan and those premium supports would be risk-adjusted so that more is given to sicker beneficiaries. The premium support would be equal to the cost of the second-least expensive plan in a beneficiary's area. Beneficiaries would have the option of using their premium support to enroll in traditional Medicare. If a beneficiary chooses a plan that costs less than the premium support he or she would then pocket the difference. If the beneficiary chooses a more expensive plan he or she would pay the difference.[2]

The Ryan-Wyden plan has much to offer. It uses competition among insurance companies to keep Medicare costs down, something that has proven effective in the Medicare Part D prescription drug program. According to the Congressional Budget Office the Ryan-Wyden plan would reduce Medicare costs 14 percent by 2030.[3]

Unfortunately, handing Medicare over to health insurance companies is likely a political non-starter. Insurance companies are not popular among the public, and opponents of the Ryan-Wyden plan will use that to their advantage. The opponents will use the fact that Medicare money is going to insurance companies to distort the facts about the Ryan-Wyden plan—witness the commercial run against Ryan's initial Medicare plan in which a Ryan look-alike pushes a little old lady in a wheelchair over a cliff. Such attacks are unfair, but fairness and effectiveness are often mutually exclusive in political fights. Expect more of the same should

Congress or a president advance the Ryan-Wyden plan seriously. Such attacks against unpopular insurance companies are likely to torpedo the Ryan-Wyden plan.

Even if the plan became law, many of Medicare's policies that create victims would likely remain in place. Ryan-Wyden would likely keep the coding system that is helping to drive primary care physicians away from Medicare. Nor would the plan likely cover treatments that Medicare does not, so that future Clay Bells would have to wait and hope that a judge would reverse a denial of coverage ruling. Finally, insurance companies that cover Medicare beneficiaries unfortunately wouldn't be serving merely those beneficiaries. Their livelihood will also depend on staying in the good graces of Congress. That means insurers involved in Medicare will lobby Congress for their own benefit possibly to the detriment of Medicare patients. For example, industries often lobby for laws that make it more difficult for new companies to start up and compete. Less competition would benefit the insurance companies already in Medicare, but it will not be helpful (and could be harmful) to Medicare beneficiaries.

Medicare Reform

This book proposes a different approach to reform Medicare. It starts with the basic principle that Medicare reform should result in Medicare's money going directly into the hands of the beneficiaries. That is, beneficiaries should exercise ultimate control over how Medicare funds are spent. Following that principle, this reform does away with Medicare Parts A and B and instead sets up two Medicare accounts—a Basic Account and a Major Medical (MM) Account—for each beneficiary to purchase medical care. The amounts in these accounts will be renewed every year, although the amounts will not accumulate over time.

Reform should mimic the way we buy other goods and services. If an individual spends money on a computer, he saves money if he chooses a cheaper unit over a pricier one. The money he saves can either be spent on something else or saved for a later date.

That is how Social Security works. Beneficiaries receive their checks from the Social Security Administration each month and then have complete discretion over how to spend it: housing, groceries, gas, entertainment or gifts for their grandchildren. They can spend it on just about anything legal, and what they don't spend they can save.

Medicare should work similarly but with the stipulation that the money must be spent on medical care. The legislation instituting this reform should define medical care as broadly as possible, so that beneficiaries have a lot of leeway in finding treatments that work for them. Obviously, there must be some limits—Medicare money shouldn't be spent on quack treatments. But those limits should be few and clearly defined.

With that proviso in mind, under this reform Medicare will credit each Basic Account with $5,000 annually. At the end of the year, the beneficiary gets to keep 10 percent of what remains in the account. Thus, if he has $4,000 left, he gets to keep $400 to be spent as he wishes.

Of the roughly 37.7 million people on traditional Medicare in 2012 (i.e., they are not in Medicare Advantage), about 25.5 million have annual Medicare expenses under $5,000.[4] If beneficiaries use their Basic Accounts as health care consumers to shop around for the best deal for their medical needs, and if providers respond by lowering prices and improving quality, then there is great potential for savings in Medicare.

The MM Account will provide coverage for those with serious medical expenses, such as treating a chronic condition, surgery, cancer treatment or emergency situations. Medicare will credit each MM Account with $70,000. A beneficiary only gains access to this account if he spends all of the money in the Basic Account. If he has money left over in the MM Account at the end of the year, he gets to keep 1 percent to spend on whatever he wishes.

To see how this would work, consider "John Smith." By the middle of the year, Mr. Smith has spent $1,000 of his Basic Account. He then has to have an operation that will cost $12,000. To pay for it, he must spend the remaining $4,000 in the Basic Account and then $8,000 of the MM Account. Let's say he has $2,000 worth of follow up medical expenses after the operation, which will also be paid out of the MM Account. At the end of the year, he will have $60,000 left in the MM Account, of which he gets to keep 1 percent, or $600.

The combined $75,000 in annual coverage should prove sufficient for most Medicare beneficiaries. About 3.9 million beneficiaries had Medicare expenses over $25,000 in 2012, and the average expense among those beneficiaries was just under $57,000.[5]

What about those who have medical costs above $75,000? To start with, Medicare will pay for expenses over $75,000 for people who are disabled and seniors whose annual incomes are less than 150 percent of the federal poverty level.

For everyone else, they will have to purchase a private Medigap plan to cover expenses over $75,000. This will be the new role of Medigap plans. Instead of covering coinsurance on physician visits, tests and hospital stays, they will now pay for truly catastrophic costs. Money in the Basic and MM Accounts cannot be used to pay for Medigap premiums.

One other expense that the Basic and MM Accounts cannot be used for is prescription drugs. Prescription drugs will still be covered by Medicare Part D, which will be kept separate from Basic and MM Accounts. However, the insurance companies that administer Part D will be given the freedom to experiment with similar accounts for prescription drugs. Medicare Advantage will also be left in place. Beneficiaries who wish to receive their benefits through a private insurance company will continue to be able to do so.

Otherwise, beneficiaries can use the Medicare Accounts for visits to physicians and other health care providers, tests, therapy, durable medical equipment, hospital, hospice and nursing-home stays, emergency care, minor and major surgery, and cancer treatment.

One might reasonably ask, instead of two accounts, wouldn't it be simpler to just have one large account? The problem with doing that is that one large account provides much less incentive to people who have relatively small amounts of medical expenses to be frugal. To see this, suppose that beneficiaries have access to one large account of $75,000 and they would get to keep 1.5 percent of anything they didn't spend. Now suppose that an individual spent $2,000 of his account. At the end of the year he would keep $1,095 ($73,000 multiplied by 1.5 percent.) Now suppose he spent $4,000, in which case he would keep $1,065 ($71,000 multiplied by 1.5 percent.) Thus, he keeps only $30 more if he spends $2,000 less.

Compare that to the Basic Account of $5,000 in which an individual keeps 10 percent of anything he doesn't spend. If he spends $2000, he gets to keep $300 at the end of the year. If he spends $4,000, he keeps $100. That's a difference of $200. Obviously, $200 provides much more incentive to keep costs down than does $30. Hence the two accounts instead of one large account.

There are some other policy changes that will have to be made before this system can work.

The first is "dual-eligibles." These are the people who receive Medicare but are poor enough to qualify for Medicaid that pays for Medicare's cost sharing. In 2011 Medicaid spent about $143 billion on dual-eligibles. About $81 billion of that was federal money, money that should be redirected into Medicare Accounts.[6] But what about the $62 billion spent by the state on Medicaid for dual-eligibles? Should that money now be rolled into Medicare to help fund Medicare Accounts? That issue will have to be resolved.

Second, if this reform achieves savings in the disability part of Medicare, a portion of the savings should be used to reduce the two-year waiting period over time until it is no more than six months long at most. This way, patients like Sean Plomann will have to wait less time for coverage.

Third, Congress must repeal the prohibitions on physician ownership of hospitals. Medicare beneficiaries must be free to choose what type of hospital they wish to patronize regardless of who owns it. Physicians are often in the best position to improve hospitals since they spend much of their careers working in them. The best way they can improve hospitals is if they own them. Denying physicians ownership of hospitals denies patients an important source of cost-effective, quality care.

Fourth, every Medicare recipient will have to fill out two small forms when they enroll in Medicare. The first will designate the heir of the left-over funds in the year the recipient dies. So, if a beneficiary dies with $4,000 left in his Basic Account, the 10 percent savings, or $400, will go to the designated heir. The heir can be a family member, friend, charity—pretty much whomever the beneficiary chooses. The second will be a form that authorizes another person to manage a beneficiary's Basic and MM Accounts should the beneficiary be unable to manage the accounts himself. It will also spell out how any left-over funds are to be used at the end of the year.

Fifth, before lawmakers consider this change, they should test it with a "demonstration project." Such projects are potential Medicare reforms that are tested on a small scale before Congress considers whether to apply them to the entire Medicare system. Most Medicare demonstration projects have involved disease management, care-coordination, and value-based payments. A recent Congressional Budget Office report found that few met their goals of saving Medicare money or improving quality for patients.[7]

These projects fail, economist John Goodman explains, because Medicare tries to take the place of health care entrepreneurs. "Successful innovations are produced by entrepreneurs, *challenging* conventional thinking—not by bureaucrats *trying to implement* conventional thinking."[8] In a normal market, entrepreneurs are free to experiment in order to find what most satisfies their customers. In demonstration projects, Medicare dictates to hospitals and other market participants the parameters of the experimentation, limiting their freedom of action. A system of Basic and MM Accounts avoids that problem. Physicians, hospitals, and other providers will have the freedom to try new approaches to providing care, patients will be free to accept or reject those approaches, and Medicare bureaucrats will not interfere.

Next, should Congress adopt this reform, the change will turn health care, at least for Medicare beneficiaries, into a relatively free market. The consumers—the patients—will be paying physicians, hospitals, and other providers directly for their care. This, of course, depends on the ability of Medicare patients to behave like consumers. Then why is emergency care included in the care that Medicare accounts will pay for? Obviously, in emergency situations patients cannot consider their options, compare prices and do all the other things consumers normally do. Emergency care is included because making it an exception would prove too tempting for the lobbyists of provider groups. Every group would want their care to be classified as "emergency" since it would mean they could lobby Congress for better payment. The more care that gets classified as emergency, the less market pressure is brought to bear on it, with the undesirable result that reducing the costs and improving the quality of that care becomes far more difficult.

Finally, if Congress enacts these changes into law, it must allow at least five years to elapse before the changes take effect and allow current beneficiaries the choice of remaining with the current system or switching to the new one. This will give both beneficiaries and providers time to adjust to the coming changes. Once the changes take effect, all beneficiaries entering into Medicare after that point will be in the new system.

Can Medicare Patients Buy Cancer Treatments?

For markets to work in health care, patients must behave as consumers. They must be rational enough to shop around, compare prices, consider quality and so on. However, in many cases, patients facing a crippling or potentially fatal illness can be emotionally overwrought. Are these patients capable of being rational consumers of medical care?

Professors Mark A. Hall and Carl E. Schneider claim that they can't. They argue that "illness can cripple the patient as a consumer" because illness disables, causes pain, exhausts, erodes control, enforces dependence, disorients, baffles, terrifies and isolates. They ask, "Who, so beset, can muster the energy and acuity to buy a telephone sensibly, much less medical care? How can patients be the consumer a market needs?"[9]

Obviously, Hall and Schneider are painting with far too broad a brush. Many patients are not rendered completely helpless by illness. But their description undoubtedly fits some patients, such as those with cancer.

Dr. Daniel Fass is director of the Institute for Image-Guided Radiotherapy in Rye, New York, about 30 miles north of New York City. He's a highly regarded radiation oncologist with over 20 years of experience treating cancer patients. He specializes in a type of cancer treatment known as "tomotherapy." It employs a machine that enables the physician to view the tumor as a three-dimensional image. The physician can then target the radiation more directly on the tumor, avoiding the irradiation of surrounding healthy tissue.

Fass views many of his cancer patients the way Hall and Schneider view patients more generally. He often sees patients about a week after they are first diagnosed with cancer. Regarding their emotional state, he says, "Some of them seem like they've been hit by a train. Many of them are teary."

When asked if they'd make good consumers of medical care he responds:

> When I see them, usually they are overwhelmed. Some of them have the concern that this treatment might bankrupt them because they don't know what their insurance benefits are. And it can be difficult to find out. Sometimes they call their insurers and can't get a straight answer. We try to deal with that. We have someone on site who sits with them and works with them to let them know what their benefits are, what is covered and what their out-of-pocket costs will be. But it's difficult for patients to do that because most of them are devastated. Of all the things that you could be told that are wrong

with you, probably the worst is cancer. Often times, I'll sit with my patients and take the time to explain to them what they have and how the treatment will work. They leave my office, and they haven't heard a thing I've said. That's the kind of emotional state they are in.

In his view, such patients are in no condition to be shopping around, comparing prices or researching information on the quality of physicians and treatment facilities.

Yet on the wall outside of Dr. Fass's office is an article from the *Greenwich Time*, a local newspaper, about his practice.[10] It describes the treatment that one patient, Andrew Fenning, received from Dr. Fass's practice. What's remarkable is Fenning had to fly roughly 3,400 miles to see Dr. Fass.

In 2007, Fenning was in the process of leaving his home in Connecticut to move to London to head up the European division of a U.S.-based company. He was already in Europe when he was diagnosed with prostate cancer.

He researched his options, including surgery and brachytherapy, another form of radiation treatment. To Fenning, tomotherapy seemed the most promising. In February 2008, he temporarily moved back to the U.S. to receive a nine-week course of treatment from Dr. Fass. If Fenning was emotionally crippled by his diagnosis, the article doesn't mention it. Indeed, he seemed to take the news in stride and was able to calmly evaluate his options.

When asked about Fenning, Dr. Fass replies, "Oh, he was fine. You do have a spectrum of reactions. You just can't expect all of the patients to make rational, cost-effective decisions because there is too much on the line."

So how many patients can make that type of rational decision?

"Oh, probably about 30 percent," Fass replied.

Fortunately, that is more than enough for a market to work in cancer treatment, as well as health care more broadly. A common misperception about markets is that they work because they are filled with consumers eagerly searching out the best deal. In fact, markets work because only a small percentage of people, sometimes called "marginal consumers," behave that way.

These "marginal consumers" are anything but. They seek out new products, better quality, more features and lower prices than the alternatives. They drive markets by spurring producers to find ways to reduce costs and improve quality.

Take, for example, the market for automobiles. "Mr. Jones" may be so satisfied with his Honda Civic that he will never consider buying any other type of car. But there are consumers who would also consider a Ford, Hyundai or Nissan. These consumers push Honda and their competitors to make cars with better gas mileage, safety aspects and a host of other features while also keeping the cost down. One benefit of markets is that producers are unable to produce one product for marginal consumers and a different product for everyone else. Every drop in price and improvement in quality driven by a marginal consumer is available to all consumers. Thus, Mr. Jones, along with all the other committed Civic buyers, will benefit when they buy another Civic.

A market for health care would work the same way. In the case of Medicare, those beneficiaries who are marginal consumers will look for lower prices and better quality from physicians, hospitals, outpatient clinics, etc., and those providers will respond with more cost-effective care. Even in the case of cancer treatment, a small percentage of beneficiaries will be the ones seeking out the best care for the best price. Those patients who are too emotionally devastated will benefit from the decisions made by the small percentage who are not. In the case of Dr. Fass, his patients who are emotionally crippled will receive the same quality treatment that marginal consumers like Andrew Fenning push Dr. Fass to provide.

Trade-Offs

Any type of reform entails trade-offs. While we gain in some areas, we will lose in others. The best any reform can do is maximize the benefits while minimizing the costs. Below is a list of benefits and costs that will allow the reader to make a more fully informed decision about the pros and cons of changing Medicare into a system of Basic and Major Medical Accounts.

Benefits:

Better Care For Patients. Medicare beneficiaries will be given wide latitude on the type of medical care they can purchase with the Accounts. Patients like Clay Bell will be able to decide how much physical therapy they want and need without worrying about Medicare regulations. Patients who want to try a new treatment that they and their physician think will help will be able to do so without having to worry about whether CMS has given its approval. While no government program can eliminate the meddling of politicians and bureaucrats, a system of Basic and MM Accounts has the best chance of reducing it.

Less Medical Debt. Patients like Francine English will no longer have to worry about Medicare cost sharing since they will pay the full amount out of their accounts. The medical debt such beneficiaries will carry will be reduced if not eliminated.

Reduced Wait Time. Since part of any savings achieved in the disability part of Medicare will go toward reducing the wait time between receiving Social Security Disability Insurance and receiving Medicare, patients like Sean Plomann will spend less time struggling with their illnesses and get access to care quicker. It will also mean that such beneficiaries will be less likely to accumulate medical debt, since the time they will spend without any means of paying for care other than what they receive from Social Security will be reduced.

Greater Freedom For Physicians and Other Health Care Providers. Physicians will have to deal with far less coding since the patient, and not Medicare, will reimburse them. Less coding means they will save more money and time, time that can be better spent with the patient. Dr. Slatosky will be able to see more Medicare patients, since he will no longer have to worry about the overhead due to coding. Dr. Juliette Madrigal-Dersch will no longer have to require her Medicare patients to sign contacts every two years, since Medicare will now be set up so that her patients will be paying her directly. Physicians will also have to worry less about whether Medicare will reimburse the treatments they prescribe. Instead, they will be free to experiment with different treatments for their patients. Physicians such as Dr. Slatosky and Dr. Saghafi will be able to price their services at the rate that their patients value them, not by some price control set by Medicare.

Improved Quality. Patients (or, at least those who are "marginal consumers") are going to be far more concerned about the quality of their medical care when they are paying for it directly than when a third party pays for it. Better quality will mean fewer visits to the physician, hospital and other medical facilities for patients. Hospitals will be far more concerned about their reputations, resulting in fewer deaths due to hospital-acquired infections, to name just one likely result. There will probably be more physicians like Dr. Saghafi, since patients who find it difficult to move around and like the convenience are willing to pay a little extra to have a physician who makes house calls. Ultimately, with patients paying for care directly and providers responding directly to their needs and wants—and not those of CMS—quality will improve in ways that we can barely begin to foresee.

Better Use Of Health Care Resources. Our health care system will have less unnecessary treatment because Medicare patients will have an incentive to ask questions like, "Is this test really necessary?" or "Do I need to see the doctor again?" Doing so will mean more money that they get to keep at the end of the year. Tragedies like those of Selma Hartmann will be less likely to happen because people in her position will now have a financial incentive to question the necessity of a colonoscopy. It also means that some people who could treat their conditions with medication instead of an operation will do so, now that avoiding an operation will mean greater savings. Most importantly, though, the decision about what medical care is waste and what is not will be left up to the patient, who has the greatest stake in the outcome, and not to an appointed panel whose members pay no cost if they are wrong.

Taking Care Of Health = Saving Money. For many Medicare beneficiaries, taking care of their heath will mean more money they can keep from their accounts at the end of the year. Thus, people with chronic conditions such as diabetes or heart disease will have even more incentive to follow regimens that keep them healthy and out of the hospital. The more they keep their costs down, the more money they get to keep at the end of the year.

Care Coordinators. Care coordination for Medicare beneficiaries is poor because Medicare does not pay anyone to do it. Beneficiaries will, if they think they need it, be able to pay for coordination of their care out of their accounts. This may results in new services, where physicians and other providers include care coordination as part of a package that helps beneficiaries monitor which physicians they need to see, which tests they've had recently, which medications they need to take and help each physician know what the other physicians involved in the beneficiary's care are doing. Other beneficiaries may prefer to pay a fee to a private company that will help them coordinate their care. Still other beneficiaries may prefer to use a computer service that includes an application that they can download to their cell phones that their physicians can access when they visit them. Now that beneficiaries can pay for care coordination directly, many new ways of providing that service are sure to appear.

Price Transparency. A system of Basic and MM Accounts will incentivize physicians, hospitals and other providers to provide "price transparency." In other words, physicians, hospitals, and other providers will have to make the prices for their services easily accessible to patients. Price transparency could take many forms, such as providing a list of prices in a physician's office or on a hospital's website. At present, with third parties paying most health care costs, there is little incentive for health care providers to give patients easy access to their prices. Faced with millions of Medicare beneficiaries with Basic and MM accounts, though, providers will have a big incentive to post their prices in order to attract those beneficiaries.

Saving Taxpayers Money. When people have an incentive to monitor how much health care they consume and how much they pay for it, they save money. One of the earliest demonstrations of this was an experiment conducted by Harvard economist Joseph Newhouse, who put large groups of people into different types of insurance. Those put into an insurance plan with the largest cost sharing achieved reductions in health care spending of 40 percent.[11] More recently, insurance plans with high deductibles coupled with tax-free Health Savings Accounts have reduced spending by 12 percent.[12] As will be examined in more detail below, an insurance plan using "reference pricing" achieved a 37 percent reduction in the price of knee and hip replacements.[13] A system of Basic and MM accounts has great potential to reduce the amount Medicare spends on health care, thereby reducing the unfunded liability that future taxpayers would otherwise have to bear.

Costs:

The Last Dollars Of The Basic Account. The accounts do create some incentives for wasteful care. Specifically, beneficiaries who are down to the last dollars in their Basic Accounts near the end of a year will have an incentive to spend those down so they can get to the MM Account. For example, consider a beneficiary who has only $400 left in his Basic Account in, say, November. If he has no more medical expenses, he'll get 10 percent, or $40, to keep at the end of the year. But if he spends down that last $400, he'll get to the $70,000 in the MM account. He'll get one percent of that at the end of the year, or $700. That beneficiary will thus have an incentive to burn through that last $400, spending it on care that provides marginal to no benefit. Obviously, that will happen in some cases, but as long as it does not offset the savings that come from other areas of the system, then it is a cost that is worth tolerating.

Saving Money When You Really Need Care. Unfortunately, there are some beneficiaries who will try to save money when they really do need care— care that could save their lives or at least prevent a serious illness. In some cases such care might reduce or eliminate larger expenses later on. That is inevitable with Basic and MM Accounts. Yet even in today's world that is dominated by third-party payers, people still put off seeking care until it is too late. Would the increase in that behavior be so severe that it would offset the health improvements and savings that the Basic and MM Accounts would create elsewhere? That is a question that could be best answered with a demonstration project. However, evidence from the private insurance market suggests that is highly unlikely. People who have private insurance that requires considerable out-of-pocket costs, such as policies that include Health Savings Accounts, do have slightly lower rates of health care use than people with traditional insurance. For the most part, though, the difference is small, and some of it comes in the form of less wasteful consumption of care, such as fewer emergency room visits.[14] In fact, people with Health Savings Accounts are more likely to participate in wellness programs, such as weight loss and smoking cessation, than people with other types of insurance.[15]

Coding and Claims Processing Jobs. The massive number of codes that physicians and hospitals have to include in their paperwork has spawned an entire industry devoted to training people how to become medical coders. To see this, simply type "medical coding" into an internet search engine like Google or Yahoo. Medicare also hires large companies such as Blue Cross/Blue Shield to process the claims that physicians and hospitals submit to get paid by Medicare. When patients pay providers directly, providers will no longer have to get their reimbursement from CMS, which will mean they won't have to file Medicare claims or worry about coding. Over time, medical-coding and claims-processing jobs will decline. Of course, businesses involved in those areas will not take such change lying down.

Other Opposition. Any group that would see their wallets get lighter as a result of reform would surely oppose it. Both the AARP and the insurance industry make a great deal of money off Medigap plan sales. If reform reduces the amount of Medigap coverage that beneficiaries need, then Medigap sellers will lose money and will oppose reform. Also, the AARP may oppose reform for "ideological" reasons. The AARP is headed by people who think that Medicare beneficiaries are unable to make proper medical decisions on their own. They "need" the help of supposedly "unbiased" experts at the AARP and other groups who will push for government policies that supposedly protect Medicare beneficiaries. Another group that will see its finances take a hit is the American Medical Association. The AMA owns exclusive copyrights to the Current Procedural Terminology (CPT) Codes. As reform will reduce the need for coding, there will be less demand for CPT codebooks and software that the AMA sells. Some accounts claim that the AMA now makes more money from CPT Codes than it does from membership dues.[16] If so, the AMA would be a vociferous opponent.

Are We Willing To Make Trade-Offs For Ourselves? We cannot avoid trade-offs in life. The only question is who will be making the trade-offs—will we make our own or will we let someone else make them for us? Unfortunately, we have become accustomed to a health care payment system that largely insulates us from considering the price of our medical care. Rather, the job of worrying about payments has been left to a system of third-party payers, both public and private. The trade-off is that we lose much control over our medical care decisions because that third party has a vested interest in how money is spent on medical care. Regardless, we have become accustomed to that system. What are the chances that Medicare beneficiaries, accustomed to that system most of their lives, would be willing to make such a substantial change?

A recent article in the *New York Times* examined physicians in New York City who have stopped taking insurance and switched to cash-only practices. Consider the response of one patient to the change:

> Since her doctor stopped accepting her insurance, Kathryn Vanasek, 43, a mother of two in Manhattan, hasn't been back for a checkup or preventive screenings, relying on a new walk-in clinic for urgent problems like an ear infection.
>
> Her annual physical would cost at least $250 out of pocket, Ms. Vanasek said, but she would not get any money back from her insurer until she met the deductible.
>
> "You are making a decision between preventive medicine and reactive medicine," she said.[17]

Perhaps Ms. Vanasek is struggling financially and $250 is a considerable expense. But if we assume that she is doing quite well, is $250 really too much money to spend on a checkup? We often pay that much and more on items that, while important, are seldom as important as medical care. Cell phones, personal computers, wide-screen televisions, DVD players, the occasional expensive night out—all of these can easily cost $250 or more. Paying that much for such things directly has become almost routine. But doing the same for medical care is apparently controversial enough to merit the attention of the *New York Times*. It is not that there is anything inherently wrong with paying that much directly for care. Indeed, paying directly would produce far more benefits than routinely using third parties. The controversy arises from the fact that paying directly is still unusual.

Is it possible that we have become so accustomed to third parties paying for our care that we prefer not to even consider the cost? That was the finding of a recent study of the attitudes of people toward health care and costs. The study found "four times as many negative comments as...positive ones on the theme of willingness to discuss [health care] costs."[18] Rather, most participants insisted on getting the best care regardless of cost. That attitude appeared to stem from an "inexperience with making trade-offs between health and money,"[19] no doubt the result of our third-party payer system.

The third-party payer system may also be limiting the proliferation of policies that would help reduce costs and improve quality, such as Medicare Medical Savings Accounts (MSAs). An MSA-eligible policy for an individual must come with a deductible of no less than $2,100 and a maximum of $4,200 in out-of-pocket costs. An MSA is a tax-savings account in which an individual can deposit money tax-free to help pay for both his expenses under the deductible and additional out-of-pocket costs.

Yet MSA policies have had little success in the Medicare market. MSA policies receive very good quality ratings, on average, from the people who have them.[20] Yet only about 5,850 MSA policies were sold in 2013, out of a total of 14.8 million enrollees in Medicare Advantage plans.[21] Some blame this on private insurance companies that do not market MSA plans. They are usually buried in the back of booklets that insurers send to beneficiaries. Insurers, it appears, make more money on other types of plans. While that's one possible reason, another is that MSAs do not appeal to people who are accustomed to a third party paying their bills. Both reasons probably explain much of the lackluster interest in MSA policies.

Other research, however, suggests people are willing to make trade-offs between getting health care and saving money. For example, almost one-third of employees with health insurance now have plans that have a deductible of at least $1,000.[22] In other words, they have to pay nearly $1,000 out of pocket for most care before their insurance plans start paying for their care.

In 2011, the health plan for members of the California Public Employees' Retirement System (CalPERS) instituted a system of reference pricing in which members seeking knee or hip replacement were limited to only $30,000 coverage for hospital charges. CalPERS identified 48 California hospitals in which knee and hip replacements cost $30,000 or less. If a retiree received his joint replacement in one of those "approved" hospitals, CalPERS would pay the entire cost. If he went to a different hospital, he would pay for any expenses above $30,000. From 2011-2012, almost four in 10 CalPERS members who received a knee or hip replacement went to a hospital other than one of the 48 approved ones.[23] Strikingly, hospitals that were not among the approved 48 dropped their prices for knee and hip replacements for CalPERS members from an average of $43,308 in 2010 to $27,149 in 2012, a decline of 37 percent. Prices dropped because CalPERS patients "undoubtedly told the providers they had only $30,000 to spend."[24]

Most of the CalPERS patients were in their 50s and, therefore, probably accustomed to a third-party payer system. Thus, it is possible for people to move from a third-party payer system to one in which they pay for their health care directly and save money in the process. Would Medicare beneficiaries be willing to switch to such a system? It may be the only way to both save taxpayers money and, most importantly, put Medicare beneficiaries in charge of their health care.

ABOUT THE AUTHOR

David Hogberg is a senior fellow for health care policy at the National Center for Public Policy Research. He has previously worked at *Investor's Business Daily*, the Office of Representative Jeff Fortenberry, the Capital Research Center and the Public Interest Institute. His work has been published in National Review Online, The American Spectator, The Daily Caller, The Federalist, The Washington Examiner, The Washington Times, The New Individualist and The Omaha World-Herald. He holds a B.A. from California State University, Sacramento, an M.A. from the University of Missouri-Columbia, and a Ph.D. from the University of Iowa, all in political science.

He lives in Maryland with his wife, two dogs and a cat. He is an avid poker player. He can be reached at dwhmedicare@gmail.com.

APPENDIX

Table 1: New Medicare Benefits Added By Congress, 1965-2015	
New Medicare Benefit(s)	**Year Congress Approved**
Outpatient physical therapy.	1967
Added disabled to Medicare.	
Allowed beneficiaries to get Medicare coverage from HMOs.	
Outpatient kidney dialysis.	1972
Speech therapy.	
Outpatient chiropractic services.	
Eliminated the limit on home health visits.	
Eliminated prior hospitalization requirement for home health visits.	1980
Hospice benefit for terminally ill; benefit would expire on Sept. 30, 1986.	1982
Barred hospitals from billing Medicare patients more than what is authorized under Medicare.	1983
Pays for supplies for hemophiliacs.	
Hepatitis immunization for kidney disease patients.	1984
Made hospice care benefit for terminally ill permanent.	
One year of coverage of immunosuppressive drugs for organ-transplant patients	1986
Medicare Catastrophic Coverage Act passed. Reduced coverage gaps, added prescription drug benefit, but taxed seniors to pay for it. (Later repealed).	1988

Table 1--Continued	
New Medicare Benefit(s)	Year Congress Approved
Medicaid must cover part B premiums for Medicare beneficiaries between 100% and 120% of federal poverty level Routine mammogram every two years for women age 65 and older.	1990
Coverage of oral drugs for cancer that also have an injectable form	1993
Coverage of immunosuppressive drugs expanded to three years.	1995
Glucose monitoring equipment and instruction for diabetics. Annual prostate cancer screenings for Medicare beneficiaries over age 55. Coverage of FOBT screenings for colon cancer. Limited coverage of sigmoidoscopies and colonoscopies. Medicare Part C expanded to include PPOs and POSs in addition to HMOs, what later became known as Medicare Advantage.	1997
Glaucoma screening. Lifetime coverage of immunosuppressive drugs (for transplants). Colonoscopy once every ten years for all beneficiaries.	2000
Prescription drug benefit (Part D). Medicare Part C became Medicare Advantage Initial wellness exam.	2003
No co-pays for wellness exams, preventive colonoscopies, and mammograms. Reduction of the Part D "donut hole."	2010

Table 8.2: Medicare Pay and Recommended Minutes for Home Visits, 2015				
	New Patient:		Established Patient:	
Visit	Pay	Minutes	Pay	Minutes
Level I	$53.67	20	$54.30	15
Level II	$78.27	30	$82.30	25
Level III	$127.68	45	$125.40	40
Level IV	$178.55	60	$173.64	60
Level V	$216.22	75	-	-
Sources: CMS, Hospice Medicare Director Billing Guide				

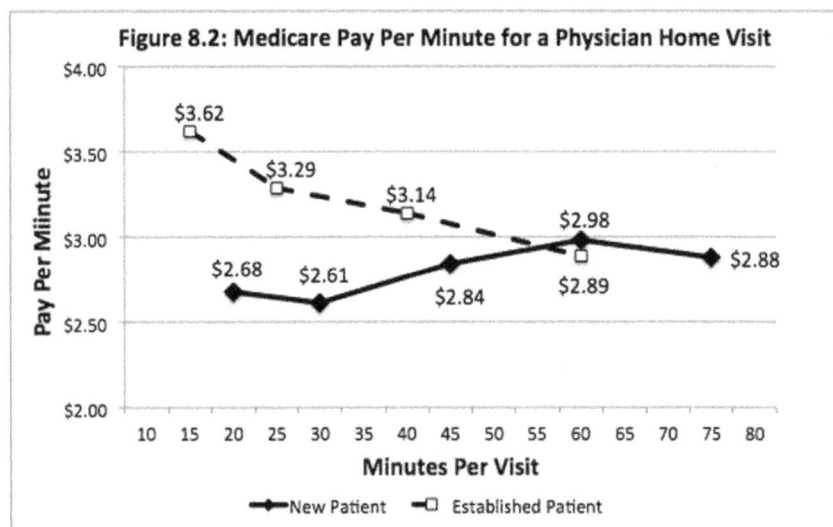

Figure 8.2: Medicare Pay Per Minute for a Physician Home Visit

Table 9.2: General Hospitals in the McManis Case Studies--Then And Now			
Hospital:	Profit Rate in 2013-2014:	Number of Beds in:	
		2002-2003*	2014
Kansas			
Wesley Medical Center	3.0%	469	520
Via Christi - St. Francis	3.5%	965	1268
Via Christi - Pittsburg	0.5%	**	
Oklahoma			
OU Medical Center	0.9%	727	750
INTEGRIS Baptist Medical Center	3.6%	469	579
INTEGRIS Southwest Medical Center	1.0%	351	389
Mercy Health Center	0.5%	416	349
St. Anthony Hospital	-4.9%	428	615
Deaconess Hospital	-0.5%	313	238
Norman Regional Hospital	0.6%	297	324
Midwest Regional Medical Center	0.7%	247	254
Nebraska			
BryanLGH	7.7%	563	252
Saint Elizabeth Regional Medical Center	8.0%	240	265
South Dakota			
Rapid City Regional Hospital	8.9%	282	417
Lookout Memorial Hospital***	10.7%	40	40

*Time period examined in McManis Case Studies
**Via Christi at Pittsburg and St. Francis are a joint venture
***Lookout Memorial is now Spearfish Regional
Source: McManis Case Studies and American Hospital Directory

Table 9.3: Quality Measures of Hospital in McManis Case Studies, 2013-2014			
General Hospitals:	Avg. Length of Stay in Days	Patients Giving Highest Rating	Patients Who Would Definitely Recommend
Kansas	4.9	68%	70%
Wesley Medical Center	4.8	67%	70%
Via Christi - St. Francis	3.5	70%	65%
Via Christi - Pittsburg			
Oklahoma	6.2	66%	67%
OU Medical Center	6.9	79%	81%
INTEGRIS Baptist Medical Center	4.7	68%	67%
INTEGRIS Southwest Medical Center	5.2	73%	78%
Mercy Health Center	5.5	81%	82%
St. Anthony Hospital	5.1	66%	68%
Deaconess Hospital	3.6	73%	73%
Norman Regional Hospital	4.2	48%	48%
Midwest Regional Medical Center			
Nebraska	5.6	NA	NA
BryanLGH	3.9	77%	80%
Saint Elizabeth Regional Medical Center			
South Dakota	5.7	67%	68%
Rapid City Regional Hospital	2.9	73%	71%
Lookout Memorial Hospital*			
Average of General Hospitals	4.8	70%	71%
*Lookout Memorial is now called Spearfish Regional			

268

APPENDIX

Table 9.3--Continued			
Physician-Owned Specialty Hospitals:	Avg. Length of Stay in Days	Patients Giving Highest Rating	Patients Who Would Definitely Recommend
Kansas			
Kansas Heart Hospital	4.4	89%	91%
Galichia Heart Hospital	4.4	NA	NA
Kansas Surgery and Recovery Center	2.2	83%	86%
Oklahoma			
Northwest Surgery Hospital	2	86%	86%
Lakeside Women's Hospital	4.3	75%	80%
Surgical Hospital of Oklahoma	1.9	77%	80%
Oklahoma Spine Hospital	2.5	90%	91%
South Dakota			
Black Hills Surgery Center	2.7	93%	95%
Average of PSHs	**3.1**	**85%**	**87%**

Source: McManis Case Studies and American Hospital Directory

Index

S

T

Notes

Chapter 1: Introduction

[1] Carlene A. Muto, John A, Jernigan, Belinda E. Ostrowsky, Herve M. Richet. William R. Jarvis, John m. Boyce, and Barry M. Farr, "SHEA Guideline for Preventing Noscomail Transmission of Multidrug-Resistant Strains of *Staphylococcus aureaus* and *Enterococcus*," *Infection Control and Hospital Epidemiology*, May 2003, Vol. 24, No. 5, p. 362.

[2] United States Dept. of Health and Human Services, Center for Medicare and Medicaid Services, "42 CFR Parts 411, 412, 413, and 489 Medicare Program; Changes to the Hospital Inpatient Prospective Payment Systems and Fiscal Year 2008 Rates; Final Rule," *Federal Register*, August 22, 2007, p.47218.

[3] United States Dept. of Health and Human Services, Center for Medicare and Medicaid Services, "42 CFR Parts 411, 412, 413, 422, and 489 Medicare Program; Changes to the Hospital Inpatient Prospective Payment Systems and Fiscal Year 2009 Rates; Payments for Graduate Medical Education in Certain Emergency Situations; Changes to Disclosure of Physician Ownership in Hospitals and Physician Self-Referral Rules; Updates to the Long-Term Care Prospective Payment System; Updates to Certain IPPS-Excluded Hospitals; and Collection of Information Regarding Financial Relationships Between Hospitals; Final Rule," *Federal Register*, August 19, 2008, pp.48483-4.

[4] Grace M. Lee, Ken Kleinman, Stephen B. Soumerai, Alison Tse, David Cole, Scott K, Fridkin, Teresa Horan, Richard Platt, Charlene Gay, William Kassler, Donald A. Goldman, John Jernigan, and Ashish K. Jha,

"Effect of Nonpayment for Preventable Infections in U.S. Hospitals," *The New England Journal of Medicine*, October 11, 2012, Vol. 367, No. 15.

[5] Jennifer A. Meddings, Heidi Reichert, Mary A.M. Rogers, Sanjay Saint, Joe Stephansky, and Laurence F. McMahon Jr., "Effect of Nonpayment for Hospital-Acquired, Catheter-Associated Urinary Tract Infection," *Annals of Internal Medicine*, September 4, 2012, Vol. 157, No.2.

[6] President Lyndon B. Johnson, "President Lyndon B. Johnson's Remarks With President Truman at the Signing in Independence of the Medicare Bill," Lyndon Baines Johnson Library and Museum, National Archives and Records Administration, at http://www.lbjlib.utexas.edu/johnson/archives.hom/speeches.hom/650730.asp (November 19, 2011).

[7] Robert Weissman, "We Still Need Medicare-for-All," Public Citizen, CitizenVox, June 28, 2012, at http://www.citizenvox.org/2012/06/28/supreme-court-obamacare-public-citizen/ (May 20, 2014.)

Chapter 2: Greenspring Votes

[1] Theodore R. Marmor, *The Politics of Medicare*, 2nd edition, New York: Aldine De Gruyter, 2000.

[2] Marilyn Moon, *Medicare: A Policy Primer*, Washington, D.C.: The Urban Institute Press, 2006, p.48.

[3] Sue A. Blevins, *Medicare's Midlife Crisis*, Washington, D.C.: The Cato Institute, 2001.

[4] David Blumenthal and James Monroe, "The Lessons of Success— Revisiting the Medicare Story," *The New England Journal of Medicine*, November 27, 2008, Vol. 359, No. 22, p. 2385.

[5] Ibid., p. 2386.

[6] Ibid.

[7] Ibid, p.2386.

[8] Ibid, p.2387.

[9] See Belvins, p.55.

[10] Ilya Shapiro, "Supreme Court Snubs Citizens Whose Social Security Will Be Confiscated If They Refuse Government Health Care," *Cato At Liberty*, January 25, 2013, http://www.cato.org/blog/supreme-court-snubs-citizens-whose-social-security-will-be-confiscated-they-refuse-government (June 5, 2014).

[11] See Blevins, p.72.

[12] See Blevins, p.42

[13] Phill Galewitz, "Study: Nearly A Third Of Doctors Won't See New Medicaid Patients," *Kaiser Health* News, August 6, 2012, at http://www.kaiserhealthnews.org/stories/2012/august/06/third-of-medicaid-doctors-say-no-new-patients.aspx (June 6, 204).

[14] Virginia State Board of Election, "Election Results," at http://sbe.virginia.gov/index.php/resultsreports/election-results/ (June 1, 2014).

[15] Medicare as percent of GDP and of federal budget based on author's calculations using data from Office of Management and Budget, Table 3.1—Outlays by Superfunction and Function, at http://www.whitehouse.gov/omb/budget/historicals (February 5, 2015).

Chapter 3: Medicare's Second-Class Citizens

[1] "House Passes Welfare Reform, Senate Delays Action," *Congressional Quarterly Almanac*, 27th Annual, 92nd Congress, 1971, pp.519-20.

[2] "Social Security Amendments Of 1971," Hearings Before The Committee On The Finance, U.S. Senate Ninety-Second Congress, First Session, On H.R. 1 To Amend The Social Security Act To Increase Benefits And Improve Eligibility And Computation Methods Under That OASDI Program, To Make Improvements In The Medicare, Medicaid, and Maternal And Child Health Programs With Emphasis On Improvements In Their Operating Effectiveness, To Replace The Existing Federal-State Public Assistance Programs With A Federal Program Of Adult Assistance And A Federal Program If Benefits To Low-Income Families With

Children With Incentives And Requirements For Employment And Training To Improve The Capacity For Employment Of Members Of Such Families, And For Other Purposes, Part 2 of 6, July 27, 29, August 2 and 3 1971, p.44

[3] Gina Livermore, David Stapleton, and Henry Claypool, "Costs and Benefits of Eliminating the Medicare Waiting Period for SSDI Beneficiaries," Center for Studying Disability Policy, *Disability Policy Research Brief*, No. 09-02. March 2009.

[4] Stacy Berg Dale and James M. Verdier, "Elimination of Medicare's Waiting Period for Seriously Disabled Adults: Impact on Coverage and Costs," Issue Brief, Commonwealth Fund, July 2003; and "Budget Options Volume I: Health Care," Congressional Budget Office, December 2008.

[5] Bob Williams, Adrianne Dulio, Henry Claypool, Michael J. Perry, and Barbara S. Cooper, "Waiting For Medicare: Experiences of Uninsured People With Disabilities in the Two-Year Waiting Period for Medicare," The Commonwealth Fund and the Christopher Reeve Paralysis Foundation, October 2004.

[6] Robert M. Hayes, Deane Beebe, and Heidi Kreamer, "Too Sick To Work, Too Soon For Medicare: The Human Cost Of The Two-Year Medicare Waiting Period For American With Disabilities," April 2007, The Commonwealth Fund, at http://www.commonwealthfund.org/publications/publications_show.htm?doc_id=473514 (December 2, 2010).

[7] Bob Williams, Adrianne Dulio, Henry Claypool, Michael J. Perry, and Barbara S. Cooper, "Waiting For Medicare: Experiences of Uninsured People With Disabilities in the Two-Year Waiting Period for Medicare," The Commonwealth Fund and the Christopher Reeve Paralysis Foundation, October 2004.

[8] Robert M. Hayes, Deane Beebe, and Heidi Kreamer, "Too Sick To Work, Too Soon For Medicare: The Human Cost Of The Two-Year Medicare Waiting Period For American With Disabilities," April 2007, The Commonwealth Fund, at

http://www.commonwealthfund.org/publications/publications_show.htm?d oc_id=473514 (December 2, 2010).

[9] Gerald F. Riley, "Health Insurance and Access to Care among Social Security Disability Insurance Beneficiaries during the Medicare Waiting Period," *Inquiry*, Vol. 43, Fall 2006.

[10] Gina Liverpool, David Stapleton, and Henry Claypool, "Health Insurance and Health care Access Before and After SSDI Entry," The Commonwealth Fund, May 2009.

[11] Riley, p. 225.

[12] Livermore, et al., p. 24.

[13] Gerald F. Riley, "The cost of eliminating the 24-month Medicare waiting period for Social Security disabled-worker beneficiaries," Medical Care, Vol. 42, No. 4, April 2004; and Gina Livermore, David Stapleton, and Henry Claypool, "Costs and Benefits of Eliminating the Medicare Waiting Period for SSDI Beneficiaries," Disability Policy Research Brief, Center for Studying Disability Policy, No. 09-02, March 2009.

[14] Dale and Verdier, July 2003.

[15] Senator Max Baucus, "Call To Action: Health Reform 2009," November 12, 2008, p. 14.

[16] Douglas W. Elmendorf, "Letter to the Honorable Charles B. Rangel," Congressional Budget Office, July 17, 2009.

[17] "Budget Options Volume I: Health Care," Congressional Budget Office, December 2008.

[18] Jennifer C. Day and Avalaura L. Gaither, "Voting and Registration in the Election of November 1988," Population Characteristics, Current Population Reports, U.S. Census Bureau, P20-523RV, August 2000.

[19] Judith Waldrop and Sharon M. Stern, "Disability Status: 2000," Census 2000 Brief, U.S. Census Bureau, C2KBR-17, March 2003, 2000; Amie Jamieson, Hyon B. Shin, and Jennifer Day, "Voting and Registration in the Election of November 2000," Population Characteristics, Current Population Reports, U.S. Census Bureau, P20-542, February 2002; and Lisa Schur, Todd Shields, Douglas Kruse and Kay Schriner, "Enabling

Democracy: Disability and Voter Turnout," *Political Research Quarterly*, Vol. 55, No. 1, March 2002.

[20] U.S. Government Accountability Office, "Federal Disability Assistance: Wide Array of Programs Needs to be Examined in Light of 21st Century Challenges," Report to Congressional Committee, GAO-05-626, June 2005.

[21] Becky Bruce Stuart, Jalpa Doshi, and Sachin Kamal-Bahl, "Medicare's Disabled Beneficiaries: The Forgotten Population In The Debate Over Drug Benefits," The Commonwealth Fund and the Henry J. Kaiser Family Foundation, September 2002.

[22] Marsha Gold and Beth Stevens, "Medicare's Less Visible Population: Disabled Beneficiaries under Age 65," Operational Insights: Monitoring Medicare + Choice, Mathematica Policy Research, Inc., May 2001, No. 2, at http://www.mathematica-mpr.com/PDFs/opinsights2.pdf, (December 6, 2010).

[23] Kristina W. Hanson, Patricia Neuman, David Dutwin, and Judith D. Kasper, "Uncovering The Health Challenges Facing People With Disabilities: The Role Of Health Insurance," *Health Affairs*, Web Exclusive, November 19, 2003.

[24] "Medicare And Nonelderly People With Disabilities," *Medicare Fact Sheet*, The Henry J. Kaiser Foundation, September 2010.

[25] Ibid.

[26] David and O'Brien, Summer 1996.

[27] Cubanski and Neuman, September 2010.

[28] Hanson, et al., November 19, 2003, pp. W3-562 – W3-563.

Chapter 4: Donut Hole

[1] "'Buried In The Archives,' The Original Town-Hall Battle," August 10, 2009, at http://www.youtube.com/watch?v=qre7DzEtxyc (April 17, 2011).

[2] Richard Himmelfarb, *Catastrophic Politics. The Rise and Fall of the Medicare Catastrophic Coverage Act of 1988*, University Park, Pennsylvania: The Pennsylvania State University Press, 1995, p.44.

[3] Congressional Budget Office, "The Medicare Catastrophic Coverage Act of 1988," Staff Working Paper, October 1988, p.8.

[4] Himmelfarb, p.45.

[5] David A. Hyman, *Medicare Meets Mephistopheles*, Washington, D.C.: Cato Institute, 2006, Chp. 4.

[6] Robert Pear and Walt Bogdanich, "Some Successful Models Ignored As Congress Works on Drug Bill," The New York Times, September 4, 2003, p.A1.

[7] Dennis Hastert, interview by author, tape recording, Washington, DC, October 21, 2010.

[8] Ibid.

[9] Jack Hoadley, Elizabeth Hargrave, Juliette Cubanski, and Tricia Neuman, "Specialty Tiers," *Medicare Part D 2009 Data Spotlight*, June 2009.

[10] Ibid.

[11] John E. Calfee, *Prices, Markets, and the Pharmaceutical Revolution*, AEI Press, Washington, D.C., 2000, p.7.

[12] Aaron Catlin, Cathy Cowan, Micah Hartman, Stephen Heffler, and the National Health Expenditure Accounts Team, "National Health Spending In 2006: A Year Of Change For Prescription Drugs," *Health Affairs*, January/February 2008, Vol. 27, No. 1, p.15.

[13] Calfee, 2000.

[14] Ibid, p.10.

[15] Usha Sambamoorthi, Dennis Shea, and Stephen Crystal, "Total and Out-of-Pocket Expenditures for Prescription Drugs Among Older Persons," *The Gerontologist*, June 2003, Vol. 43, No. 3.

[16] Usha Sambamoorthi, Ayse Akincigil, Wenhui Wei, and Stephen Crystal, "National trends in out-of-pocket prescription drug spending among elderly medicare beneficiaries," *Expert Review of Pharmacoeconomics & Outcomes Research*, June 2005, Vol. 5, No. 3.

[17] Barents, LLS, WESTAT, and The Henry J. Kaiser Foundation, "How Medicare HMO Withdrawals Affect Beneficiary Benefits, Costs, and Continuity of Care," The Henry J. Kaiser Foundation, November 1999.

[18] American Academy of Actuaries Medicare Supplement Insurance Work Group, "Report To The National Association Of Insurance Commissioners," June 8, 2000, at http://www.actuary.org/pdf/medicare/naicrptjune00fin.pdf (June 25, 2011).

[19] Robin Toner, "Bitter Partisan Fight Brewing Over Medicare Drug Benefits," *The New York Times*, April 5, 2000, p.A1.

[20] Robert Pear and Elisabeth Bumiller, "The President's Proposals: On The Road; Doubts Are Emerging as Bush Pushes His Medicare Plan," *The New York Times*, January 30, 2002, p.18A.

[21] Robert Pear, "Bush May Link Drug Benefit In Medicare To Private Plans," *The New York Times*, January 24, 2002, p.1A.

[22] Dennis Hastert, *Speaker: Lessons From Forty years In Coaching And Politics*, Regnery Publishing, Inc., Washington, D.C., 2004, p. 265.

[23] Edward Epstein, "Democrats Decry Republican Tactics in Marathon Vote / GOP Leadership Abused Rules, Twisted Arms in Late-Night Session, Pelosi Says," *San Francisco Chronicle*, December 9, 2003, at http://articles.sfgate.com/2003-12-09/news/17521950_1_medicare-vote-voting-rules-angry-house-democrats (June 7, 2011).

[24] Vicki Kemper, "Medicare Drug Benefit Plan to Far Exceed Cost Estimate," *Los Angeles Times*, January 30, 2004, at http://articles.latimes.com/2004/jan/30/nation/na-medicare30 (June 7, 2011).

[25] Emily Heil, "Medicare Actuary Details Threats Over Estimates," *CongressDaily*, March 25, 2005, at http://www.govexec.com/dailyfed/0304/032504cdam1.htm (June 7, 2011).

[26] Center for Medicare and Medicaid Services, LIS Enrollment By Plan, "2015 LIS Enrollment By Plan," at http://www.cms.gov/Research-Statistics-Data-and-Systems/Statistics-Trends-and-Reports/MCRAdvPartDEnrolData/LIS-Enrollment-by-Plan.html (April 10, 2015).

[27] Laura Summer, Jack Hoadley, and Elizabeth Hargrave, "The Medicare Part D Low-Income Subsidy Program: Experience to Date and Policy Issues for Consideration," *The Medicare Drug Benefit*, The Henry J. Kaiser Foundation, September 2010.

[28] Patricia Neuman, Michelle Kitchman Strollo, Stuart Guterman, William H. Rogers, Angela Li, Angie Mae C. Rodday, and Dana Gelb Safran, "Medicare Prescription Drug Benefit Progress Report: Findings From A 2006 National Survey Of Seniors," *Health Affairs*, August 21, 2007, Web Exclusive, p.w638

[29] Walid F. Gellad, Haiden A. Huskamp, Kathryn A. Phillips, and Jennifer S. Haas, "How The New Medicare Drug Benefit Could Affect Vulnerable Populations," *Health* Affairs, January/February 2006, Vol. 25, No. 1, p.252.

[30] Nueman et al., August 21, 2007.

[31] Dana Gelb Safran, Patricia Neuman, Cathy Schoen, Michelle S. Kitchman, Ira B. Wilson, Barbara Cooper, Angela Li, Hong Change, and William H. Rogers, "Prescription Drug Coverage And Seniors: Findings From A 2003 National Survey," *Health Affairs*, Web Exclusive.

[32] "The Medicare Prescription Drug Benefit Fact Sheet," The Henry J. Kaiser Foundation, November 19, 2013.

[33] Ibid.

[34] The Board of Trustees, Federal Hospital Insurance and Federal Supplementary Medical Insurance Trust Funds, "The 2013 Annual Report of the Boards of Trustees Of The Federal Hospital Insurance and Federal Supplementary Medical Insurance Trust Funds," May 31, 2013, p.111. For initial estimates see Trustees Report for 2007 p.113.

[35] Stephen B. Soumerai, Marsha Pierre-Jacques, Fang Zhang, Dennis Ross-Degnan, Alyce S. Adama, Jerry Gurwitz, Gerald Adler, and Dana Gelb Safran, "Cost-Related Medication Nonadherence Among Elderly and Disabled Medicare Beneficiaries," *Archives of Internal Medicine*, September 25, 2006, Vol. 166, No. 17.

[36] Jeanne M. Madden, Amy J. Graves, Fang Zhang, Alyce S. Adams, Becky A. Briesacher, Dennis Ross-Degnan, Jerry H. Gurwitz, Marsha

Pierre-Jacques, Dana Gelb Safran, Gerald S. Adler, Stephen B. Soumerai, "Cost-Related Medication Nonadherence and Spending on Basic Needs Following Implementation of Medicare Part D," *Journal of the American Medical Association*, April 23/30 2008, Vol. 299, No. 16.

[37] Sebastian Schneeweiss, Amanda R. Patrick, Alexd Pedan, Laleh Varasteh, Raisa Levin, Nan Liu, and William H. Shrank, "The Effect Of Medicare Part D Coverage On Drug Use And Cost Sharing Among Seniors Without Prior Drug Benefits," *Health Affairs*, February 3, 2009, Web Exclusive.

[38] Madden et al., April 23/30, 2008.

[39] Yuting Zhang, Julie Marie Donohue, Jospeh P. Newhouse, and Judith R. Lave, "The Effects Of The Coverage Gap On Drug Spending: A Closer Look At Medicare Part D," *Health Affairs,* February 3, 2009, Web Exclusive.

[40] Susan L. Ettner, Neil Steers, O. Kenrik Duru, Norman Turk, Elaine Quiter, Julie Schmittdiel, and Carol M. Mangione, "Entering and Exiting the Medicare Part D Coverage Gap: Role of Comorbidities and Demographics," *Journal of General Internal Medicine*, June 2010, Vol. 25, No. 6.

[41] Zhang et al., February 3, 2009.

[42] Jack Hoadley, Elizabeth Hargrave, Juliette Cubanski and Tricia Neuman, "The Medicare Part D Coverage Gap: Costs and Consequences In 2007," *The Medicare Drug Benefit*, The Henry J. Kaiser Foundation, August 2008.

[43] Schneeweiss et al., February 3, 2009.

[44] "Designing A Twenty-First Century Medicare Prescription Drug Benefit," Hearing Before the Subcommittee on Health of the Committee on Energy and Commerce, House of Representatives One Hundred Eight Congress, First Session, April 8, 2003, p.29.

[45] See Earl P. Steinberg, Benjamin Gutierrez, Aiman Momani, Jospeh A. Boscarino, Patricia Neuman, and Patricia Deverka, "Beyond Survey Data: A Claims-Based Analysis Of Drug Use And Spending By The Elderly," *Health Affairs*, March/April 2000, Vol. 19, No. 2; and Wenke Hwang,

Wendy Weller, Henry Ireys, and Gerard Anderson, "Out-Of-Pocket Medical Spending For Care Of Chronic Conditions," *Health Affairs*, November/December 2001, Vol. 20, No. 6.

[46] Bruce Stuart and James Grana, "Ability to Pay and the Decision to Medicate," *Medical Care*, February 1998, Vol. 36, No. 5.

[47] Dana Gelb Safran, Patricia Neuman, Cathy Schoen, Jana E. Montgomery, Wenjun Li, Ira B. Wilson, Michelle S. Kitchman, Andrea E. Bowen, and William H. Rogers, "Prescription Drug Coverage And Seniors: How Well Are States Closing The Gap?" *Health Affairs*, July 31, 2002, Web Exclusive; and C1

[48] Emily R. Cox, Cindy Jernigan, Stephen Joel Coons, and JoLaine R. Graugalis, "Medicare Beneficiaries' Management of Capped Prescription Benefits," *Medical Care,* March 2001, Vol. 39, No. 3.

[49] Michele Heisler, Kenneth M. Langa, Elizabeth L. Eby, A Mark Fendrick, Mohammed U. Kabeto, and John D. Piette, "The Health Effects of Restricting Prescription Medication Use Because of Cost," *Medical Care*, July 2004, Vol. 42, No. 7.

[50] Robyn Tamblyn, Rejean Laprise, James A. Hanely, Michael Abrahamowicz, Susan Scott, Nancy Mayo, Jerry Hurley, Roland, Grad, Eric Latimery, Roberty Perreault, Allen Huang, Pierre Larochell, and Louise Mallet, "Adverse Events Associated With Prescription Drug Cost sharing Among Poor and Elderly Persons," *Journal of the American Medical Association*, January 24/31, 2001, Vol. 285, No.4

[51] Stephen B. Soumerai, Dennis Ross-Degnan, Jerry Avorn, Thomas J. McLaughlin and Igor Choodnovskiy, "Effects of Medicaid Drug-Payment Limits On Admission To Hospitals And Nursing Homes," *The New England Journal Of Medicine*, October 10, 1991, Vol. 325, No. 15.

[52] Stephen B. Soumerai, Thomas J. McLaughlin, Dennis Ross-Degnan, Christina S. Casteris, and Paola Bollini, "Effects Of Limiting Medicaid Drug-Reimbursement Benefits On The Use Of Psychotropic Agents And Acute Mental Health Services By Patients With Schizophrenia," *The New England Journal Of Medicine*, September 8, 1994, Vol. 331, No. 10.

[53] Dennis Hastert, interview by author, tape recording, Washington, DC, October 21, 2010.

[54] Robert Pear and Robin Tower, "Despite High Hopes, Drug Plan May Be Disappointing to Elderly," *New York Times*, July 22, 2001, p.1.

[55] Robert Pear, "Drug Benefits Up to $2,500 Are in Plan For Medicare," *New York Times*, June 29, 1999, p.A17.

[56] Voter Consumer Research, "Senior Impressions of Medicare Part D," November 6, 2007, at http://www.medicaretoday.org/pdfs/2007Survey.pdf (June 25, 2011).

[57] Hoadley, et al., September 2010, Schneeweiss et al., February 3, 2009, and Ettner et al., June 2010.

[58] "HHS News Release: Nearly 4 million Medicare beneficiaries received help with prescription drug cost under Affordable Care Act," Q1Medicare.com, Medicare Part D Blog, March 22, 2011, at http://www.q1medicare.com/q1group/MedicareAdvantagePartD/Blog.php ?blog=HHS-News-Release:-Nearly-4-million-Medicare-beneficiaries-receive-help-with-prescription-drug-cost-under-Affordable-Care-Act&blog_id=158&category_id=9&start=0&arcyear=2014&arcmonth=m &curyear=2014&curmonth=3&curday=d (July 8, 2014).

[59] Centers for Medicare & Medicaid Services, "Press release: 7.9 million people with Medicare saved over $9.9 billion on prescription drugs," March 21, 2014.

[60] Alan Fram, "Big Pharma Wins Big With Health Care Reform Bill," The Huffington Post, March 29, 2011, http://www.huffingtonpost.com/2010/03/29/big-pharma-wins-big-with_n_516977.html (January 10, 2015).

Chapter 5: Too Small, Too Sick, Too Transient

[1] *Medicare Benefit Policy Manual*, Chapter 15—Covered Medicare Services and Other Health Services, November 11, 2011, p.168.

[2] United States General Accounting Office, 'Medicare: Rehabilitations Service Claims Paid Without Adequate Information," GAO/HRD-87-91, July 1987, p.2.

[3] Marc. B. Reitberg, Dina Brooks, Bernard M.J. Uitdenhaag, and Gert Kwakkel, "Exercise Therapy For Multiple Sclerosis," *Cochrane Database of Systematic Reviews*, January 1, 2005, Issue 1.

[4] Fary Khan, Bhasker Amatya, and Lynne Turner-Stokes, "Symptomatic Therapy and Rehabilitation in Primary Progressive Multiple Sclerosis," *Neurology Research International*, 2011, Vol. 2011, No. 740505, at http://www.hindawi.com/journals/nri/2011/740505/ (July 30, 2012).

[5] Nancy A. Baker, and Linda Tickle-Degnen, "The Effectiveness of Physician, Psychological, and Functional Interventions in Treating Clients With Multiple Sclerosis: A Meta-Analysis," *The American Journal of Occupational Therapy*, May/June 2001, Vol. 55, No. 3.

[6] Fary Khan, Lynne Turner-Stokes , Louisa Ng, Trevor Kilpatrick, and Bhasker Amatya, "Multidisciplinary Rehabilitation For adults With Multiple Sclerosis," *Journal of Neurology, Neurosurgery and Psychiatry*, 2008, Vol. 79, No. 114.

[7] Massimo Venturelli, Renato Scarsini, and Federic Schena, "Six-Month Walking Program Changes Cognitive and ADL Performance In Patients With Alzheimer," *American Journal of Alzheimer's Disease & Other Dementias*, August 2011, Vol. 26, No. 5.

[8] Gustavo Christofoletti, Merlyn Mercia Oliani, Sebastiao Gobbi, Florinda Stella, Lilian Teresa Bucken Gobbi, and Paulo Renato Canineu, "A Controlled Clinical Trial on the Effect of Motor Intervention on Balance and Cognition in Institutionalized Elderly Patients With Dementia," *Clinical Rehabilitation*, July 2008, Vol. 22, No. 7.

[9] Danielle N. Ripich and Jennifer Homer, "The Neurodegenerative Dementias: Diagnoses and Interventions," *The ASHA Leader*, April 27, 2004. See especially "Selected Essential References: Intervention," at http://www.asha.org/Publications/leader/2004/040427/f040427a.htm#3 (August 2, 2012).

[10] Medicare Benefit Policy Manual, Chapter 15, p. 168.

[11] United States General Accounting Office, "Subject: Outpatient Rehabilitation Therapy Caps Are Important Controls But Should Be Adjusted for Patient Need," October 8, 1999, GAO/HEHS-00-15R.

[12] United States Government Accounting Office, "Medicare: Tighter Rules Needed To Curtail Overcharges for Therapy in Nursing Homes," March 1995, GAO/HEHS-95-23, pp. 5-6.

[13] Ibid., p.10

[14] United States Government Accountability Office, "Medicare: Little Progress Made in Targeting Outpatient Therapy Payments to Beneficiaries' Needs," November 2005, GAO-06-59, p. 6.

[15] Ibid., p. 5

[16] Ibid., p. 15.

[17] Department of Health and Human Services, Center for Medicare & Medicaid Services, *CMS Manual System,* Pub. 100-04 Medicare Claims Processing, Transmittal 855, February 15, 2006.

[18] Department of Health and Humans Services, Center for Medicare and Medicaid Services, "Medicare Program; Revisions to Payment Policies Under the Physician Fee Schedule, DME Face to Face Encounters, Elimination of the Requirement for Termination of Non-Random Prepayment Complex Medical Review and Other Revisions to Part B for CY 2013; Hospital Outpatient Prospective and Ambulatory Surgical Center Payment Systems and Quality Reporting Programs; Electronic Reporting Pilot; Inpatient Rehabilitation Facilities Quality Reporting Program; Quality Improvement Organization Regulations; Proposed Rules," Federal Register, Monday, July 30, 2012, Vol. 77, No. 146, p.44764.

[19] *Medicare Claims Processing Manual*, Chapter 5—Part B Outpatient Rehabilitation and CORF/OPT Services, October 27, 2011, p. 10.

[20] Medicare Benefit Policy Manual, Chapter 15, p. 168.

[21] Medicare Claims Processing Manual, Chapter 5, p. 11.

[22] Ibid., p. 12.

[23] Gill Deford, Margaret Murphy, and Judith Stein, "How the 'IMPROVEMENT STANDARD' Improperly Denies Coverage to

Medicare Patients with Chronic Conditions," *Clearinghouse Review Journal of Poverty and Law and* Policy, January-February 2010, Vol. 43, Nos. 9-10, p. 423.

[24] Center for Medicare Advocacy, Inc., "Lawsuit Filed To Block Illegal Denials of Services To Medicare Patients With Chronic Illness: Center for Medicare Advocacy Lead Counsel in National Class-Action Suit," January 18, 2011, at

http://www.medicareadvocacy.org/Media/PressReleases/2011/11_01.18.I mprovementSuit.htm (August 1, 2012).

[25] Daniel E. Ciolek and Wenke Hwang, "Feasibility and Impact Analysis: Application of Various Outpatient Therapy Service Claim HCPCS Edits. *Final Report*," Centers for Medicare and Medicaid Services, November 15, 2004. See Appendices H, I and J.

[26] Daniel E. Ciolek and Wenke Hwang, "Short Term Alternatives for Therapy Services (STATS) Task Order: CY 2008 Outpatient Therapy Utilization Report," Centers for Medicare and Medicaid Services, June 4, 2010.

[27] Kaveh G. Shojania, Kathryn McDonals, Robert M. Wachter, Douglas K. Owens, *Closing the Quality Gap: A Critical Analysis of Quality Improvement Strategies. Volume 7—Care Coordination.* Perpared for the Agency for Healthcare Research and Quality, June 2007, AHRQ Publication No. 04(07)-0051-7, p.v.

[28] Christopher O. Phillips, Scott M. Wright, David E. Kern, Ramesh M. Singa, Sasha Shepperd, Haya R. Rubin, "Comprehensive Discharge Planning With Postdischarge Support for Older Patients With Congestive Heart Failure: A Meta-analysis," *Journal of the American Medical Association*, March 17, 2004, Vol. 291, No. 11.

[29] Kaveh G. Shojania, Sumant R. Ranji, Kathryn M. McDonald, Jeremy M. Grimshaw, Vandana Sundaram, Robert J. Rushakoff, and Douglas K. Owens, "Effects of Quality Improvement Strategies for Type 2 Diabetes on Glycemic Control: A Meta-Regression Analysis," *Journal of the American Medical Association*, July 26, 2006, Vol. 296, No. 4.

[30] Jody Hoffer Gittell, Kathleen M. Fairfield, Benjamin Bierbaum, William Head, Robert Jackson, Michael Kelly, Richard Laskin, Stephen Lipson, John Siliski, Thomas Thornhill and Joseph Zuckerman, "Impact of Relations Coordination on Quality of Care, Postoperative Pains and Functioning, and Length of Stay: A Nine-Hospital Study of Surgical Patients," *Medical Care*, 2000, Vol. 38, No. 8.; and Dana Beth Weinberg, Jody Hoffer Gittell, R. William Lusenhop, Cori M. Kautz, and John Wright, "Beyond Our Walls: Impact of Patient and Provider Coordination across the Continuum on Outcomes for Surgical Patients," *Health Services Research*, February 2007, Vol. 42, No. 1.

[31] Eric A. Coleman, Carla Parry, Sandra Chalmers, and Sung-joon Min, "The Care Transitions Intervention: Results of a Randomized Controlled Trial," *Archives of Internal Medicine*, September 25, 2006, Vol. 166, No. 17.

[32] Tracey E. Barnett, Neale R. Chumbler, W. Bruce Vogel, Rebecca J. Beyth, Haijin Qin, and Rita Kobb, "The Effectiveness of a Care Coordination Home Telehealth Program for Veterans With Diabetes Mellitus: A 2-Year Follow-up," *The American Journal of Managed Care*, Vol. 12, No. 8.

[33] Takahiro Higashi, Paul G. Shekelle, David H. Solomon, Eric L. Knight, Carol Roth, John T. Chang, Caren J. Kamberg, Catherine H. MacLean, Roy T. Young, John Adams, David B. Reuben, Jerry Avorn, and Neil S. Wenger, "The Quality of Pharmacologic Care for Vulnerable Older Patients," *Annals of Internal Medicine*, 2004, Vol. 140, No. 9.

[34] Craig C. Earle and Bridget A. Neville, "Under Use of Necessary Care among Cancer Survivors," *Cancer*, October 15, 2004 Vol. 101, No. 8, p. 1718.

[35] Gregg C. Fonarow, Eric E. Smith, Mathew J. Reeves, Wenqin Pan, DaiWai Olson, Adrian F. Hernandez, Eric D. Peterson, Lee H. Schwamm, "Hospital-Level Variation in Mortality and Rehospitalization for Medicare Beneficiaries With Acute Ischemic Stroke," *Stroke,* January 2011, Vol. 42. No. 1.

36 Dawn M. Bravata, Shih-Yieh Ho, Thomas P. Meehan, Lawrence M. Brass, and John Concato, "Readmission and Death After Hospitalization for Acute Ischemic Stroke: 5-Year Follow-Up in the Medicare Population," *Stroke*, May 17, 2007, at http://stroke.ahajournals.org/content/38/6/1899.full.pdf+html (July 7, 2011).

37 Gerard F. Anderson and Earl P. Steinberg, "Hospital Readmission in the Medicare Population," *New England Journal of Medicine*, November 22, 1984, Vol. 311, No. 21.

38 Stephen F. Jencks, Mark V. Williams, and Eric A. Coleman, "Rehospitalizations among Patients in the Medicare Fee-for-Service Program," *New England Journal of Medicine*, April 2, 2009, Vol. 360, No. 4, p. 1418.

39 Gerard Anderson and James R. Knickman, "Changing The Chronic Care System To Meet People's Needs," *Health Affairs*, November/December 2001, Vol. 20, No. 6, p. 147.

40 Center for Medicare & Medicaid Services, "CPT/HCPCS Codes included in Range 99210 – 99205," at http://www.cms.gov/medicare-coverage-database/staticpages/cpt-hcpcs-code-range.aspx?DocType=LCD&DocID=32007&ver=2&Group=1&RangeStart=99201&RangeEnd=99205 (July 17, 2012).

41 Gerard Anderson, "The Benefits of Care Coordination: A Comparison of Medicare Fee-for-Service and Medicare Advantage," *Report Prepared for the Alliance of Community Health Plans*, September 2009.

42 Ibid, p. 2.

43 Congressional Budget Office "Lesson's from Medicare's Demonstration Projects on Disease Management, Care Coordination, and Value-Based Payment," *Issue Brief*, January 2012.

44 Center for Medicare Advocacy, Inc. "Lawsuit Challenges Rigid Interpretation of 'Inpatient' For a Hospital Qualifying Stay," December 16, 2004, at http://www.medicareadvocacy.org/News/WeeklyAlerts/AlertPDFs/2004/CMA_Weekly_Alert_12.16.04.Landers.pdf (August 1, 2014). ; Inside CMS,

"Beneficiaries File Suit Over CMS' Three-Day Hospital Policy For SNF Care," Vol. 7, No. 27. December 30, 2004.

[45] *Estate of Landers v. Leavitt*, United State Court of Appeals for the Second Circuit, October 1, 2008.

[46] Lan Zhao, Claudia Schur, Niranjana Kowlessar, and Keith D. Lind, "Rapid Growth in Medicare Hospital Observation Services: What's Going On?", Research Report, AARP Public Policy Institute, September 2013.

[47] Zhanlian Feng, Brad Wright, and Vincent Mor, "Sharp Rise In Medicare Enrollees Being Held In Hospitals For Observation Raises Concerns About Causes And Consequences," *Health Affairs,* Vol. 31, No. 6, June 2012.

[48] Office of Inspector General, "Hospitals' Use of Observation Stays and Short Inpatient Stays for Medicare Beneficiaries," U.S. Dep.t of Health and Human Services, Report OEI-02-12-00040, July 29, 2013.

[49] Paul Span, "In the Hosptial, but Not Really a Patient, The New Old Age Blog, *New York* Times, June 22, 2012, at http://newoldage.blogs.nytimes.com/2012/06/22/in-the-hospital-but-not-really-a-patient/ (August 2, 10214).

[50] Christopher W. Baugh, Arjun K. Venkatesh, and J. Stephen Bohan, "Emergency Department Observation Units: A Clinical and Financial Benefit for Hospitals," *Health Care Management Review*, Vol. 36, No. 1, January-March 2011; and Michael F. McDermott, Declan G. Murphy, Robert J. Zalenski, Robert J. Rydman, Madelin McCarren, Dova Marder, Borko Jovanovic, Kam Kaur, Rebecca R. Roberts, Mark Isola, Edward Mensah, R. Rajendra, L. Kampe, "A Comparison Between Emergency Diagnostic and Treatment Unit Inpatient Care in the Management of Acute Asthma," *Archives of Internal Medicine*, Vol. 157, No. 18, October 13, 1997.

[51] Centers For Medicare and Medicaid Services, "Listening Session: Hospital Observation Beds," August 24, 2010, p.2, at https://www.cms.gov/Medicare/Medicare-Fee-for-Service-Payment/HospitalOutpatientPPS/downloads/94244031HosptialObservationBedsListeningSession082410.pdf (August 2, 2014).

[52] Federal Register, "Medicare Program; Hospital Inpatient Prospective Payment Systems for Acute Care Hospitals and the Long Term Care; Hospital Prospective Payment System and Fiscal Year 2014 Rates; Quality Reporting Requirements for Specific Providers; Hospital Conditions of Participation; Payment Policies Related to Patient Status; Final Rule," Department of Health and Human Services, Vol. 78, No. 160, August 19, 2013, p.50506.

[53] Jeffrey Lord, "ObamaCare Takes A Life," The American Spectator, April 1, 2014, at http://spectator.org/articles/58588/obamacare-takes-life (August 2, 2014).

[54] Ibid.

[55] Ibid.

[56] Centers for Disease Control and Prevention, "Leading Causes of Death," *FastStats*, at http://www.cdc.gov/nchs/fastats/lcod.htm/ (July 17, 2012).

[57] Andrew Owen, "Life Expectancy of elderly and very elderly patients with chronic heart failure," *American Heart Journal*, June 2006, Vol. 151, No. 6.; and Bao C. Huynh, Aleksandr Rovner, and Michael W. Rich, "Long-term survival in elderly patients hospitalized for heart failure: 14-year follow-up from a prospective randomized trial," *Archives of Internal Medicine*, September 25, 2006, Vol. 166, No. 17.

[58] Robert Pear, "Settlement Eases Rules for Some Medicare Patients," *New York Times*, October 22, 2012, at http://www.nytimes.com/2012/10/23/us/politics/settlement-eases-rules-for-some-medicare-patients.html (May 22, 2013).

Chapter 6: What Is "Waste"?

[1] Peter Cram, Mark Fendrick, John Inadomi, Mark E. Cowen, Daniel Carpenter and Sandeep Vijan, "The Impact of a Celebrity Promotion Campaign on the Use of Colon Cancer Screening: The Katie Couric Effect," *Archives of Internal Medicine*, July 14, 2003, Vol. 163, No. 13.

[2] Cary P. Gross, Martin S. Andersen, Harlan M. Krumholz, Gail J. McAvay, Deborah Proctor and Mary E. Tinetti, "Relation Between Medicare Screening Reimbursement and Stage at Diagnosis for Older Patients With Colon Cancer," *Journal of the American Medical Association*, December 20, 2006, Vol. 296, No. 23.

[3] "Medicare Leading Part B Procedure Codes Based on Allowed Charges Calendar Year 2000," Centers for Medicare and Medicaid Services, Data Compendium, 2002 Edition, Part V. Utilization, http://www.cms.gov/Research-Statistics-Data-and-Systems/Statistics-Trends-and-Reports/DataCompendium/20_2002_Data_Compendium.html (January 29, 2013).

[4] "Medicare Leading Part B Procedure Codes Based on Allowed Charges Calendar Year 2002," Centers for Medicare and Medicaid Services, Data Compendium, 2002 Edition, Part V. Utilization, http://www.cms.gov/Research-Statistics-Data-and-Systems/Statistics-Trends-and-Reports/DataCompendium/19_2003DataCompendium.html (January 29, 2013).

[5] "Table V.6a: Medicare Leading Part B Procedure Codes Ranked by Allowed Charges Calendar Year 2009," Centers for Medicare and Medicaid Services, Data Compendium, 2010 Edition, Part V. Utilization, at http://www.cms.gov/Research-Statistics-Data-and-Systems/Statistics-Trends-and-Reports/DataCompendium/14_2010_Data_Compendium.html, (January 29, 2013).

[6] Gross, et al., 2006, p.2819.

[7] "Deaths Final Data for 2000," Centers for Disease Control, *National Vital Statistics Reports*, September 16, 2002, Vol. 50, No. 15, p. 32; and "Deaths: Final Data for 2009," Centers for Disease Control, *National Vital Statistics Reports*, December 29, 2011, Vol. 60, No. 3, p. 36.

[8] James S. Goodwin, Amanpal Sing Nischita Reddy, Taylor S. Riall and Yong-Fang Kuo, "Overuse of Screening Colonoscopy in the Medicare Population," *Archives of Internal Medicine*, August 8, 2011, Vol. 171, No. 15.

[9] Pignone, et al., 2002.

298

[10] Alfred I. Neuget and Kenneth A. Forde, "Screening Colonoscopy: Has The Time Come?" *The American Journal of Gastroenterology*, March 1988, Vol. 83, No. 3.

[11] Gregory Warner, "Should the colonoscopy be the 'gold standard'?" *National Public Radio*, August 18, 2010, at http://www.marketplace.org/topics/life/health-reform/should-colonoscopy-be-gold-standard, (May 10, 2013).

[12] Alfred I. Neuget and Kenneth A. Forde, "Colonoscopy vs Sigmoidoscopy; Getting It Right," *Journal of the American Medical Association*, July 28, 2010, Vol. 304, No. 4, p.461.

[13] John E. Wennberg and Alan Gittelsohn, "Health Care Delivery in Maine I: Patterns of Use of Common Surgical Procedures," *The Journal of the Maine Medical Association*, May 1975, Vol. 66, No. 5; and John E. Wennberg and Alan Gittelsohn, *The Journal of the Maine Medical Association*, "Health Care Delivery in Maine II: Conditions Explaining Hospital Admission," October 1975, Vol. 66, No. 10

[14] John E. Wennberg, *Tracking Medicine: A Researcher's Quest To Understand Health Care*, Oxford: Oxford University Press, 2010, p.25.

[15] For more on HRRs see Wennberg, *Tracking Medicine*, 2010, pp. 271-272.

[16] Elliott S. Fisher, David E. Wennberg, Thérése A. Stukel, Daniel J. Gottlieb, F. L. Lucas and Étoile L. Pinder, "The Implications of Regional Variations in Medicare Spending. Part 1: The Content, Quality, and Accessibility of Care," *Annals of Internal Medicine*, February 18, 2003a, Vol. 138, No. 4.

[17] John E. Wennberg, Elliot S. Fisher, Thérése A. Stukel, Jonathan S. Skinner, Sandra M. Sharp and Kristen K. Bronner, "Use of hospitals, physician visits, and hospice care during the last six months of life among cohorts loyal to highly respected hospitals in the United States," *British Medical Journal*, March 13, 2004, Vol. 328, No. Issue 7440.

[18] Elliott S. Fisher, David E. Wennberg, Thérése A. Stukel, Daniel J. Gottlieb, F. L. Lucas and Étoile L. Pinder, "Use Of Medicare Claims Data

To Monitor Provider-Specific Performance Among Patients With Severe Chronic Illness," *Health Affairs*, Web Exclusive, October 7, 2004.

[19] Elliott S. Fisher, David E. Wennberg, Thérése A. Stukel, Daniel J. Gottlieb, F. L. Lucas and Étoile L. Pinder, "The Implications of Regional Variations in Medicare Spending. Part 2: Health Outcomes and Satisfaction with Care," *Annals of Internal Medicine*, February 18, 2003b, Vol. 138, No. 4.

[20] Jonathan S. Skinner, Douglas O. Staiger and Elliott S. Fisher, "Is Technological Change In Medicine Always Worth It? The Case Of Acute Myocardial Infarction," *Health Affairs*, March 2006, Vol. 25, No. 2.

[21] Katherine Baicker and Amitabh Chandra, "Medicare Spending, The Physician Workforce, And Beneficiaries' Quality Of Care," *Health Affairs*, Web Exclusive, April 7, 2004.

[22] Elliott S. Fisher and H. Gilbert Welch, "Avoiding the Unintended Consequences of Growth in Medical Care," *Journal of the American Medical Association*, February 3, 1999, Vol. 281., No. 5.

[23] Skinner, et al., 2001, p. ii.

[24] Fisher, et al., 2003a.

[25] Ibid., p. W97.

[26] Fisher, et al., 2003a; and Fisher, et al. 2003b.

[27] Peter R. Orszag, "Increasing the Value of Federal Spending on Health Care," Statement before the Committee on the Budget of the U.S. House of Representative, Congressional Budget Office, July 16, 2008, p.4.

[28] Fisher, *Tracking Medicine*, 2010, p.159.

[29] Elliot S. Fisher, Mark B. McClellan, John Bertko, Steven M. Lieberman, Julie J. Lee, Julie L. Lewis and Jonathan S. Skinner, "Fostering Accountable Health Care: Moving Forward In Medicare," *Health Affairs*, January 27, 2009, Web Exclusive, p. W220 and w230.

[30] For pro-ACO views see Anna Wilde Mathews, "Can Accountable-Care Organizations Improve Health Care While Reducing Costs?" *Wall Street Journal*, January 23, 2012, at http://online.wsj.com/article/SB10001424052970204720204577712890171 4576054.html (February 7, 2012); and Niyum Gandhi and Richard Weil,

"The ACO Surprise," Oliver Wyman, 2012, at
http://www.oliverwyman.com/the-aco-surprise.htm#.UZfBR0SMByh
(May 11, 2013). For those who are skeptical see Lawton R. Burns and
Mark V. Pauly, "Accountable Care Organizations May Have Difficulty
Avoiding The Failures Of Integrated Delivery Networks Of The 1990s,"
Health Affairs, November 2012, Vol. 31, No. 11; and Scott Gottlieb,
"Accountable Care Organizations: The End of Innovation in Medicine?"
Health Policy Outlook, American Enterprise Institute, February, 2011, No.
3.
[31] Robert Kocher, Ezekiel J. Emanuel and Nancy-Ann M. DeParle, "The
Affordable Care Act and the Future of Clinical Medicine: The
Opportunities and Challenges," *Annals of Internal Medicine*, October 19,
2010, Vol. 153, No. 8, p. 538.
[32] Mathews, 2012.
[33] U.S. Department of Health & Human Services, "Medicare's delivery
system reform initiatives achieve significant savings and quality
improvements—off to a strong start," January 30, 2014, at
http://www.hhs.gov/news/press/2014pres/01/20140130a.html (August 21,
2014).
[34] David Hogberg, "ObamaCare's ACOs Saving Medicare A Pittance,"
Amy Ridenour's National Center Blog, September 22, 2014, at
http://www.conservativeblog.org/amyridenour/2014/9/22/obamacares-
acos-saving-medicare-a-pittance.html (February 11, 2015).
[35] Mark McLellan, S. Lawrence Kocot and Ross White, "Early Evidence
On Medicare ACOs And Next Steps For The Medicare ACO Program
(Updated)," Health Affairs Blog, January 22, 2015, at
http://healthaffairs.org/blog/2015/01/22/early-evidence-on-medicare-acos-
and-next-steps-for-the-medicare-aco-program/ (February 11, 2015).
[36] Lawrence P. Casalino, MichaelF. Pesko, Andrew M. Ryan, Jayme L.
Mendelsohn, Kennon R. Copeland, Patricia Pamela Ramsay, Xuming Sun,
Diane R. Rittenhouse and Stephen M. Shortell, "Small Primary Care
Physician Practices Have Low Rates of Preventable Hospital Admissions,"
Health Affairs, September 2014, Vol. 33, No. 9.

[37] Wennberg, *Tracking Medicine*, 2010, pp.268-269.

[38] Ibid., p.269.

[39] Peter Orszag, "To Save Money, Save the Health Care Act," *The New York Times*, November 3, 2010, at http://www.nytimes.com/2010/11/04/opinion/04orszag.html (April 9, 2011).

[40] Peter Orszag, "Too Much of a Good Thing," *The New Republic*, September 14, 2011, at http://www.newrepublic.com/article/politics/magazine/94940/peter-orszag-democracy# (December 4, 2011).

[41] 42 U.S.C. § 1395kkk (g)(2)(C).

[42] Ibid., (h)(1) and (2).

[43] Ibid., (c)(5).

[44] Ibid., (c)(2)(A)(ii) and (iii).

[45] Ibid., (f).

[46] Diane Cohen and Michael F. Cannon, "The Independent Payment Advisory Board PPACA's Anti-Constitutional and Authoritarian Super-Legislature," Cato Institute, *Policy Analysis*, June 14, 2012, No. 700.

[47] Selina McKee, "NICE says 'no' again to Roche's Avastin for ovarian cancer," *Pharma Times*, March 26, 2013, at http://www.pharmatimes.com/article/13-03-26/NICE_says_no_again_to_Roche_s_Avastin_for_ovarian_cancer.aspx (May 5, 2013); and Rebecca Smith, "Bowel cancer drug Avastin turned down by Nice," August 20, 2010, at http://www.telegraph.co.uk/health/healthnews/7959762/Bowel-cancer-drug-Avastin-turned-down-by-Nice.html (May 5, 2013).

[48] Sarah Boseley, "Drug company attacks Nice for rejecting new lupus treatment," *The Guardian*, April 26, 2012, at http://www.guardian.co.uk/business/2012/apr/27/drug-company-nice-lupus-reject (May 5, 2013); "Liver cancer drug not recommended for the NHS," National Institute for Health and Care Excellence," May 25, 2010, at http://www.nice.org.uk/proxy/?sourceUrl=http%3a%2f%2fwww.nice.org.

uk%2fmedia%2fD00%2fF8%2f2010058SorafenibForAdvancedHCCFinal Guidance.pdf (September 29, 2014); "Two breast cancer drugs not cost effective, says final NICE guidance," National Institute for Health and Care Excellence, June 26, 2012 at https://www.nice.org.uk/News/Press-and-Media/two-breast-cancer-drugs-not-cost-effective-says-final-nice-guidance (September 29, 2014); and Kate Kelland, "NICE rejects Novartis kidney cancer drugs," *Reuters*, July 2, 2010, at http://uk.reuters.com/assets/print?aid=UKTRE6605NN20100701 (May 5, 2013).

[49] "Exceptional Progress? Assessing the progress made in improving access to treatment for people with rarer cancers," Rare Cancers Forum, March 2010.

[50] Jenny Hope, "Ex-MP in drug fight to save her sight," *The Daily Mail*, January 29, 2007, at http://www.dailymail.co.uk/news/article-432334/Ex-MP-drug-fight-save-sight.html (May 5, 2013).

[51] "Former MP advised to give up Lucentis fight," *Optician*, March 16, 2007, at http://www.opticianonline.net/Articles/2007/03/16/18028/Former+MP+advised+to+give+up+Lucentis+fight.htm (May 5, 2013).

[52] Vivian Y. Wu and Yu-Chu Shen, "The Long-Term Impact of Medicare Payment Reductions On Patient Outcomes," NBER Working Paper Series, Working Paper 16859, March 2011.

[53] Melissa Attias, "Medicare Boars Still a Long Way Off," *CQ Weekly*, October 6, 2012.

[54] Gina Kolata, "Patients In Florida Lining Up For All That Medicare Covers," *The New York Times*, September 13, 2003, at http://www.nytimes.com/2003/09/13/us/patients-in-florida-lining-up-for-all-that-medicare-covers.html (June 7, 2011).

[55] Gina Kolata, "Law May Do Little to Help Curb Unnecessary Care," *The New York Times*, March 29, 2010, at http://www.nytimes.com/2010/03/30/health/30use.html (June 7, 2011).

[56] Richard A. Cooper, "States With More Health Care Spending Have Better Quality Health Care: Lessons About Medicare," *Health Affairs*,

January/February 2009, Vol. 28, No. 1; also see Richard A. Cooper "States With More Physicians Have Better-Quality Health Care," *Health Affairs,* January/February 2009, Vol. 28, No. 1.

[57] Katherine Baicker and Amitabh Chandra, "Cooper's Analysis Is Incorrect," *Health Affairs,* January/February 2009, Vol. 28, No. 1.

[58] Louise Sheiner, "Why The Geographic Variation in Health Care Spending Can't Tell Us Much About the Efficiency or Quality of our Health Care System," Federal Reserve Board of Governors, December 20, 2012, at

http://www.federalreserve.gov/pubs/feds/2013/201304/201304pap.pdf (March 15, 2013).

[59] Jeffery H. Silber, Robert Kaestner, Orit Even-Shoshan, Yanli Wang and Laura J. Bressler, "Aggressive Treatment Style and Surgical Outcomes," *Health Services Research,* December 2010, Volume 45, No. 6.2.

[60] Micahel K. Ong, Carol M. Mangione, Patrick S. Romanao, Qiong Zhou, Andrew D. Auerbach, Alein Chun, Bruce Davidson, Theodore G. Ganiats, Sheldon Greenfield, Michael A. Gropper, Shaista Malik, J. Thomas Rosenthal and José J. Escarce, "Looking Forward, Looking Back: Assessing Variations in Hospital Resource Use and Outcomes for Elderly Patients With Heart Failure," *Circulation: Cardiovascular Quality and Outcomes,* November 2009, Vol. 2, No. 6.

[61] Amber E. Barnato, Chung-Chou H. Chang, Max H. Farrell, Judith R. Lave, Mark S. Roberts and Derek C. Angus, "Is Survival Better at Hospitals With Higher 'End-of-Life' Treatment Intensity," *Medical Care,* February 2010, Vol. 48, No. 2.

[62] Stephen Zuckerman, Timothy Waidmann, Robert Berenson and Jack Hadley, "Clarifying Source of Geographic Differences in Medicare Spending," *The New England Journal of Medicine,* July 1, 2010, Vol. 363, No. 1.

[63] Robert Kaestner and Jeffrey H. Silber, "Evidence of the Efficacy of Inpatient Spending on Medicare Patients," *The Milibank Quarterly,* December 2010, Vol. 88, No. 4, p. 581.

[64] Interview with author, December 17, 2012.

[65] David C. Goodman, Amos R. Esty, Elliot S. Fisher and Chiange-Hua Chang, "Trends and Variation in End-of-Life Care for Medicare Beneficiaries with Severe Chronic Illness," *A Report of the Dartmouth Atlas Project*, The Dartmouth Institute foe Health Policy and Clinical Practice, April 12, 2011, p8.

[66] Fisher, et al., 2003a, p. 273

[67] Interview with author, December 17, 2012.

[68] James D. Reschovsky, Jack Hadley, Cynthia B. Saiontz-Martinez and Ellyn R. Boukus, "Following the Money: Factors Associated with the Cost of Treating High-Cost Medicare Beneficiaries," *Health Services Research*, August 2011, Vol. 46, No. 4, p. 1001.

[69] Brownlee, *Overtreated*, 2007, p. 5.

[70] "Part B Spending Per Decedent, By Interval Before Death and Type of Service," SSM DePaul Health Center, 2001-2005, The Dartmouth Atlas of Health Care, at http://www.dartmouthatlas.org/data/table.aspx?ind=13&tf=1&ch=1,4&loc=7160&loct=5&addn=ind-19_ch-5_tf-1&fmt=25 (May 2, 2013).

Chapter 7: The Next Exodus

[1] David Olmos, "Mayo Clinic in Arizona to Stop Treating Some Medicare Patients," *Bloomberg*, December 31, 2009, at http://www.bloomberg.com/apps/news?pid=newsarchive&sid=aHoYSI84VdL0 (Jan. 7, 2011).

[2] Todd Ackerman, "Texas Doctors Fleeing Medicare In Droves," *Houston Chronicle*, May 18, 2010, at http://www.chron.com/news/houston-texas/article/Texas-doctors-fleeing-Medicare-in-droves-1718866.php (Feb. 4, 2011).

[3] "Survey of Texas Physicians: Preliminary Research Findings," Texas Medical Association, March 2010.

[4] Ellyn Boukus, Alwyn Cassil, and Ann S. O'Malley, "A Snapshot of U.S. Physicians: Health Tracking From the 2008 Health Tracking Physician

Survey," Center for Studying Health System Change, Data Bulletin, No. 35, September 2009, p.7.

[5] Sandra L. Decker, "In 2011 Nearly One-Third of Physicians Said They Would Not Accept New Medicaid Patients, But Rising Fees May Help," *Health Affairs*, August 2012, Vol. 31, No. 8; and "A Survey Of America's Physicians: Practice Patterns And Perspectives," The Physicians' Foundation, September 2012.

[6] "The Physicians' Perspective: Medical Practice in 2008," The Physicians' Foundation, Survey Summary and Analysis, October 2008.

[7] "The Impact of Medicare Physician Payment on Seniors Access' to Care," American Medical Association, AMA Online Survey of Physicians, May 2010.

[8] Data downloaded from "HSCdataOnline – Physician Survey," at http://hscdataonline.s-3.com/psurvey_r5.asp (March 10, 2012).

[9] "The Impact of Medicare Physician Payment on Seniors Access' to Care," May 2010.

[10] Boukus, et al., p.7.

[11] "Medicare SGR Survey," Texas Medical Association, August 2011, p.3.

[12] "Opt-Out – Physician – standard Physicians Contract," Association of American Physicians and Surgeons, at http://www.aapsonline.org/sampleforms/optout02.pdf (March 14, 2012).

[13] "Opt-Out – Patient – standard Patient Contract," Association of American Physicians and Surgeons, at http://www.aapsonline.org/sampleforms/optout03.pdf (March 14, 2012).

[14] Miriam J. Laugesen, Roy Wada, and Eric M. Chen, "In Setting Doctor's Medicare Fees, CMS Almost Always Accepts The Relative Value Update Panel's Advice On Work Values," *Health Affairs*, May 2012, Vol. 31, No. 5; and Joe Eaton, "Little-Known AMA Group Has Big Influence On Medicare Payments," Center for Public Integrity, October 27, 2010, at http://www.kaiserhealthnews.org/Stories/2010/October/27/AMA-center-public-integrity.aspx (August 4, 2011).

[15] Eaton, October 27, 2010.

[16] Ibid.

[17] Anna Wilde Mathews, "Dividing the Medicare Pie Pits Doctor Against Doctor," *The Wall Street Journal*, April 7, 2011, at http://online.wsj.com/article/SB10001424052702303341904575576480649488148.html (April 19, 2012); also see Anna Wilde Mathews and Tom McGinty, "Physician Panel Prescribes the Fees Paid by Medicare," *The Wall Street Journal*, October 26, 2010, at http://online.wsj.com/article/SB100014240527487046573045755404401737721102.html (April 19, 2012).

[18]"Physicians Fee Schedule Search," Center for Medicare & Medicaid Services, at https://www.cms.gov/apps/physician-fee-schedule/overview.aspx (September 10, 2014).

[19] Eaton, October 27, 2011.

[20] Federal Register, "Part II, Department of Health and Human Services," Friday, December 8, 1995, pp. 63162-63164; Federal Register, "Part, III Department of Health and Human Services," Friday, October 31, 1997, pp. 59085-59088; Federal Register, "Part II, Department of Health and Human Services," Monday, November 2, 1998, pp. 58889-58890; Federal Register, "Part III, Department of Health and Human Services," Tuesday, November 2, 1999, pp. 63162-63164; Federal Register, "Part II, Department of Health and Human Services," Wednesday, November 1, 2000, pp. 65421-65423; Federal Register, "Part II, Department of Health and Human Services," Tuesday, December 31, 2002, pp. 80002-80005; Federal Register, "Part II, Department of Health and Human Services," Friday, November 7, 2003, pp. 63233-63235; Federal Register, "Part III, Department of Health and Human Services," Monday, November 15, 2004, pp. 66365-66368; Federal Register, "Part II, Department of Health and Human Services," Monday, November 21, 2005, pp. 70277-70280; Federal Register, "Part II, Department of Health and Human Services," Tuesday, November 27, 2007, pp. 66365-656368; Federal Register, "Part II, Department of Health and Human Services," Wednesday, November 19, 2009, pp. 69883-69890; and Federal Register, "Part II, Department of Health and Human Services," Wednesday, November 25, 2009, pp. 61950-

61953; Federal Register, "Part II, Department of Health and Human Services," Monday, November 29, 2010, pp. 73342-73349.

[21] Medicare Program; Revisions to Payment Policies and Five-Year Review of and Adjustments to the Relative Value Units Under the Physician Fee Schedule for Calendar Year 1997, Final Rule, Federal Register, November 22, 1996, p. 59721.

[22] Medicare Program; Revisions to Payment Policies, Five-Year Review of Work Relative Value Units, Changes to the Practice Expense Methodology Under the Physician Fee Schedule, and Other Changes to Payment Under Part B; Revisions to the Payment Policies of Ambulance Services Under the Fee Schedule for Ambulance Services; and Ambulance Inflation Factor Update for CY 2007, Final Rule, Federal Register, December 1, 2006, pp.69735-69736

[23] Roy Poses, "Conflicts of Interest Among The RUC's Members," *Care and Cost*, April 28, 2011, at http://careandcost.com/2011/04/28/conflicts-of-interests-among-the-rucs-members/ (April 19 2012).

[24] Jerry Cromwell, Nancy McCall, Kathleen Dalton and Peter Brau, "Missing Productivity Gains in the Medicare Physician Fee Schedule: Where Are They?" *Medical Care Research and Review*, November 2010, Vol. 67, No. 6.

[25] "Report to Congress: Medicare Payment Policy," Medicare Payment Advisory Commission, MedPAC, March 2006, p. 142; "Medicare Program; Five-Year Review of Work Relative Value Units Under the Physician Fee Schedule and Proposed Changes to the Practice Ex0pense Methodology, Proposed Notice," Federal Register, June 29, 2006, pp. 37174-37188; and "Medicare Program; Five-Year Review of Work Relative Value Units Under the Physician Fee Schedule, Proposed Notice" Federal Register, June 6, 2011, pp. 32423-32427.

[26] Brian Keppler and David C. Kibbe, "Quit The RUC," *Kaiser Health News*, January 20, 2011, at http://www.kaiserhealthnews.org/Columns/2011/January/012111kepplerkibbe.aspx (April 19, 2012).

[27] Brian Klepper, Paul Fischer and Kathleen Anne Behan, "Stifling Primary Care: Why Does CMS Continue To Support The RUC?" *Health Affairs Blog*, May 24, 2011, http://healthaffairs.org/blog/2011/05/24/stifling-primary care-why-does-cms-continue-to-support-the-ruc/ (April 19, 2012).

[28] "AAFP Opts to Remain in the RUC: Academy Vows to Advocate Change, Frequently Reassess Involvement," AAFP News Now, American Association of Family Physicians, March 13, 2012, at http://www.aafp.org/online/en/home/publications/news/news-now/inside-aafp/20120313rucdecision.html (April 19, 2012).

[29] "Plumber with shattered arm left horrifically bent out of shape has operation 'cancelled four times'," *The Daily Mail*, Octber 8, 2009, at http://www.dailymail.co.uk/news/article-1218927/Plumber-shattered-arm-left-horrifically-bent-shape-operation-cancelled-times.html (May 10, 2010).

[30] Lawrence P. Casalino, Sean Nicholson, David N. Gans, Terry Hammons, Dante Morra, Theodore Karrison and Wendy Levinson, "What Does It Costs Physician Practices To Interact With Health Insurance Plans?" *Health Affairs,* July/August 2009, Vol. 28, No. 4.

[31] "ICD-10 Cost Estimates Increases for Most Physicians," American Medical Association, February 12, 2014, at http://www.ama-assn.org/ama/pub/news/news/2014/2014-02-12-icd10-cost-estimates-increased-for-most-physicians.page (September 10, 2014).

[32] "ICD10Data.com," at http://www.icd10data.com/ (February 13, 2015).

[33] Ibid.

[34] Martin Libicki and Irene Brahmamulam, "The Costs and Benefits of Moving to the ICD-10 Code Sets," Technical Report, RAND Corporation, March 2004.

[35] "The Impact of Medicare Physician Payment on Seniors Access' to Care," May 2010.

[36] "Medicare SGR Survey," August 2011.

[37] Donald K. Cherry, Catharine W. Burt, and David A. Woodwell, "National Ambulatory Medical Care Survey: 2001 Summary," Centers For

Disease Control, Advanced Data From Vital and Health Statistics, No. 337, August 11, 2003.

[38] Sandra L. Decker, "In 2011 Nearly One-Third Of Physicians Said They Would Not Accept New Medicaid Patients, But Rising Fees May Help," *Health Affairs*, August 2012, Vol. 31, No. 8.

[39] Gail Wilensky, "Reforming Medicare's Physician Payment System," *The New England Journal of Medicine*, February 12, 2009, Vol. 360, No. 7, p.654.

[40] Robert Pear, "Medicare to Cut Payment To Doctors 4.4% Next Year," *The New York Times*, December 21, 2002 Section A, p. 14.

[41] Aparna Narayanan, "Medicare, Medicaid funding problems," *Asbury Park Press*, March 20, 2003, Section 18, p.18.

[42] "Physicians Fee Schedule Search."

[43] "Medicare SGR Survey," August 2011.

[44] "The Impact of Medicare Physician Payment on Seniors Access' to Care," May 2010

[45] Douglas Iliff, "Does Primary Care Need Medicare'" *Family Practice Magazine,* January 2008, Vol. 15, No. 1, at http://www.aafp.org/fpm/2008/0100/p7.html (March 2, 2012).

[46] Barbara Starfield, Klaus W. Lemke, Terence Bernhardt, Steven S. Foldes, Christopher B. Forrest, and Jonathan P. Weiner, "Comorbidity: Implications for the Importance of Primary Care in 'Case' Management," *Annals of Family Medicine*, May/June 2003, Vol. 1, No. 1; and Thomas Bodenheimer, Edward H. Wagner, and Kevin Grumbach, "Improving Primary Care For Patients With Chronic Illness," *Journal of the American Medical Association*, October 9, 2002, Vol. 288, No. 14.

[47] Barbara Starfield, Leiyu Shi, and James Macinko, "Contributions of Primary Care to Health Systems and Health," *The Milbank Quarterly*, 2005, Vol. 83, No. 3; and Kevin Grubach and Thomas Bodenheimer, "A Primary Care Home for Americans: Putting the House in Order," *Journal of the American Medical Association*, August 21, 2002, Vol. 288, No. 7.

Chapter 8: How to Not Be Rewarded for Making Patients Healthier

[1] Michael F. Cannon, "Pay-for-Performance: Is Medicare A Good Candidate?" *Yale Journal of Health Policy, Law, and Ethics*, 2007, Vol. 2, No. 1, p.4.

[2] William C. Hsiao, Peter Braun, Douwe Yntema and Edmund R. Becker, "Estimating Physicians' Work For A Resource-Based Relative-Value Scale," *The New England Journal of Medicine*, September 29, 1988, Vol. 319, No. 13, pp. 836-837.

[3] William C. Hsiao, Peter Braun, Edmund R. Becker and Stephen R. Thomas, "The Resource-Based Relative Value Scale: Toward the Development of an Alternative Physician Payment System," Journal of the American Medical Association, August 14, 1987, Vol. 258, No. 6, p.799.

[4] Hsiao, Braun, Yntema and Becker, 1988, p.835.

[5] William C. Hsiao and Daniel L. Dunn, "The Resource-based Relative Value Scale for Pricing Physicians' Services," in *Regulating Doctor's Fees: Competition, Benefits, and Controls under Medicare*, ed. H.E. Frech III, Washington, D.C., AEI Press, 1991, p.234.

[6] Robert E. Moffit and Edmund F. Haislmaier, "The Medicare Relative Value Scale: Comparable Worth For Doctors," *Backgrounder*, The Heritage Foundation, October 25, 1989, No. 732. p.2.

[7] William C. Hsiao and William B. Stason, "Toward Developing a Relative Value Scale for Medical and Surgical Services," Health Care Financing Review, Fall 1979, Vol. 1, No. 2, p.35.

[8] Bruce H. Chamberlain, "Hospice Medical Director Billing Guide," American Academy of Hospice and Palliative Medicine, 2006, p.13.

[9] Dan-Avi Landau, Yaacov G. Bachner, Keren Elishkewitx, Liav Goldstein and Erez Barneboim, "Patients' Views on Optimal Visit Length in Primary Care," *Journal of Medical Practice Management*, July/August 2007, Vol. 23, No. 1.

[10] David A. Gross, Stephen J. Zyzanski, Elaine A. Borawski, Randall D. Cebul and Kurt C. Strange, "Patient Satisfaction with Time Spent with Their Physician," *Journal of Family Practice*, August 1998, Vol. 47, No. 2.

[11] Estella M. Geraghty, Peter Franks and Richard L. Kravitz, "Primary Care Visit Length, Quality, and Satisfaction for Standardized Patients with Depression," *Journal of General Internal Medicine*, December 2007, Vol. 22, No. 12.

[12] Leone Ridsdale, Maria Carruthers, Richard Morris and Jane Ridsdale, "Study of the effect of time availability on the consultation," *Journal of the Royal College of General Practitioners*, December 1989, Vol. 39, No. 329.

[13] Karen Scott Collins, Cathy Schoen and David R. Sandman, "The Commonwealth Fund Survey of Physician Experiences with Managed Care," The Commonwealth Fund, March 1, 1997.

[14] Sally Trude, "So Much to Do, So Little Time: Physician Capacity Constraints, 1997-2001," Center for Studying Health System Change, May 2003, Tracking Report, No. 8.

[15] JSK Watanabe and Daniel P. Sulmasy, "The Changing Times: Patient Visit Duration With Internists, 1980-1996," 1998 National Research Service Award (NRSA) Trainees' Research Conference, Washington, DC, July 20, 1998.

[16] Lena M. Chen, Wildon R. Farwell and Ashish K. Jha, "Primary Care Visit Duration and Quality. Does Good Care Take Longer?" *Archives of Internal Medicine*, Nov. 9, 2009, Vol. 169, No. 20; and David Mechanic, Donna D. McAlpine, and Marsha Rosenthal, "Are Patients' Office Visits With Physicians Getting Shorter?" *The New England Journal of Medicine*, January 18, 2001, Vol. 344, No. 3.

[17] Leslie L. Barton, "Changes in the Lengths of Office Visits," *The New England Journal of Medicine*, May 10, 2001, Vol. 344, No. 19.

[18] Ha T. Tu and Paul B. Ginsburg, "Losing Ground: Physician Income, 1995-2003," Center for Studying Health System Change, Tracking Report, No. 15, June 2006.

312

[19] Carry Mira Renders, Gerlof D. Vlak, Simon J. Griffin, Edward Wagner, Jacques Thm van Eijk and Willem J.J. Assendelft, "Interventions to improve the management of diabetes mellitus in primary care, outpatient and community settings (Review)," *The Cochrane Library*, 2009, Issue 1.

[20] "Physician – Neurology – U.S. National Averages, as of February 2015," *Salary Wizard*, at http://www1.salary.com/neurologist-Salary.html (February 17, 2015).

[21] Cannon, 2007, p.3.

[22] "Physician Quality Reporting System and Electronic Prescribing (eRx) Incentive Program: 2012 Reporting Experience Including Trends (2007-2012)," Centers for Medicare and Medicaid Services, March 14, 2014, pp.ix-x.

[23] Ibid., p.x.

[24] "2012 Physician Quality Reporting System (Physician Quality Reporting) Measures List," Centers for Medicare and Medicaid Services, Version 6.2, December 23, 2011, p.1.

[25] Ibid.

[26] "2012 Physician Quality Reporting System. Measure Specifications Manual for Claims and Registry Reporting of Individual Measures," Centers for Medicare and Medicaid Services, December 23, 2011, Version 6.2, pp.15-17.

[27] Ibid., pp.30-33.

[28] "2012 Physician Quality Reporting System (Physician Quality Reporting) Measures List," p.34.

[29] Physician Compare, Medicare.gov, at http://www.medicare.gov/physiciancompare/search.html (September 18, 2014).

[30] Laura A. Petersen, LeChauncy D. Woodard, Tracy Urech, Christina Daw and Supicha Sooknan, "Does Pay-for-Performance Improve the Quality of Health Care?" *Annals of Internal Medicine*, August 15, 2006, Vol. 145, No. 4.

[31] "High Blood Pressure—Medicines to Help You," U.S. Food and Drug Administration, U.S. Department of Health and Human Services, at

http://www.fda.gov/forconsumers/byaudience/forwomen/ucm118594.htm (November 10, 2012).

[32] Mary E. Tinetti, Sidney T. Bogardus and Joseph V. Agostini, "Potential Pitfalls of Disease-Specific Guidelines for Patients with Multiple Conditions," *The New England Journal of Medicine*, December 30, 2004, Vol. 351, No. 27, p. 2872.

[33] "SGR Repeal and Medicare Provider Payment Modernization Act, Section by Section," House Ways and Means Committee, pp. 1-4, at http://waysandmeans.house.gov/uploadedfiles/hr_1470_section_by_sectio n.pdf (March 25, 2015).

[34] David Hogberg, "Medicare Doc Fix Bill Is IPAB-Lite," *The Daily Caller*, April 13, 2015, at http://dailycaller.com/2015/04/13/medicare-doc-fix-bill-is-ipab-lite/ (April 13, 2015).

[35] "Lessons from Medicare's Demonstration Projects on Disease Management, Care Coordination, and Value-Based Payment," Congressional Budget Office, Issue Brief, January 2012.

[36] Lyle Nelson, "Lessons from Medicare's Demonstration Projects on Disease Management and Care Coordination," Congressional Budget Office, Working Paper 2012-01, January 2012, p. 26. Also see Lyle Nelson, "Lessons from Medicare's Demonstration Projects on Value-Based Payment," Congressional Budget Office, Working Paper 2012-02, January 2012.

[37] John C. Goodman, *Priceless: Curing The Healthcare Crisis*, 2012, Oakland: The Independent Institute, p. 74.

[38] "Our Mission," Center for Medicare and Medicaid Innovation, Centers for Medicare and Medicaid Services, at http://www.innovations.cms.gov/About/Our-Mission/index.html (November 13, 2012).

Chapter 9: The Big Hospital Lobby

[1] Medicare Payment Advisory Commission, "Report To Congress: Physician-Owned Specialty Hospitals," March 2005.

[2] Regina E. Herzlinger, "Specialization and Its Discontents: The Pernicious Impact of Regulations Against Specialization and Physicians Ownership on the US Healthcare System," *Circulation*, 2004, Vol. 109, No. 20, pp. 2376-8.

[3] Mark Sherman, "Medicare bill clamps down on physician-owned specialty hospitals," *Associated Press*, November 26, 2003.

[4] Rick Pollack, "Statement on GAO Report – Niche Providers," *Press Releases & Statement*, American Hospital Association, May 15, 2003.

[5] Charles N. Kahn III, "Intolerable Risk, Irreparable Harm: The Legacy Of Physician-Owned Specialty Hospitals," *Health Affairs*, January/February 2006, Vol. 25, No. 1, p. 130.

[6] American Hospital Association, "Self-referral to Physician-owned Hospitals: What The Research Says," April 17, 2008, at http://www.American Hospital Association.org/American Hospital Association/trendwatch/2008/twapr2008selfreferral.pdf (October 25, 2010).

[7] Jack Hadley and Stephen Zuckerman, "Physician-Owned Specialty Hospitals: A Market Signal For Medicare Payment Revisions," *Health Affairs*, October 25, 2005, Web Exclusive.

[8] United States General Accounting Office, "Medicare: Referring Physicians' Ownership of Laboratories and Imaging Centers," Statement of Michael Zimmerman, Director of Medicare and Medicaid Issues, Human Resources Division, June 8, 1989; and United States General Accounting Office, "Physicians Who Invest in Imaging Centers Refer More Patients for More Costly Services," Statement of Janet L. Shikles, Director, Health Financing and Policy Issues, April 20, 1993.

[9] Jane M. Orient, M.D. *Your Doctor Is Not In: Healthy Skepticism About National Health Care*, 1994, New York: Crown Publishers, Inc., p. 113.

[10] Campaign For America's Future conference call, December 16, 2008.

[11] David Burda, "Looking at bans in a different light: Efforts to end self-referrals are more turf battles than altruistic crusades," *Modern Healthcare*, May 31, 1993, p.25.

[12] "Two-pronged attack seeks to end physician self-referral," *Medical Laboratory Observer*, April 1, 1989, Vol. 21, No. 4, p. 21.

[13] Burda, 1993, p. 21.

[14] David Schactman, "Specialty Hospitals, Ambulatory Surgery Centers, And General Hospitals: Charting A Wise Public Policy Course," *Health Affairs*, May/June 2005, vol. 24, No. 3, p. 871.

[15] Kahn, p. 130.

[16] David Ansley, "Hospitals: Physicians Joint Venture Offers Luxury For Less," *San Jose Mercury News*, June 19, 1992.

[17] Raquel Santiago, "Hospital Group Seeks 2-Year Building Ban," *Crain's Cleveland Business*, December 1, 1997, p. 1.

[18] Ibid.

[19] Troy May, "Hospital Association seeks hiatus on new construction," *Business First-Columbus*, December 5, 1997, Vol. 14, No. 15, p. 3.

[20] Bureau of Labor Statistics, Occupational Employment Statistics, May 2013 National Industry-Specific Occupational Employment and Wage Estimates, "NAICS 622100 - General Medical and Surgical Hospitals (including private, state, and local government hospitals)," April 1, 2014, at http://www.bls.gov/oes/current/naics4_622100.htm (January 15, 2015).

[21] Joseph Conn, "Heavy heart; Stark prompts inspector general study of MedCath hospital," *Modern Physician*, October 1, 2000, p.2.

[22] Patrick Reilly, "AMERICAN HOSPITAL ASSOCIATION's specialty hospital task force suggests changes; Physician investors consider proposals unfair control of competition," *Modern Healthcare*, December 16, 2002.

[23] Roger Yu, "Bypassing hospitals; As surgery centers pop up, critics complain not all is well; Doctor's ownership, reimbursement rates under examination," *Dallas Morning News*, May 4, 2003, p. 1D.

[24] Conn, 2000, p.2.

[25] Chip Kahn, "GAO: Physician-Owned Boutique Hospitals Harmful To Competitors," Federation of American Hospitals, October 22, 2003.

[26] United States General Accounting Office, "Specialty Hospitals: Information on National Market Share, Physician Ownership, and Patients Served," April 18, 2003, GAO-03-683R

[27] Pollack, 2003.

[28] Chip Kahn, "GAO Report Provides Important Guidance About 'Boutique Hospitals'," Federation of American Hospitals, May 15, 2003.

[29] Amy Goldstein, "Medicare Law Stunts Hospital Rival; Growth of Specialty Care Centers Slowed While Impact Studied," *Washington Post*, December 16, 2003, Section A, p. A35.

[30] Sherman, 2003.

[31] *Inside CMS*, "Hospital Groups Respond To Grassley\ Request For Support," September 25, 2003, Vol. 6, No. 20.

[32] United States General Accounting Office, "Specialty Hospitals. Geographic Location, Services Provided, and Financial Performance," Report to Congressional Requesters, October 2003, GAO\-04-167.

[33] Ann L. Hendrick and Nelson Lee, "Intra-unit patient transports: time, motion, and cost impact on hospital efficiency," *Nursing Economics*, July-August 2005, Vol. 23, No. 4, pp.157-64.

[34] Vivian G. Valdmanis, Michael D. Rosko and Ryan L. Mutter, "Hospital Quality, Efficiency, and Input Slack Differentials," *Health Services Research*, October 2008, Vol. 43, No. 5, Part II, pp. 1830-48.

[35] Ritu Agarwal, Daniel Z. Sands, Jorge Diaz Schneider and Detlev H. Smaltz, "Quantifying the Economic Impact of Communication Inefficiencies in U.S. Hospitals," *Journal of Healthcare Management*, July-August 2010, Vol. 55, No. 4, pp. 265-81.

[36] Douglas Gregory, Walter Baigelman and Ira B. Wilson, "Hospital Economics of the Hospitalist," *Health Services Research*, June 2003, Vol. 38, No. 3, pp. 905-18.

[37] Mary E. Deily and Niccie L. McKay, "Cost inefficiency and mortality rates in Florida hospitals," *Health Economics*, 2006, Vol. 15, No. 4, pp. 419-31.

[38] American Hospital Association, *Hospital Statistics*, 2001.

[39] The Synthesis Project, "How has hospital consolidations affected the price and quality of hospital care?" Robert Wood Johnson Foundation, *Policy Brief*, February 2006, No. 9.

[40] Cory Capps and David Dranove, "Hospital Consolidation And Negotiated PPO Prices," *Health Affairs*, March/April 2004, Vol. 23, No. 2, pp.175-81.

[41] The United States Senate Committee on Finance, "Grassley, Baucus Urge Colleagues to Support Bill Reining in Doctor-Owned Specialty Hospitals," June 8, 2005.

[42] The United States Senate Committee on Finance, "Sens. Grassley, Baucus raise questions about Medicare payment at specialty hospital in West Texas," February 8, 2007.

[43] Ibid.

[44] Ibid.

[45] *Inside CMS*, "OIG Report On Specialty Hospitals Refuels Call To Curb Facilities," January 24, 2008, Vol. 11, No. 2.

[46] Office of the Inspector General, Department of Health and Human Services, "Physician-Owned Specialty Hospitals' Ability To Manage Medical Emergencies," January 2008, OEI-02-06-00310.

[47] *Inside CMS*, "Specialty Hospitals Refute OIG Report On Emergency Capabilities," January 24, 2008, Vol. 11, No. 2.

[48] *Inside CMS*, "OIG Report On Specialty Hospitals Refuels Call To Curb Facilities," January 24, 2008, Vol. 11, No. 2.

[49] McManis Consulting, "Impact of Physician-owned Limited-service Hospitals: Wichita, KS Cast Study" February 16, 2005, at http://www.American Hospital Association.org/American Hospital Association/content/2005/pdf/Wichita%20Final%20PDF.pdf (October 25, 2010); and "Impact of Physician-owned Limited-service Hospitals: Oklahoma City Case Study," February 16, 2005, at http://www.American Hospital Association.org/American Hospital Association/content/2005/pdf/Oklahoma%20Final%20PDF.pdf (October 25, 2010).

[50] McManis Consulting, "Impact of Physician-owned Limited-service Hospitals: Black Hills Case Study," November 18, 2004, p.31, at http://www.American Hospital Association.org/American Hospital Association/content/2005/pdf/Black%20Hills%2011%2019%20FINAL.pdf (October 25, 2010).

[51] McManis Consulting, "Impact of Physician-owned Limited-service Hospitals: Lincoln Case Study," February 16, 2005, p. 17, at http://www.American Hospital Association.org/American Hospital Association/content/2005/pdf/Lincoln%20Final%20PDF.pdf (October 25, 2010).

[52] Ibid, p. 18.

[53] American Hospital Association, "Self-referral to Physician-owned Hospitals: What The Research Says," p. 1.

[54] American Hospital Association, "The State of America's Hospitals – Taking the Pulse. A Chart Pack: Findings from the 2006 AHA Survey of Hospital Leaders," 2006, at http://www.aha.org/aha/content/2006/.../StateHospitalsChartPack2006.PPT (December 22, 2010); and Maggie Fox, "U.S. hospitals fall to zero," *Thomson Reuters*," March 2, 2009, at http://www.reuters.com/article/idUSTRE5216G320090302 (December 22, 2010).

[55] Medicare Payment Advisory Commission, "Physician-Owned Specialty Hospitals Revisited," *Report To Congress*, August 2006, pp. 24-5; Center for Studying Health System Change, "General Hospitals, Specialty Hospitals and Financially Vulnerable Patients," *Research Brief*, April 2009, No. 11; and United States Government Accountability Office, "General Hospitals. Operational and Clinical Changes Largely Unaffected by Presence of Competing Specialty Hospitals," *Report to the Chairman, Committee on Ways and Means, House of Representatives*, April 2006, GAO-06-520.

[56] American Hospital Association, "Impact of Limited-service Providers on Communities and Full-service Hospitals," *Trendwatch*, Vol. 6, No. 2, September 2004, at http://www.American Hospital

Association.org/American Hospital
Association/trendwatch/2004/040924_twvol6no2limitedserv.pdf (October
26, 2010).
[57] Al Dobson, "A Comparative Study of Patient Severity and Quality of
Care between MedCath Heart Hospitals and Peer Hospitals for 2005
Discharges. Executive Summary," The Lewin Group, September 2006, at
http://www.medcathpartners.com/Portals/MP/Lewin-executive-
summary%209-30-06.pdf, (October 31, 2010).
[58] Jean M. Mitchell, "Effects Of Physician-Owned Limited-Service
Hospitals: Evidence From Arizona," *Health Affairs*, October 25, 2005, pp.
W5-481-90.
[59] Allen Dobson and Randall Haught, "The Rise Of The Entrepreneurial
Physician," *Health Affairs*, October 25, 2005, p. W5-494.
[60] Peter Cram. M.D., M.B.A., Gary E. Rosenthal, M.D. and Mary S.
Vaughan-Sarrazin, Ph.D., "Cardiac Revascularization in Specialty and
General Hospitals," *The New England Journal of Medicine*, April 7, 2005,
Vol. 352, No. 14, pp. 1454-62; Brahmajee K. Nallamothu, M.D., M.P.H.,
Mary A.M. Rogers, Ph.D., Michael E. Chernes, Ph.D., Harlan M.
Krumholz, M.D., S.M., Kim A. Eagle, M.D. and John D. Birkmeyer,
M.D., "Opening of Specialty Cardiac Hospitals and Use of Coronary
Revascularization in Medicare Beneficiaries," *Journal of the American
Medical Association*, March 7, 2007, Vol. 297, No. 9, pp. 962-68.
[61] Nallamothu, et al., pp. 967-68.
[62] Centers for Medicare & Medicaid Services, "Study of Physician-owned
Specialty Hospitals Required in Section 507(c)(2) of the Medicare
Prescription Drug, Improvement, and Modernization Act of 2003," May
2005, p.ii, at http://www.cms.hhs.gov/MLNProducts/Downloads/RTC-
StudyofPhysOwnedSpecHosp.pdf (October 26, 2010).
[63] Ibid, p. 26.
[64] Centers for Medicare & Medicaid Services, pp. 41-8 and 66-8.
[65] Leslie Greenwald, Jerry Cromwell, Walter Adamache, Shulamit
Bernard, Edward Drozd, Elizabeth Root and Kelly Devers, "Specialty
Versus Community Hospitals: Referrals, Quality, And Community

Benefits," *Health* Affairs, January/February 2006, Vol. 25, No. 1, pp. 106-18.

[66] Medicare Payment Advisory Commission, "Report To Congress: Physician-Owned Specialty Hospitals," March 2005, p.16; and Medicare Payment Advisory Commission, "Report To Congress: Physician-Owned Specialty Hospitals Revisited," August 2006, pp. 9-10.

[67] See Table 9.3 in Appendix.

[68] Centers for Medicare & Medicaid Services, p. 53.

[69] Greenwald, et al., p.115

[70] Centers for Medicare & Medicaid Services, p. 52.

[71] Greenwald, et al., p.115

[72] Centers for Medicare & Medicaid Services, p. 51.

[73] Ibid.

[74] David Whelan, "Bad Medicine," *Forbes Magazine*, February 14, 2008, at http://www.forbes.com/forbes/2008/0310/086.html (October 31, 2010).

[75] Centers for Medicare & Medicaid Services, p. 58.

[76] Greenwald, et al., p.116.

[77] Medicare Payment Advisory Commission, March 2005, p. 19.

[78] Medicare Payment Advisory Commission, March 2006, p. 5.

[79] United States General Accounting Office, "Specialty Hospitals. Geographic Location, Services Provided, and Financial Performance," Report to Congressional Requesters, October 2003, GAO-04-167, p. 21.

[80] Medicare Payment Advisory Commission, August 2006, p. 8.

[81] Ibid, p. 15.

[82] Ibid, p. 17.

[83] Centers for Medicare & Medicaid Services, p. 31; and Greenwald, et al., p. 112.

[84] Centers for Medicare & Medicaid Services, p. 30.

[85] Sean Parnell, "Innovations in the Business of Health Care. The Role of Specialty Hospitals," The Texas Public Policy Foundation, Center for Health Care Policy, May 2008. pp. 10-11, at http://www.texaspolicy.com/pdf/2008-05-RR03-specialtyhospitals-parnell.pdf (October 27, 2010).

[86] Medicare Payment Advisory Commission, August 2006, p. 19.

[87] Jean M. Mitchell, "Utilization Changes Following Market Entry by Physician-owned Specialty Hospitals," *Medical Care Research and Review*, August 2007, Vol. 64, No. 4, pp. 395-415; Jean M. Mitchell, "Effect of Physician Ownership of Specialty Hospitals and Ambulatory Surgery Centers of Frequency of Use of Outpatient Orthopedic Surgery," *Archives of Surgery*, August 2010, Vol. 145, No. 8, pp. 732-38.

[88] Jeffrey Stensland and Ariel Winter, "Do Physician-Owned Cardiac Hospitals Increase Utilization?" *Health Affairs*, January/February 2006, Vol. 25, No. 1, pp. 119-29; G. William Woods, Daniel P. O'Connor, and Peggy Pierce, "Orthopedic Surgeons Do Not Increase Surgical Volume After Investing In A Specialty Hospital," *Journal of Bone and Joint Surgery*, June 2005, Vol. 87-A, No. 6, pp. 1185-90.

[89] Medicare Payment Advisory Commission, 2006, p.23; United States General Accounting Office, October, 2003.

[90] Lawrence P. Casalino, Kelly J. Divers, and Linda R. Brewster, "Focused Factories? Physician-Owned Specialty Facilities," *Health Affairs*, November/December 2003, Vol. 22, No. 6, p. 61.

[91] Medicare Payment Advisory Commission, March 2005, p. 7.

[92] David Hogberg, "ObamCare Will Effectively Bar New Physician-Owned Hospitals," *Investor's Business Daily*, March 24, 2010, at http://www.investors.com/NewsAndAnalysis/Article.aspx?id=528337 (December 3, 2010).

[93] Hogberg, 2010.

[94] Interview with author, September 1, 2010.

[95] Hogberg, 2010.

[96] Department of Health and Human Services, "Medicare Program: Hospital Outpatient Prospective Payment System and CY 2011 Payment Rates; Ambulatory Surgical Center Payment System and CY 2011 Payment Rates; Payments to Hospitals for Graduate Medical Education Costs; Physician Self-Referral Rules and Related Changes to Provider Agreement Regulations; Payment for Certified Registered Nurse Anesthetist Services Furnished in Rural Hospitals and Critical Access

Hospitals," *Federal Register, The Daily Journal of the United States Government*, November 24, 2010, at http://www.federalregister.gov/articles/2010/11/24/2010-27926/medicare-program-hospital-outpatient-prospective-payment-system-and-cy-2011-payment-rates-ambulatory (December 23, 2010).

[97] Interview with author, September 1, 2010.

[98] David Hogberg, "Congress should repeal limits on doctor-owned hospitals," *The Washington Examiner*, March 6, 2013, at http://www.washingtonexaminer.com/op-ed-congress-should-repeal-limits-on-new-doctor-owned-hospitals/article/2523441 (January 5, 2014).

[99] Steven Tavares, "Stark's Hilarious Mailer Skewering Swalwell's Inexperience Also Shows Fundraising Strength," *East Bay Citizen*, October 8, 2012, at http://www.ebcitizen.com/2012/10/starks-hilarious-mailer-skewering.html (February 18, 2015).

[100] Cheryl Clark, "Doctor-owned Hospitals Worried Reform Will Cripple Them," *Health Leaders Media*, December 17, 2009, at http://www.healthleadersmedia.com/content/PHY-243676/Doctorowned-Hospitals-Worried-Reform-Will-Cripple-Them#%23 (December 3, 2010).

[101] Interview with author, February 3, 2009.

[102] Centers for Medicare & Medicaid Services, 2005, p. 26.

[103] Todd H. Wagner and Lisa Smith Wagner, "Who Gets Second Opinions?" *Health Affairs*, September/October 1999, Vol. 18, No. 5, pp. 137-45.

Chapter 10: Trade-Offs

[1] The Board of Trustees, Federal Hospital Insurance and Federal Supplementary Medical Insurance Trust Funds, "2014 Annual Report of the Boards of Trustees of the Federal Hospital Insurance and Federal Supplementary Medical Insurance Trust Funds," Washington, D.C., July 28, 2014, p. 229.

[2] The House Committee on the Budget, "The Path To Prosperity. A Blueprint For American Renewal," Fiscal Year 2013 Budget Resolution, March 20, 2012.

[3] Congressional Budget Office, "The Long-Term Impact of Paths for Federal Revenues and Spending Specified by Chairman Ryan," March 2012, p. 8.

[4] Medicare enrollment and utilization data at Centers for Medicare & Medicaid Services, "Medicare & Medicaid Statistical Supplement, 2013 Edition," Tables 2.1 and 3.6; Medicare Advantage enrollment data at Marsha Gold, Gretchen Jacobson, Anthony Damico and Tricia Neuman, "Medicare Advantage 2012 Data Spotlight: Enrollment Market Update," Data Spotlight, Kaiser Family Foundation, May 31, 2012.

[5] Centers for Medicare & Medicaid Services, Table 3.6.

[6] Judy Feder, Lisa Clemans-Cope, Teresa Coughlin, John Holahan and Timothy Waidmann, "Refocusing Responsibility For Dual Eligibles: Why Medicare Should Take The Lead," Urban Institute, October 2011.

[7] Congressional Budget Office, "Lessons from Medicare's Demonstration Projects on Disease Management, Care Coordination, and Value-Based Payment," January 18, 2012.

[8] John C. Goodman, *Priceless: Curing The Healthcare Crisis*, Oakland, California: The Independence Institute, 2012 p. 74.

[9] Mark A. Hall and Carl e. Schneider, "Patients As Consumers: Courts, Contracts, And The New Medical Marketplace," *Michigan Law Review*, February 2008, Vol. 106, No. 4, pp. 650-51.

[10] Camilla A. Herrera, "Cancer Blasting, " Greenwich Time, May 13, 2008, at http://www.instituteigrt.com/pdf/Greenwich_Time5_13_08.pdf.

[11] Joseph P. Newhouse and the Insurance Experiment Group, *Free For All? Lessons From The RAND Health Insurance Experiment*, Cambridge, Massachusetts: Harvard University Press, 1993.

[12] "Consumer Driven Health Care Plans Can Help Consumers Reduce Health Care Spending and Make Positive Behavior Changes," PR Newswire, June 13, 2012, at http://www.prnewswire.com/news-releases/consumer-driven-health-care-plans-can-help-consumers-reduce-

health-care-spending-and-make-positive-behavior-changes-158848095.html (June 15, 2012).

[13] James C. Robinson and Timothy T. Brown, "Increases In Consumer Cost Sharing Redirect Patient Volumes And Reduce Hospital Prices For Orthopedic Surgery," *Health Affairs*, August 2013, Vol. 32, No. 8.

[14] United States Government Accountability Office, "Consumer-Directed Health Plans: Health Status, Spending, and Utilization of Enrollees in Plans Based on Health Reimbursement Arrangements," Report to Congressional Requesters, GAO-10-616, July 2010.

[15] Greg Scandlen, "Working as Intended: What We Have Learned About Consumer Driven Health Care," Consumers For Health Care Choices, November 2007, at http://www.hii.org/documents/859.pdf (October 6, 2013).

[16] Avik Roy, "Why the American Medical Association Had 72 Million Reasons to Shrink Doctors' Pay," The Apothecary, Forbes, November 28, 2011, at http://www.forbes.com/sites/theapothecary/2011/11/28/why-the-american-medical-association-had-72-million-reasons-to-help-shrink-doctors-pay/ (November 10, 2013).

[17] Roni Caryn Rabin, "When Doctors Stop Taking Insurance," *New York Times*, October 1, 2012, at http://well.blogs.nytimes.com/2012/10/01/when-doctors-stop-taking-insurance/ (November 7, 2012).

[18] Roseanna Sommers, Susan Dorr Goold, Elizabeth A. McGlynn, Steven D. Pearson and Marion Danis, "Focus Groups Highlight That Many Patients Object To Clinicians' Focusing On Costs," *Health Affairs*, February 2013, Vol. 32, No. 2, p.339.

[19] Ibid, p.340.

[20] Centers For Medicare and Medicaid Services, "Part C and D Performance Data: 2013 Part C & D Medicare Star Ratings Data," December 13, 2012, at http://www.cms.gov/Medicare/Prescription-Drug-Coverage/PrescriptionDrugCovGenIn/PerformanceData.html (October 5, 2013).

[21] Centers For Medicare and Medicaid Services, "Details by Title: Monthly Enrollment by Plan," September 2013, at http://www.cms.gov/Research-Statistics-Data-and-Systems/Statistics-Trends-and-Reports/MCRAdvPartDEnrolData/Monthly-Enrollment-by-Plan-Items/Monthly-Enrollment-by-Plan-2013-09.html (October 20, 2013).

[22] Greg Scandlen, "Nearly One-Third of All Workers Now In Consumer-Driven Health Plans," John Goodman's Health Policy Blog, October 25, 2011, at http://healthblog.ncpa.org/nearly-one-third-of-all-workers-now-in-consumer-driven-health-plans/ (August 10, 2013).

[23] Robinson and Brown, 2013.

[24] John C. Goodman, "Stunning Results from California," John Goodman's Health Policy Blog, August 7, 2013, at http://healthblog.ncpa.org/stunning-results-from-california/ (August 8, 2013).

www.ingramcontent.com/pod-product-compliance
Lightning Source LLC
Chambersburg PA
CBHW031953190326
41520CB00007B/229